Contributions to Economics

More information about this series at http://www.springer.com/series/1262

Anastasios Karasavvoglou • Dimitrios Kyrkilis •
Georgios Makris • Persefoni Polychronidou
Editors

Economic Crisis, Development and Competitiveness in Southeastern Europe

Theoretical Foundations and Policy Issues

Springer

Editors
Anastasios Karasavvoglou
Eastern Macedonia and Thrace
Institute of Technology
Kavala, Greece

Dimitrios Kyrkilis
University of Macedonia
Thessaloniki, Greece

Georgios Makris
University of Macedonia
Thessaloniki, Greece

Persefoni Polychronidou
Eastern Macedonia and Thrace
Institute of Technology
Kavala, Greece

ISSN 1431-1933 ISSN 2197-7178 (electronic)
Contributions to Economics
ISBN 978-3-319-40321-2 ISBN 978-3-319-40322-9 (eBook)
DOI 10.1007/978-3-319-40322-9

Library of Congress Control Number: 2016951307

Printed on acid-free paper

This Springer imprint is published by Springer Nature
The registered company is Springer International Publishing AG Switzerland

Contents

About the Book

Since the beginning of the current decade, i.e. 2010, the Balkans and the Southeastern Europe at large have been suffering from the continuation of the 2007–2008 world financial crisis as sovereign debt crisis in Greece and other south eurozone countries triggered by coexisting fiscal and external imbalances. The crisis turned to a prolonged fiscal crisis, a bank confidence crisis, and economic recession. European and national authorities sought ways to resolve the crisis in a context of non-pre-existing institutional and policymaking arrangements while policy measures actually taken after tedious deliberations generated internal conflicts both within the nation states and the eurozone as a whole. The eurozone economic crisis was and still is complicated by geopolitical tensions in Ukraine, Turkey, and the Middle East while geopolitical risks around the world are increasing, e.g. North Korea, while structural transformations and problems in China feed world economic instability and risk. At the same time, the dramatic fall in international oil prices raises stability concerns for neighbouring oil producing countries, casts sustainability doubts on plans for energy transmission networks in the broader area, and calls for reconsidering national roles and cross-border arrangements.

The macroeconomic outlook of the broader Southeastern Europe seems uncertain with mixed GDP growth rates and directions, while any positive growth rates seem anaemic and their sustainability is questionable. Deflation has been established as a widespread trend, and high unemployment rates persist, although the European Central Bank (ECB) has been running a quantitative easing monetary policy that it expects to maintain until September 2016 at least. At the same time, in some cases foreign debts are increasing, cross-border financial flows including worker remittances are highly volatile, credit expansion is insufficient to mobilise the economy, and the non-performing share of loans is growing. Many of these problems pre-existed the 2007–2008 world financial crisis, but they became more acute calling for immediate resolutions after the eruption of the eurozone crisis while policies implemented ever since seem ineffective in easing them.

It is the continuation of the crisis in many aspects, especially in the form of deflation, unemployment, and low and unstable economic growth that sets the question: is there any scope of changing the policy mix? The question needs urgent answers especially in the eurozone where the single currency does not allow any currency value realignment, a powerful instrument of remedying national competitiveness deficiencies, and it dictates a single monetary policy designed and implemented by the European Central Bank that lacks flexibility, and thus, it cannot serve individual member country needs which in many cases are conflicting to each other due to national asymmetries and structural divergences. Although there are arguments that the policies of fiscal consolidation and economic thrift implemented as a general and iron law managed to end the crisis and set the economies on a growth path, from another point of view these same policies have failed to improve economic structures and achieve convergence, and instead they contributed to a spiral of recession and/or low-level stationarity and divergence. Policymakers in many countries in the area seek policy measures for advancing the economic competitiveness of their countries as a means to secure economic growth and improve standards of living for their populations. However, the problem of what constitutes economic competitiveness and about policies and structures economic, institutional, and others that improve competitiveness demands both theoretical and empirical foundations; therefore, further research is needed.

The 7th Economies of Balkan of Eastern Europe Countries (EBEEC) Conference which was organised jointly by the TEI of Eastern Macedonia and Thrace, Department of Accounting and Finance, and the University of Macedonia, Department of Balkan, Slavic and Oriental Studies in Kavala, Greece, May 8–10, 2015, aimed to present research papers making propositions from both the theoretical and empirical point of view about the foundations and means of overcoming the crisis in the broader area, the concept, determinants, and policies of competitiveness, and other relevant issues. The current volume contains a number of papers presented at the conference and chosen according to a peer-review process.

The papers report research related to the themes referred above, making significant contributions to their investigation.

The volume is organised into two parts. The first part contains papers taking a rather macroeconomic and more theoretical approach of analysing the issues in question and establishing relevant propositions. The second part consists of papers exploring specific policies for improving competitiveness and boosting economic growth, and they take a rather empirical approach in doing so.

Part one begins with Professor Heiner Flassbeck's paper titled "**Macroeconomic theory and macroeconomic logic—the case of the Euro crisis**". Heiner Flassbeck makes a very interesting effort to analyse from a macroeconomic point of view the roots of the economic crisis in the eurozone and to point out the reasons for the economic recession persisting across Europe. The issues of wage flexibility vs. inflexibility and its consequences, those of real wage growth and its relation to domestic demand, and the question of nominal vs. real convergence are some that have a key role in pursuing this study. Additionally, the author discusses the case for monetary cooperation and the core monetary principles of the European Monetary Union (EMU). The author argues that there is a strong and stable positive relationship between the growth rate of unit labour costs (ULC) and the inflation rate, on the one hand, and the growth rate of real wages and domestic demand, on the other. Under such connections, ECB's inflation targeting at 2 % monetary policy is ineffective to the extent that at least one country, i.e. Germany, pursues a ULC below 2 %. ECB has to lower its inflation target in line with Germany's ULC, in which case all other countries would have to moderate their ULCs. But any accruing advantage towards emerging markets, e.g. China, would be lost due to the adjustment of the exchange rate of the Euro to the lower inflation rate. Ultimately, that means that across the eurozone policy of cutting ULCs is useless in terms of improving competitiveness but effective in terms of stagnating or even lowering domestic demand and increasing unemployment. The paper concludes that there is a considerably strong connection between the adjustments demanded by the European institutions at the national level and the economic recession in peripheral EMU countries. The author notes "In a monetary union, a country with a low export share and facing a huge current-account deficit and financing problems due to an implicitly overvalued currency would be trapped. Downward adjustment of wages, sometimes erroneously called "internal devaluation", would be no solution as it would destroy both domestic demand and output before it could bring some relief through rising exports........ (eurozone) countries with a huge gap of competitiveness against Germany would have to go through an extended period of catching-up in terms of price competitiveness......(current account) deficit countries have to dive below the German UCL path for a long time to regain some of the losses they have experienced in the first 10 years of EMU."

Dimitrios Kyrkilis, Georgios Makris, and Konstantinos Hazakis in their paper "**Economic crisis and national economic competitiveness: Does labour cost link the two? The case of the south eurozone states**" reach similar conclusion arguing that the ULC is not the most significant determinant of national competitiveness. They base their analysis on, first, the Ricardian theory of comparative advantages and the neoclassical theory of international trade, pointing out that the first sources the root of comparative advantages on labour productivity differentials due to technological differences among nations while the second sources the basis of comparative advantages on the relative abundance of production factors. They analyse the concept of competitiveness and its differences between the micro- and macro-levels, and they argue that ULC is inappropriate for approaching competitiveness at the macro-level because it fails to capture the connection between investments, the main determinant of competitiveness through its influence on labour productivity and profits, the latter being a function of the distribution of income between labour and capital. Such connections require the introduction of the real wage instead of its nominal value in the analysis on the one hand, and it leads to the conclusion that any reduction of the ULC either has to be followed by a reduction of prices, i.e. deflation not having that way any impact on the investment activity, or if prices do not follow suit, price competitiveness does not improve. In any case, the paper concludes similarly to Flassbeck's paper that the policy of domestic devaluation, at least as it has been implemented in the south eurozone countries, has led to GDP depression but not to restoring competitiveness.

Nikitas-Spiros Koutsoukis and Spyros Roukanas in their paper "**Compulsory' economic deflation turned political risk: Effects of austere decision-making on Greece's 'true' economy (2008–2015) and the 'Eurozone or default' dilemma**" analyse the consequences on the Greek society of the economic austerity measures taken under the internal devaluation strategy adopted by the national authorities. These policies provoked a socio-humanitarian crisis, political populism, and polarisation. The authors seek to investigate the key factors of the political and economic degradation by focusing on high-level shifts of the Greek economy and its institutions. Elements of political risk and progression are used in order to demonstrate how the bailout program designed and implemented by the European institutions influences the ability of Greece to handle the crisis. In conclusion, authors state that economic adjustment programmes caused a severe hike of political risk with negative consequences for the valued solidarity not only in Greece but in all members' state of the eurozone.

Edgar Saucedo and Jesus Diaz in their paper "**Theory of optimum currency area and the Balkans**" construct a framework to examining the consequences for the Balkan countries of introducing regional single currency against those introducing the Euro. Specific theoretical elements of the theory of optimum currency have been employed for running simulations for groups of Balkans countries. For the purpose of the analysis, innovative criteria have been used such as the criterion of co-movement and the criterion of political proximity. In addition, the criteria of trade integration and inflation have also been included. The results indicate that countries introducing the euro would enjoy more benefits against countries introducing a regional single currency.

Elena Spasova in the paper titled "**The balance of payments constrained model in a transitional economy: The case of Bulgaria**" makes an effort to analyse the growth dynamics of the Bulgarian economy within a time period of 20 years using the balance-of-payments (BOP) constrained growth model established by Anthony Thirwall and known as Thirlwall's Law. The paper attempts to control for the suitability of this framework to explain the growth rates of the Bulgarian economy in the last 20 years. For the purpose of the study, an econometric model has been estimated for establishing the Bulgarian economy's equilibrium growth rate as it would have been achieved according to the BOP constraint on growth and after that the results have been compared with the real registered levels of economic growth. According to the author, specific features of the Bulgarian economy cause inefficiencies of the external trade sector resulting in constraining the country's growth and impeding its economic convergence with the developed countries.

Finally, Ozcan Karahan and Olcay Colak in the paper "**The nexus between imports and national income in Turkey**" address the issue of the relationship between imports and national income in Turkey. The authors present the contradictory approaches of Keynesian Multiplier Theory and Endogenous Growth Models concerning the connection between import-led economic shrinkage and import-led economic growth, respectively. Based on this methodological framework, they aim at examining these arguments regarding the effect of imports on

Turkish economy. For testing this relationship, they use a time-series econometric analysis for the period 2002–2014 based on the Johansen co-integration and Granger causality tests in addition to Innovation Accounting Techniques. The results show that the argument of the Endogenous Growth Model is confirmed in the case of Turkey. Empirical results demonstrate a strong causality linkage between imports and economic growth in Turkey with the causality running from imports to economic growth.

The second part starts with the paper "**Interaction between competitiveness and innovation: Evidence from South-Eastern European countries**" by Jelena Stankovic, Vesna Jankovic-Milic, and Marija Dzunic. The paper refers to the relationship between innovation activities and the improvement of competitiveness examining the impact of indicators of innovative activities on the competitiveness of certain Balkan countries through a comparative analysis. An empirical survey has been conducted on innovation activities of firms in Serbia using the method of dependency and correlation analysis. According to the authors, there is a limited innovation activity in Serbian enterprises resulting in their low competitiveness. The results demonstrate the immediate development of macroeconomic environment and the enforcement of innovation activities in order to improve the competitiveness of enterprises in the Balkans.

In the second paper of the part titled "**Testing uncovered interest parity for structural breaks: A developing country perspective**", Srdan Marinkovic, Ognjen Radovic, and Zeljko Sevic construct a single-country model for uncovered interest parity (UIP). The UIP test is widely applied in international finance. In this paper, the UIP test is based on high-frequency data. For the purpose of the analysis, the EGARCH analysis of statistical properties of time series of deviations from UIP and the Markov Switching model have been used. EGARCH analysis is responsible for predicting future volatility of the tested variable. According to the authors, the model was able to demonstrate correctly the *ex ante* identified structural break caused by crisis incidents, but was unsuccessful to separate the pre- and post-liberalisation periods.

In the last paper "**Adult education; A vehicle for economic development**", Pantelis Sklias and the Giota Chatzimichailidou attempt to investigate in depth the effect of adult education on economic development. The paper shows how education programmes concerning political, social, and economic issues motivate citizens to play a vital role in the societal development and consequently in economic progress. The authors employ the methodological framework of International Political Economy in a comparative context as opposed to the building of Human Capital Model in order to examine the correlation between economic development and adult education in the developed countries. Their findings indicate that the advancement of adult education programs is considered central for securing the societal consistency and therefore to the economic development.

Part I

Macroeconomic Theory and Macroeconomic Logic: The Case of the Euro Crisis

Heiner Flassbeck

Abstract The last 7 years have been a tumultuous period for Europe and the unrest is far from over. The global crisis that began in 2007 led to a sharp financial shock in 2008–9, which ushered in a recession across the world. Europe—including Germany—was hit hard as credit contracted and international trade shrunk. The real crisis in Europe, however, commenced in 2009–10 as the recession induced a worsening of public finances that triggered off a gigantic crisis in the Eurozone.

1 No End to the Crisis

There is little doubt at the beginning of 2015 that the crisis of the European Economic and Monetary Union (EMU) has not gone away. Unorthodox measures by the European Central Bank, in particular its promise to do "whatever it takes" to stabilise the currency system in 2012, have calmed the financial markets and provided space for economic policy to act in a stabilising way.

However, the majority of the political players, and among them the most important ones in the large countries of the Eurozone, especially those with surpluses, are still struggling to find adequate answers to the challenges raised by the sudden appearance of huge splits and divergences in a formerly homogeneous currency system. The political discourse is dominated by the attempt to convince the deficit countries to follow the path laid down by the surplus countries. Neither the obvious fallacy of composition in policy making (i.e., that all countries taken together could replicate what a single country might be able to do), nor the threat of forcing the whole Eurozone into deflation has yet permeated through the thick

H. Flassbeck
Flassbeck-Economics, Wolfersweiler, Germany
e-mail: hflassbeck@gmail.com

A. Karasavvoglou et al. (eds.), *Economic Crisis, Development and Competitiveness in Southeastern Europe*, Contributions to Economics,
DOI 10.1007/978-3-319-40322-9_1

layers of political prejudice that have prevented a reasonable and constructive political debate among member states since the beginning of the crisis.

Nevertheless, at the level of the European institutions awareness appears to be mounting that radical changes are needed to make the system more resilient. And even beyond the traditional obsession with fiscal deficits and government debt the adoption of an early warning mechanism that could deal with the core of the trouble has proceeded quite quickly. The introduction of the Macroeconomic Imbalance Procedure (MIP), aimed at dealing with existing and future current account balances and guiding member states towards more balanced trade, has marked some progress toward understanding that a currency union requires, above all, coordination of price and wage evolution.

1.1 The Case for Monetary Cooperation

It has been argued elsewhere that monetary union in Europe was not necessarily a bad idea from the outset.[1] Its likely failure in the future would reflect, first, a lack of sound economic reasoning behind the politically motivated decision to accelerate European integration and, second, the emergence of strong economic and social interests within core countries—primarily Germany—which have hardened the disastrous path of the EMU.

The launching of EMU could be considered as the final step on the way towards lasting exchange rate stability after a long period during which the members of the European Monetary System (EMS) had attempted to operate systems of fixed but managed exchange rates. After the breakdown of Bretton Woods in 1971–3, many smaller countries across the world quite sensibly refused to adopt a system of fully flexible (market determined) exchange rates. For smaller countries in Europe, monetary cooperation has been an important way of avoiding falling victim to the vagaries of the financial markets, typically followed by the harsh 'conditionality' imposed as part of a 'rescue' delivered by the international organisations of the Washington Consensus. Most European countries, in particular the smaller ones, understood quickly that monetary independence would not necessarily be to their advantage. They recognised that for small open economies tying one's hands could be an optimal solution in monetary affairs.

In the presence of extremely volatile exchange rates, small open economies do not have monetary autonomy, because their monetary authorities are obliged to respond to the pressures of currency markets. The formal autonomy of a central bank (i.e., no obligation to intervene) lacks a material basis.[2] Obviously, countries

[1]See Flassbeck and Lapavitsas (2013).

[2]Even so, the bulk of the academic literature still relies in one way or another on the OCA-theory, or on the so-called 'policy trilemma' of open economies, i.e., their inability to achieve at once stability of the exchange rate, freedom of capital flows and monetary autonomy. In a system of floating rates the trilemma is a dilemma; see, Flassbeck (2001).

under this constraint would have to cooperate with other countries to achieve a degree of exchange-rate stability sufficient to protect their competitiveness and to allow for balanced trade relations. From the perspective of these countries the valuation of currencies is too important to be left to the market.

In the absence of cooperation, conflict would be unavoidable, as a change in one country's exchange rate would always affect another country. For *n* countries in the world as a whole there would be *n-1* exchange rates. Consequently, the crucial question would be not about the need for international monetary cooperation, which is obvious, but about viable forms of cooperation. European monetary cooperation evolved in rather small steps over a period of 30 years before culminating in the full monetary union in 1999.

All traditional forms of international monetary cooperation—other than a full monetary union—require that one of the member countries would serve as an anchor for the system. Other countries would adjust their policies in relation to the anchor country. Successful monetary cooperation aimed at enlarging the room of manoeuvre for economic policy in a region as a whole would have to include at least one country that could act as lender of last resort in times of crisis. This need arises due to the asymmetry in the relations between countries whose currencies are under threat of depreciation and those whose currencies are under pressure to appreciate. Countries trying to avoid currency depreciation (or to stop depreciation at a certain point) have to intervene in the currency market. This means their central banks have to increase demand for their own money by selling international reserves. Since such reserves are always limited, countries that are threatened by depreciation are vulnerable to speculative attacks on their currency. The only way to fend off such an attack would be cooperation with the 'other side', i.e. with country that have appreciating currencies.

In Europe, Germany was the obvious candidate to become the anchor in regional monetary cooperation. Over several decades Germany has been the champion of price stability, as witnessed, in particular, by the smooth absorption of the inflationary consequences of the two oil price shocks. As a result of low inflation, the German currency never came under depreciation pressure but always tended to be on the appreciation side. Hence, Germany assumed the role of the European monetary anchor for good reasons.

Some smaller countries were able to copy the German inflation performance and to maintain exchange rate stability without a loss of overall competitiveness. Austria was the most impressive case in this respect. Most of the larger European economies, however, time and again had to accept depreciation against the German currency to compensate for domestic inflationary bouts. This was especially true for France and Italy, at least up to the mid-1980s. Anchoring proved to be successful in terms of the effective pressure on domestic inflation as long as exchange rate adjustments remained an option to restore unsustainable competitive positions among countries.

During the period of the European Monetary System (EMS) that preceded EMU and lasted roughly from 1980 to the end of the century, fixed exchange rates in Europe were seen as a tool to foster the completion of the single European market.

In addition, Germany, with its stable economic performance and a strongly dogmatic stance on inflation, was increasingly seen as a role model for other countries. The political will to adhere to economic policies and a monetary model similar to that pursued by Germany shaped the European debate on monetary policy and exchange rates to a very large extent.

For very small and extremely open economies, the anchor approach could work for quite some time, if the anchor country's economic policy treated the small satellites in the system with benign neglect. But for any larger group of countries and for countries of similar size and economic power, the anchor approach could only be considered as a transitional stage on the way to a full monetary union. The only way to ensure a consistent monetary policy for the group as a whole would be to form a common central bank. It is important to stress, however, that the transitional phase may last very long. From the first steps toward monetary cooperation to creating the EMU, it took Europe 30 years to accomplish that logical and consequent idea.

From a global perspective, the move towards monetary union supported by a strong political will to coordinate policies provided Europe with an enormous degree of independence vis-à-vis the rest of the world, the international financial markets and international financial organisations. With an anchor strong and stable enough to weather even big international storms the group was able to fend off strong external shocks. No single country of the EMU had to call upon the IMF to overcome problems of exchange rate misalignment and/or lack of international liquidity before the 2010 crisis broke out.

One final point to mention is that command over world money is a measure of international political power, which, in the case of the Euro and due to its creditor position, means primarily German power. It ought to be stressed that the EMU was not originally a plan to promote German ascendancy, but rather a formal, treaty-based alliance establishing rights and obligations for member-states, and relying strongly on the ideology of Europeanism. Nonetheless, for reasons that are made clear below, the Euro has rebounded strongly in favour of Germany which- after the global financial crisis—has emerged as the country able to set economic and social policy across Europe as it is the main creditor. Yet, in view of the coming clash between debtors and creditors inside the Euro area, Germany's pre-eminence remains extremely fragile.

1.2 The Core Monetary Principles of the EMU

A monetary union is first and foremost a union of countries willing to give up their own national currency for the purpose of creating a common currency. Giving up a national currency implies waiving the right of the national authorities to issue coins and notes and in this way to deploy national money (fiat money). Any decision with respect to issuing money would be delegated to a supranational institution. The decision-making organs of that institution would be designed to reflect the composition of the membership, but no single country would have a majority influence. National central banks still exist within the EMU, but the power to determine monetary policy and all related decisions has been transferred exclusively to the ECB and its Executive Board.

Entering a monetary union also implies giving up national inflation targets and agreeing on a common inflation target for the union as a whole. The Deutsche Bundesbank, the anchor of the EMS and the role model for the ECB, had established monetarism, or the so-called Quantity Theory of Money, as the leading monetary doctrine in the years prior to the EMU. For a monetary union, monetarism would hold that the common central bank would be able to contain inflation across the entire union by steering the money supply and, moreover, that inflation differentials among the member countries would not occur. On this theoretical basis, the control exercised by the ECB over the money supply was deemed sufficient to hold the actual inflation rate of the EMU close to the target set by the ECB.

Even from this questionable theoretical perspective, public budget deficits, which proved to be the most hotly contested topic in the political debate, are not supposed to influence the inflation performance of the union, for there is no systematic relationship between the size of budget deficits and the rate of inflation. For monetarists, no matter how large was the budget deficit of a country, monetary policy could always attain its inflation target by strictly adhering to "objective" rules governing the expansion of the money supply.

Monetarist theory has been based on weak empirical evidence from the very beginning. Since the 1930s the monetarist dogma has mainly relied on a kind of *post-hoc ergo propter-hoc* fallacy. Monetarists have typically insisted that without more money an inflationary acceleration would not be possible. It is, of course, true that without an expanding money supply an inflationary acceleration would be impossible, but it does not at all follow that any monetary expansion would lead to an inflationary acceleration, i.e., monetary expansion is a *necessary* but not a *sufficient* condition for inflationary acceleration. To put it plainly, while more money would be necessary to inflate the economy, it would be by no means sufficient to expand the money supply to inflate the economy.

At the beginning of the 1990s this key issue of monetary policy, i.e., the capacity of the common central bank to control inflation, was not subject to much critical analysis within the EMU. Notwithstanding some controversy about the necessary degree of independence of the central bank, the overwhelming weight of opinion agreed that control over the monetary supply would be sufficient to control inflation. In this way, price instability could be avoided and the ECB would be able to replicate what was considered the splendid performance of the Bundesbank during the preceding 20 years.

With the passage of time, however, the intellectual debate gave the cold shoulder to monetarism and adopted a fresh approach to central banking, in many ways influenced by the achievements of the US Federal Reserve System under its chairman Alan Greenspan. This was not without influence on the ECB, which has from the start been a much more open and multicultural institution than the Bundesbank. Given the failure to find convincing evidence of a strong relationship between prices and the traditional money supply aggregates, the ECB gradually deviated from the doctrine of the Bundesbank (the so-called monetary pillar) and turned towards an approach in which the central bank explicitly acts by setting the short-term interest rate in light of its judgement about macroeconomic developments.

Although this approach is more amenable to testing by using methods that go beyond the traditional money supply channel, its impact was blocked by other neoliberal doctrines that proved far too strong to be rejected even in the light of clear evidence. Both the ECB and the European Commission have been dominated by neoliberal thinking during the period that led to the outbreak of the crisis in 2008. It is mainly for this reason that the ECB, as well as the other institutions founded to govern and to protect EMU, have essentially failed in the first decade. The governing institutions of the EMU began to rise from their intellectual slumber only after the global financial crisis of 2007–9 gave international investors a major jolt concerning the ability of peripheral Eurozone members to pay back the debt they had accumulated during the first 10 years of EMU.

1.3 Wage Flexibility and Its Consequences

The clearest evidence regarding the dominant role of neoliberal thinking within the institutions of the EU has been offered by labour market theory, considered to be one of the main doctrinal pillars of the functioning of the common market and the EU as a whole. The so-called Lisbon Process and a plethora of decisions taken by the European Council demonstrate the adherence to neoliberal thinking at the top of EMU. "Labour market flexibility" and "improved competitiveness" have been (and within many circles still are) the mantras guiding the creation of the common market and the attempt to accelerate growth and job creation.

It ought to be stressed that there is little empirical evidence for the theoretical belief that flexible labour markets would automatically provide jobs for all those who are willing to work. The absence of relevant evidence on this issue is as pronounced as for the other fundamental belief in the importance of controlling the money supply and guaranteeing the independence of central banks to ensure price stability. Indeed, had some different but striking evidence been taken into account, it would have been possible to prevent both the EMU and the EU from falling victim to the financial markets and from entering the current impasse. The most important piece of evidence is the high and stable correlation between the growth rate of unit labour costs (ULC) and the inflation rate.

Unit labour costs appear to be the crucial determinant of overall price movements in national economies as well as for groups of economies. Figure 1 demonstrates this simple fact, which ought to be at core of all macroeconomic reasoning but is widely ignored, usually for ideological reasons.

The cost of labour is the most important component of the total cost of production for the economy as a whole because—in vertically integrated production

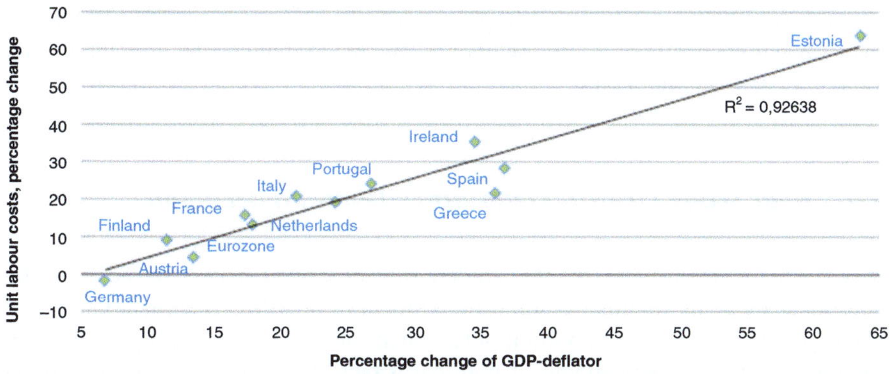

Fig. 1 ULC[1] growth rates and inflation for EMU (1999–2007)[2]. *Notes*: 1. ULC defined as gross income per capita in ECU/Euro of dependent employees divided by real GDP per total employed persons. 2. 12 countries: Belgium, Germany, Finland, France, Greece, Ireland, Italy, Luxembourg, Netherlands, Austria, Portugal, Spain. *Source*: AMECO database (as per Nov-12); own calculations

processes—labour produces final consumer goods as well as intermediate and capital goods. Unit labour costs are the perfect instrument to forecast and control inflation, especially in view of potentially strong political influence that could be exercised on wage setting and wage policy more generally. Specifically, for inflation to hit its chosen target, it would be necessary for nominal wage growth to be in line with national productivity growth plus the inflation target. Astonishingly, the doctrinaire neoliberal approach adopted by the leading institutions of the EU led to profound indifference regarding the evolution of wages and ULC over time.

If the strong correlation between ULC and inflation was acknowledged and placed at the heart of macroeconomic analysis, it would become clear that the main requirement for a successful monetary union would not be control over monetary affairs but rather the management of incomes and nominal wages. To be specific, the common inflation target for EMU was defined by the ECB as a rate close to 2 %. This implied that the *golden rule* for wage growth in each economy would be the sum of the national growth of productivity plus 2 %. By this token, large inflation discrepancies leading to competitiveness discrepancies across member countries would not occur.

There is a huge body of evidence showing that a system of fixed exchange rates could function properly only if there were wage adjustments sufficient to compensate for the loss of exchange-rate flexibility.[3] Equivalently, it has been very widely observed in systems of fixed but adjustable exchange rates that differences between domestic and international cost levels have to be corrected by changing the external value of the domestic currency (depreciation or appreciation). By this token, in a currency union the necessary adjustment of wages and prices for each member

[3]See Flassbeck (2001).

country would play an even more important role than in a system of fixed exchange rates since there would be no option of changing the exchange rate, as in the Bretton Woods system and the EMS.

1.4 Real Wage Growth Determines Domestic Demand

A wage path determined by the golden rule described above would have the additional merit of stabilising domestic demand in all EMU member states. Real wage growth is the most important determinant of domestic consumption growth, therefore systematic adjustment of nominal wages at a rate equivalent to national productivity growth plus the inflation target would stabilise domestic demand in each country, and thus demand across the union as a whole.

To eliminate the impact of unexpected and unforeseeable cyclical changes in productivity it would preferable to adjust nominal wages to the trend growth of productivity (say, average growth of productivity over the last 5 years). By taking into account the inflation *target* (rather than the actual rate of inflation) it would be possible to stabilising wage and demand growth. The reason is that short-term and one-off price shocks (for instance, sharp increases in the price of oil or other essential primary commodities) would be prevented from having a lasting inflationary impact. If, in contrast, such shocks were actually reflected in the adjustment of wages—as has been the case in backward-looking indexation mechanisms, such as the *scala mobile* in Italy in the 1970s—the rise in nominal wages would cause a rise in both ULC and the inflation rate, and would eventually command monetary tightening, i.e. the raising of interest rates, which would discourage real investment.

If wage adjustments systematically followed the golden rule, the national economies within the EMU—but also the union as a whole—would move along a stable path, led by generally stable growth of private consumption based on stable increases in incomes expected by households (at least as long as productivity growth was on a positive growth trajectory). Under these circumstances external trade would also be balanced, because the movement of ULC in tandem with the inflation target in all countries—irrespective of their national productivity paths—would imply stability of the real exchange rate, which is the most comprehensive measure of competitiveness.

It is apparent that stable growth of real wages in line with productivity growth would be in sharp contrast to the proposition that wages should be super-flexible and readily adjustable, as is envisaged by the neoclassical labour market doctrine. According to the latter, high and rising unemployment ("idiosyncratic shocks") would be impossible to cure unless wages were flexible enough to lag behind productivity for extended periods of time. Once again, however, this neoliberal this proposition is based neither on evidence nor on logic: with stable growth of domestic income (assured by the chosen adjustment path of real wages) and in the absence of external shocks that would be due to a fall in competitiveness, there would be no idiosyncratic shocks and no need at all to cut real wages.

Indeed, there are severe dangers to overly flexible labour markets. Deflationary traps are usually created by sharply rising unemployment for reasons that are unrelated to labour market developments, such as excessive increases in real wages. High unemployment as the result of a financial crisis, for example, would lead to downward pressure on wages and aggregate incomes, even if wages and incomes were depressed already before the occurrence of the crisis. The combination of high unemployment arising for such reasons together with workers trying to "price themselves flexibly back into the markets" and thus accepting lower wages would create a perfect storm for economic policy. And this is exactly what happened after the global financial crisis in 2008/2009.

With rising unemployment and renewed pressure on wages consumer spending did not recover in the way seen in former recessions. In the USA and Europe the restriction of aggregate demand caused by declining income expectations of households suffering from high levels of unemployment has dramatically prolonged the recession or stagnation. With monetary policy restricted by the lower bound of zero for interest rates, fiscal policy is needed to implement a huge stimulation programme to overcome the decline in aggregate demand in such a precarious situation. Indeed, a large part of the tendency to deflation in contemporary capitalism is the result of a dysfunctional labour market in which unemployment could rise sharply without wages being "too high". The lesson is that for a consistent critical approach to economics it is necessary to discard both the monetarist theory of inflation and the neoclassical theory of the labour market completely.

The conservative way of getting round the brutal logic of destabilising labour markets would be to hope for improved competitiveness of the economy as a whole and thus for more exports (or fewer imports). Indeed, a solution would seem to be found if a wage cut stimulated foreign demand by more than it depressed domestic demand. These conditions appear to hold for a paradoxical case such as Ireland. Given the country's export share in GDP of more than 100 %, the positive effect of wage cuts on the current account has balanced out the negative effect on domestic demand. However, Ireland is an exception and hardly relevant to normal economies, or to large groups of countries.

1.5 Real or Nominal Convergence?

It is frequently argued that countries with very different levels of wealth should not form a monetary union. Poorer countries are assumed to be incapable of competing with richer nations, and are advised to abstain from entering into a race for competitiveness. This argument, however, is not convincing.

The main analytical point in this connection is that, in any country, all groups of agents have to respect a budget restriction in making claims on the income produced in that country: no country can consume more than it produces in the long term. This is why in a normally functioning economy the claims of one group, including workers, are balanced out against the claims of other groups at a given level of total income. In an economy in which this balancing does not work, there would be a conflict over income distribution that would result in inflationary bouts and even spirals. If such an outcome was, however, avoided, the level of wages and profits would reflect exactly the level of wealth in that economy, and the wage level would reflect national productivity. Thus, low wages in the poorer countries would reflect low productivity and the opposite for rich countries.

The level of nominal unit labour costs would be the same in a poor and in a rich country, provided that in both countries a major conflict about income distribution and inflation could be avoided. Consequently, there would be no risk of large trade imbalances as a result of different levels of wealth as long as some minimum requirements regarding the structure of trade and the structure of products available to both countries would be met, meaning primarily an overlapping structure of goods produced in both countries. This was clearly the case for European countries, which had open trade relations long before entering the monetary union.

Overall, there is no reason why it should not be possible for poor as well as for rich countries to manage the ULC growth in the economy as a whole in such a way that it would be in line with a commonly agreed inflation target. This can be easily demonstrated for France and Germany in Fig. 2 below. Both countries had exactly the same starting point in terms of absolute productivity and nominal wages. However, over time nominal wages and (in this case nominal productivity) grew more in France and propelled the country into major difficulties compared to Germany, although French wages have followed a reasonable growth path never violating the golden rule for ULC growth in the monetary union:

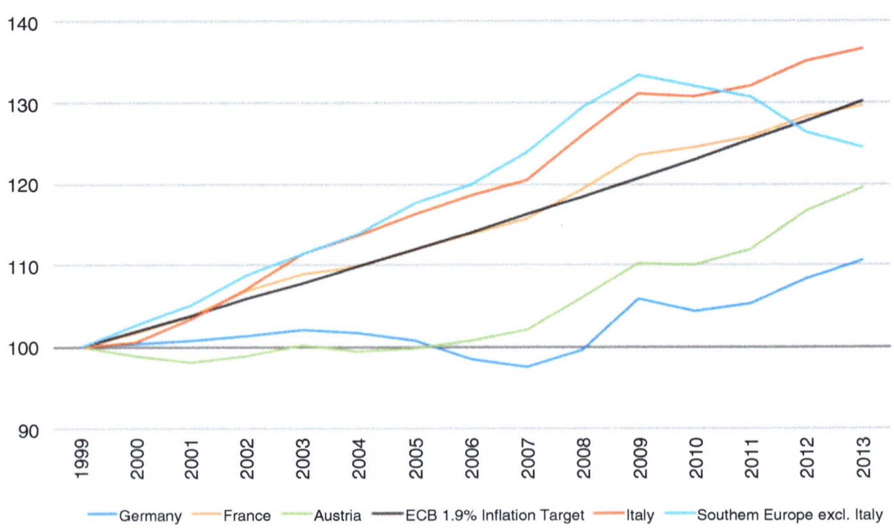

Fig. 2 ULC[1] divergence Germany and rest of EMU[2] (1999 = 100). *Notes*: 1. ULC defined as gross income per capita in ECU/Euro of dependent employees divided by real GDP per total employed persons. 2. EMU of 12 countries excluding Germany: Belgium, Finland, France, Greece, Ireland, Italy, Luxembourg, Netherlands, Austria, Portugal, Spain. *Source*: AMECO database; own calculations

The logic of a monetary union built along the lines of EMU demands that member countries must strictly accept the joint target for inflation and to preserve external equilibrium by adjusting wages to national productivity accordingly. For each country that means strict adjustment to its *own* productivity path and its *own* economic potential. Countries "living above their means" are as problematic as countries "living below their means". The requirement to live "according to its means" is as pressing as the requirement to commit to free trade for a country that enters a currency union. For, any measures to protect home-made products by imposing barriers on imports or by subsidising exports are strictly forbidden in a common market. In short, if there was no requirement to avoid "devaluation" of the real exchange rate by undercutting the inflation target through wage "moderation", the entire body of rules and regulations surrounding a monetary union would be totally useless.

1.6 Germany as the Source of the Eurozone Crisis

The preparations for EMU were deeply flawed because, instead of discussing the implications of a monetary union in detail and creating the institutions necessary to run such a union successfully, political debate and decision making in the years up to 1997—by which time the criteria for entry had to be fulfilled—actually focused on fiscal policy. Particular emphasis was laid on limiting public sector deficits to 3 % of GDP, whereas the need to avoid inflation differentials and guaranteeing the ability of member states to stick to the common inflation target over time were regarded as much less important issues for the smooth functioning of EMU. Germany, with its absolute intolerance of inflation exceeding 2 % and its dogmatic monetarist tradition, silenced any other view on inflation.

There is little doubt that the EMU obsession with fiscal targets is the direct result of the struggle between governments and markets that has dominated much of the ideological debate in the 30 years following the end of the Bretton Woods regime. Yet, there is no direct relationship between fiscal budgets and the inflation target (either empirical or theoretical) and any plausible indirect links would be very weak indeed. For, neither the current budget deficit nor the size of the public debt, has an impact on the inflationary performance of an economy. If any link could be thought of, it would be that (in line with an ancient prejudice) a highly indebted government could perhaps use inflation as a tool to reduce the real value of its debt. However, Japan during the last 25 years demonstrates that none of this holds in contemporary capitalism. With a public debt equivalent to 250 % of GDP, Japan has the highest level of public debt of all industrialised countries. And yet, despite continuous efforts, the country has not been able to get out of a deflationary trap. Japanese policymakers might dream of generating a sustainable level of inflation, but their persistent nightmare is deflation.

In the heated debate that took place in Germany about the dangers of inflationary acceleration as EMU was approached, wages or nominal unit labour costs were hardly ever mentioned. Labour costs were considered to reflect the market price for labour. The "flexibility doctrine" was the broadly accepted view in politics as well as in economics.[4] Consequently, in view of the monetary union commencing in 1999, Germany, the biggest country in the EU and the bastion of stability for several decades, decided to try out a new way of combating its high level of unemployment. In short, the government, together with the employers, started to put political pressure on labour unions in an attempt to restrict the growth of both nominal and real wages.

It ought to be stressed that Germany's vigorous attempt to tackle its persistently high unemployment rate by making its labour market more flexible was not aimed at gaining an advantage within the EMU. Rather, it was grounded in the neoliberal conviction that lower wages would result in more labour-intensive production processes across the economy. Once work-time reduction schemes had failed to deliver the expected result of reducing unemployment, labour union leaders agreed in a tripartite agreement in 1999 to abandon the formula that had hitherto been used to determine wage growth. The formula had ensured equal participation of workers in the gains from productivity growth (the golden rule mentioned above); instead, the unions agreed to "reserve productivity growth for employment".[5]

This agreement also implied that there would be a fundamental break with the German tradition of sticking to a low and stable rate of inflation. Historically, Germany had been characterised by moderate wage increases, which ensured that real wages (nominal wages adjusted for inflation) would rise in line with productivity (GDP divided by the number of hours worked). In other words unit labour costs (nominal wages divided by GDP) would generally rise in line with an inflation target of roughly 2 %. However, as monetarism became the widely accepted doctrine to tackle inflation on the approach to EMU, the new arrangement clearly meant even lower inflation, and its deflationary aspect was not even thought of.

The novel German approach to the labour market coincided with the formal introduction of the monetary union, and consequently led to huge divergences in nominal unit labour costs among the members of EMU. The main cause of these divergences was the simple fact that German nominal unit labour costs, the most important determinant of prices and competitiveness, have remained essentially flat since the start of the EMU, as is shown in Fig. 2. In contrast, most countries in southern Europe had nominal wage growth that exceeded national productivity growth plus the commonly agreed inflation target of 2 % by a small but rather stable margin. France was the only country exactly to meet the target for nominal wage growth. French wages rose in line with national productivity performance plus the ECB's inflation target of a rate close to 2 %:

Even though the annual divergence among the increases in ULC was relatively small, the dynamics of such a "small" annual divergence are able to yield dramatically large gaps over time. At the end of the first decade of EMU the cost and price

[4]The "doctrine" was clearly laid out in OECD (1994).

[5]See, Flassbeck (1997), Flassbeck and Spiecker (2005).

gap between Germany and southern Europe amounted to some 25 %, and that between Germany and France to 15 %. In other words, Germany's real exchange rate had depreciated quite significantly, even though national currencies no longer existed within the EMU. The divergence in the growth of unit labour costs was naturally reflected in equivalent price divergences. Thus, the EMU as a whole achieved the inflation target of 2 % almost perfectly, but national differences of inflation within the union were remarkable. Once again, France was by far the best performer since it succeeded in aligning its inflation rate perfectly to the EMU target. However, Germany systematically undershot the target and countries in southern Europe systematically overshot it by margins large enough to create huge gaps in competitiveness.

The cumulative gaps have meant huge absolute advantages (and thus disadvantages) in international trade for the countries of the EMU. There is little doubt about the main culprits and the extent of misbehaviour in view of the fact that the ECB's target of nearly 2 % annual inflation would only be compatible over time with a 2 % annual increase in nominal unit labour costs. Greece, for instance, was generally delinquent because annual ULC growth was roughly 2.7 %. But its violation of the rule was much less severe than that by Germany whose annual rate of ULC growth was just 0.4 %. It is even more paradoxical that Germany had explicitly agreed to the ECB target of close to 2 % because that had been its own inflation target prior to EMU. Germany was destined clearly to violate the ECB target given that its government and employers had begun to apply enormous downward pressure on wages, aiming at a different capital/labour ratio with the result of improving the country's international competitiveness.

It is undeniable that the real depreciation that has occurred in Germany has had an enormous impact on trade flows. With German unit labour costs undercutting those in the other countries by a rising margin, German exports flourished, while imports slowed down. Countries in southern Europe, but also France and Italy, began to register widening trade and current account deficits and suffered huge losses of their international markets shares. Germany, on the other hand, was able to preserve its share despite mounting global competition from China and other emerging markets. In a nutshell, Germany has operated a policy of "beggar-thy-neighbour" but only after "beggaring its own people" by essentially freezing wages.[6] This is the secret of German success during the last 15 years.

While trade within Europe had been rather balanced at the inception of the currency union and for many years before that, the EMU marked the beginning of a period of quickly growing imbalances. Even after the shock of the financial crisis and its devastating effects on global trade that are clearly visible in the German balance, the underlying trend has continued unchanged. Germany's current account has continued to rise after 2010 and even reached a new record high in 2013 (2014 will also see a current account surplus in the order of 200 billion euros or a number of close to 7 % of GDP). While the surpluses relative to the members of the

[6]See, Lapavitsas et al. (2012), pt. I.

Eurozone culminated in 2007 the surplus relative to the rest of the world increased quickly after the financial crisis.

It is obvious that immediately after the Eurozone crisis had burst out and the economies of stricken countries had began to falter, German exporters reoriented their efforts toward the rest of the world and achieved similar surpluses in those markets—still protected by the euro. With a huge accumulated margin of competitiveness in their favour and protected by the relatively low Euro exchange rate (with the exception of a few months in 2014) they could easily gain, again at the expense of other Euro members, market shares in the rest of the world. Chinese demand for automobiles in particular was the most important reason for the surge in exports.

Empirical studies sometimes fail to find evidence for an influence of prices or unit labour costs on trade flows and the current account balance.[7] This is typically due to misspecification of the study or to the uncritical use of country samples and time periods. If, for example, a study also included very small and highly specialised countries, such as Ireland or Cyprus, or poor transitional economies, such as the Baltics, the results are likely to be problematic. The production structure of these countries could not be reasonably compared to countries such as France and Germany with their highly diversified industrial base. Strong objections could also be raised against including in the sample a country such as the Netherlands, which has engaged in the German kind of "beggar-thy-neighbour" policies long before German, and was thus able to defend its current account surplus despite its unit labour cost rising more than in Germany since the beginning of EMU.

Moreover, when choosing the period of empirical analysis, it has to be taken into account that the deep recession in the deficit countries of the EMU following the financial crisis of 2008 has naturally tended to reduce the observed deficits through huge income effects that temporarily overlaid the price effects. But it is unlikely that recovery would take place in those countries without a fundamental improvement in competitiveness. The eventual revival of domestic demand, moreover, would probably bring deficits in the current account quickly back to the fore and thus restrain future growth. Even in Greece that has been devastated by the crisis and the policies imposed on it by the EU, there are signs that current account deficits are returning in 2014, i.e., as soon as the economy's contraction had ceased.

Pursuing the issue further, Figure 3 shows that among the core countries and the biggest traders of the EMU the relationship between ULC and the current account during the critical period from 1999 to 2007 is both clearly visible and negative.

The relationship would be even stronger if, instead of ULC, the movement of prices (i.e., the GDP deflator) was compared to the movement of the current account, as is shown in Fig. 4 below.

The countries included in both of these figures account for close to 80 % of overall EMU trade (internal and external). Furthermore, for Italy and France the most important competitor inside and outside EMU is Germany. To assume that an

[7]See, for instance, Gabrisch and Staehr (2014).

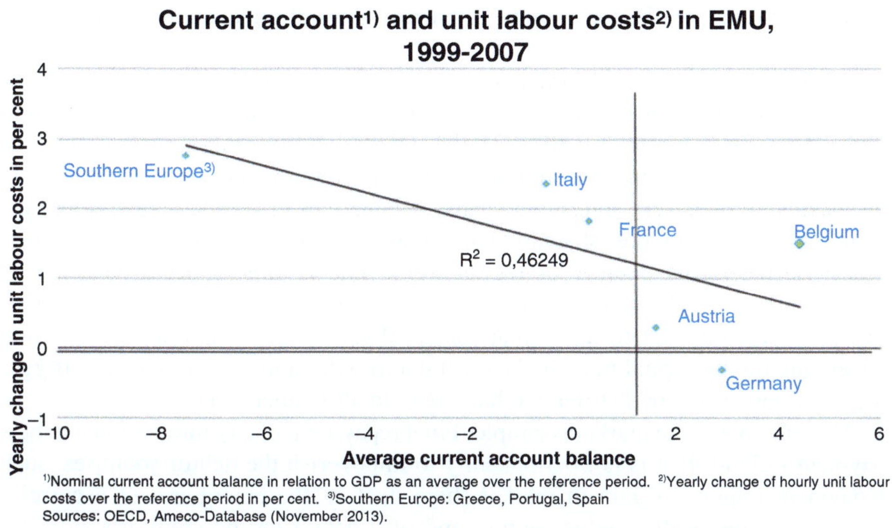

Fig. 3 Trade imbalances, prices and wages

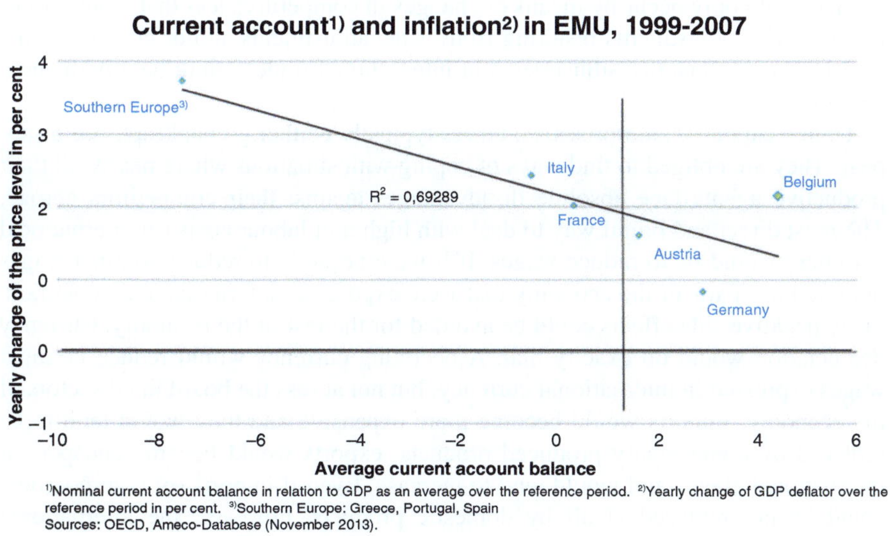

Fig. 4 Current account and inflation. *Note*: Negative values represent a current account deficit. *Source*: AMECO database (as per Nov-12); own calculations

accumulated price difference of 20–30 %, such as taken place since the start of the EMU, would not influence trade to the benefit of Germany is complete nonsense. The conclusion that "The developments in unit labour costs are endogenous and partly determined by capital flows. This may suggest that the Euro Plus Pact may have limited ability to impact unit labour costs and even if possible, this may have little effect on a possible emergence of current account imbalances", is absolutely unjustified.[8]

Finally, the need to avoid imbalances within in a currency union is not mainly about current account deficits and surpluses *per se* in a clearly defined period of time. The point is, rather, that absolute and cumulative advantages of one country or a group of countries against a similar country or group of countries are definitively unsustainable over very long time spans. A huge gap in competitiveness and the resulting losses in market shares would have to be closed at some point, because otherwise the losing country or region would find it impossible to persuade its lenders that it would be able to repay its debts at some point in the future. Whether this point will be reached in 20 years or in 40 years is not important for a nation depending on the capital market. The fact that it will happen is sufficient to trigger the reactions of the market that we have seen in all financial crises.

The calculus of the market is simple: Final repayment of any international debt is payment in kind. If it is not permanently to impoverish the debtor countries, such repayment requires a gain in market share, that is, the emergence of a current-account surplus in the debtor country and of a deficit on the creditor's side. An indebted country could only service and repay its debt over time if the surplus country allowed the deficit country to begin to register surpluses at some point. The change could only occur by means of changes in competitiveness that would occur through price adjustments resulting from wage adjustments and/or changes in the exchange rate. Quantity adjustments in international trade cannot be a permanent solution.

Unlike capitalist enterprises, countries typically neither go bankrupt, nor disappear. They are obliged to find ways of coping with situations where nearly all their productive agents face absolute disadvantages against their competitors abroad. The most direct and brutal way to deal with high unit labour costs (in international currency) would be to reduce wages. If it were possible to reduce nominal wages only in those parts of the economy that were exposed to international competition, many negative side effects could be avoided for the rest of the economy. Currency depreciation would do exactly that. A declining currency would reduce nominal wages expressed in international currency, but not across the board in all sectors of the economy. Imports would become more expensive and they would tend to be replaced by domestically produced products; exports would become cheaper for international clients and would tend to increase. Even if imports (of commodities) could be not replaced at all by domestic products, however, the international adjustment of wages would be unavoidable to allow the country to buy the necessary imports through its own exports.

[8]See, Gabrisch and Staehr (2014).

1.7 Germany Has to Adjust

It is plausible to argue (even by someone sympathetic to the views expressed in this book) that, for Germany, the strategy to contain domestic nominal wage growth was not motivated primarily by competition inside EMU but rather with emerging economies, in particular the rising industrial power of China. It might even be added that this strategy was fully in line with the general orientation of the European Union for several years, urging its members to improve their competitiveness.

Although these arguments would be intuitively attractive, they would be fallacious because they would overlook, once again, the crucial importance of the strong and stable relationship between the growth rate of unit labour costs and the inflation rate, on the one hand, and the growth rate of real wages and domestic demand, on the other. Under no circumstances should a monetary union trying to achieve an inflation rate of 2 % allow one of its member countries (particularly the biggest one) to go its own way in terms of ULC development and inflation. If Europe felt that there was a challenge from emerging markets, which had to be addressed at the macroeconomic level, it could have chosen a lower inflation rate (or even deflation) as the target of its common monetary policy. However, in that case, the exchange rate of the Euro against the Chinese Yuan, or the US Dollar, would have reflected sooner or later the lower inflation in Europe, thus destroying the advantage that Europe would have tried to obtain by pursuing a lower inflation target.

In a world of floating or adjustable exchange rates no country could gain a permanent advantage against another country, if the latter had the option of adjusting its exchange rate in accordance with inflation differentials. This means that all attempts to improve competitiveness by cutting or moderating wages for the EMU as a whole would be useless. And yet, this is precisely the approach that Europe has chosen as a way forward after the crisis. This is deeply misguided also because in most European debtor countries wage cuts would lead to severe falls in domestic demand, which is more important than external demand. In economies with an export share in GDP that was far below 50 %, wage restraint strategies would be counterproductive, since there would not be a realistic prospect of achieving a huge current account surplus over a lengthy period of time, and nor would it be possible to raise the export share in GDP beyond the 50 % mark without suffering retaliation from trading partners. Under normal circumstances, it would therefore be impossible to successfully emulate the strategy followed by Germany during the first 10 years of EMU.

Even more important than these general objections regarding German strategy, however, would be the dynamics of the overall economy. In a monetary union, a country with a low export share and facing a huge current-account deficit and financing problems due to an implicitly overvalued currency would be trapped. Downward adjustment of wages, sometimes erroneously called "internal devaluation", would be no solution as it would destroy both domestic demand and output before it could bring some relief through rising exports.

Furthermore, countries with a huge gap of competitiveness against Germany would have to go through an extended period of catching-up in terms of price competitiveness. There would be neither rapid gains in international market share, nor a lasting improvement in the current-account position, since Germany's absolute advantage would remain intact as long as the competitiveness gap was not turned into the opposite, i.e. an absolute advantage of the deficit countries. Figure 1 has already shown that deficit countries have to dive below the German UCL path for a long time to regain some of the losses they have experienced in the first 10 years of EMU.

The Achilles heel of this adjustment process is its duration. A democratic country could not possibly sustain 5–10 years of falling living standards and rising unemployment. The economic, social and political costs would be tremendous, as is made clear for Greece in this book. The process would result in social upheaval, including desperate attempts by the people to use elections to prevent what would be in their eyes a frivolous attack on their well-being.

This is why the adjustment process within the EMU would have to symmetric at the very least. This means that the country that has implicitly undervalued its exchange rate—Germany—would have to engage in a strong effort of upward adjustment, i.e. faster wage increases, while other countries would undertake a slowly downward adjustment. The most reliable yardstick for the success of the adjustment efforts on both sides would be the inflation target again. If the common inflation target was not questioned, to restore the deficit countries' international competitiveness it would be necessary to raise ULC and inflation in the surplus country up to the point where external balance on both sides over the entire life of the monetary union (the first 10 years included) would be achieved. It is enough merely to state this requirement to make its extraordinary difficulty absolutely apparent.

1.8 EMU Heads to Disaster

At the beginning of 2014 unemployment in the EU stood at more than 12 %. In Spain and Greece unemployment exceeded 25 %, while youth unemployment was above an extraordinary 55 %. More than anything else these figures show the failure of the EU tackle the problem that has emerged as the "Eurozone crisis". Indeed, while the dramatic drop in growth and employment was first caused by the global crisis of 2007–9, after 2010 the debtor nations of the EMU were deprived of the means of fighting the recession and were forced to adopt pro-cyclical policies of a scale that was last seen in the 1930s.

The German mantra of "austerity as the only solution" was applied to all countries that were forced to ask for help when their access to the global capital markets ceased, or was blocked de facto by very high interest rates.[9] Once again, obsession with apparent fiscal problems dominated the debate and the conditions

[9]See, Schäuble (2011).

that were demanded by the troika and the Eurogroup to open the coffers of the creditor nations focused on consolidating the public budgets of deficit countries at any price and as quickly as possible.

With German dominance over export markets persisting and given Germany's refusal to adjust its own economic model the future looks bleak for the Eurozone. The lack of policy instruments to tackle the recession, the conditionality attached to the adjustment programmes imposed on the crisis economies, the dysfunctional "structural" adjustment itself and the prospect of looming deflation have raised the costs of remaining within the EMU up to the point where political upheaval on the right threatens democracy and the EU. Failure to address the rate of unemployment and rising poverty has paved the way for radical right-wing and populist anti-European parties in creditor as well as in debtor countries. Against this danger, the benefits of being a member of the EMU are small and, more importantly, they are shrinking fast.

The disintegration of the capital markets in the EMU following the financial crisis has drastically reduced the benefits of belonging to the monetary union and accepting a common monetary policy. Nearly 5 years after the outbreak of the Eurozone crisis things have not changed significantly. The return of Ireland, Spain and Greece to the capital markets came at an incredibly high price, the countries having had to pay a very high rate of interest on their bonds considering that they were in recession and deflation. But even worse has been the historically unprecedented costs of the adjustment that they have had to accept to reach that point. Furthermore, the limited ability to raise funds in the capital market has not removed the constraints on domestic economic policy. For Greece in particular, and as is shown in detail in the last chapter of this book, neither fiscal policy nor any other normal economic tool is available to stimulate an economy that has gone through a great depression. At the same time, monetary conditions (interest rates and real exchange rates) are clearly worse in the deficit than in the surplus countries. Record low interest rates on government bonds in the surplus countries have laid the ground for easy consolidation of their budgets, while benign monetary conditions might begin to stimulate their economies.

For the EMU as a whole, applying "structural reforms" simultaneously to the labour markets of several countries has entailed a dramatic drop in domestic demand, and contributed to a collapse of trade flows. The effect of wage cutting in countries where domestic demand strongly exceeds foreign demand (in France, Italy, Portugal and Spain domestic demand amounts to three quarters of total demand; by contrast, in Ireland the export share of GDP is more than 100 %) has directly reduced aggregate demand. In this way, the imposed wage cuts have directly increased unemployment rather than, as the troika expected, reducing it.

Consequently, there has been a remarkably strong correlation between the adjustment demanded by the troika and economic decline in peripheral EMU countries. The more closely countries have followed the troika prescription, the more their economies have shrunk and even collapsed. France and Italy have experienced a strong deceleration of growth even with unchanged wage growth (and growth in ULC). But all countries that have actually undergone the troika "treatment" since 2010 have faced stunning decline.

Paradoxically, those countries that have gone quite a way toward improving their competitiveness by reducing wages offer the final proof that this exactly the wrong way to proceed. Indeed it is even worse than that: the brutal logic of the adjustment imposed on some smaller countries has meant that the others, including France and Italy, could not apply it without risking major political destabilisation. If France and Italy went the way of the troika, it is almost certain that the entire Eurozone would be thrown into depression resulting in a sharp drop of prices and long-lasting deflation.

It is hard to imagine that the democratic regimes in these countries would survive such an event. It is even likely that radical parties of the Right would become dominant by campaigning against Europe and the Euro. On the other hand, if France and Italy do not adjust, their economies would be destroyed in terms of competitiveness making it impossible to prosper on the basis of balanced trade. Their deficits on current account would keep on growing putting their entire economic edifice in jeopardy. But then, if France and Italy did not apply the troika adjustment programme and Germany did not change its stance, the end of the Euro as a common currency would be only a question of time.

In short, the accumulated divergences during the first years of the EMU and the terrible nature of the adjustment programmes have put the very survival of the EU in question. And yet, European policy makers appear to be oblivious to this fact. They are even less willing to engage in a policy effort to turn around the overall economy and to stop the growing divergences within the EMU. The prospect of disintegration and eventual collapse of the union can no longer be ignored.

References

Flassbeck H (1997) Und die Spielregeln für die Lohnpolitik in einer Währungsunion? Frankfurter Rundschau (31/10/1997), p 12

Flassbeck H (2001) The exchange rate: economic policy tool or market price? UNCTAD Discussion papers 157

Flassbeck H, Spiecker F (2005) Die deutsche Lohnpolitik sprengt die Europäische Währungsunion. WSI-Mitteilungen 58(12):707–713

Flassbeck H, Lapavitsas C (2013) The systemic crisis of the euro: true causes and effective therapies. Rosa Luxemburg Stiftung Studien. http://www.Rosalux.de/fileadmin/rls_uploads/pdfs/Studien/Studien_The_systemic_crisis_web.pdf

Gabrisch H, Staehr K (2014) The Euro plus pact. Cost competitiveness and external capital flows in the EU Countries. Working Paper series Nr. 1650, European Central Bank

Lapavitsas C, Kaltenbrunner A, Lambrinidis G, Lindo D, Meadway J, Michell J, Painceira JP, Powell J, Pires E, Stenfors A, Teles N, Vatikiotis L (2012) Crisis in the Eurozone. Verso, London

OECD (1994) The OECD jobs study. OECD, Paris

Schäuble W (2011) Why austerity is the only cure for the Eurozone. Financial Times (05/09/2011)

Economic Crisis and National Economic Competitiveness: Does Labor Cost Link the Two? The Case of the South Eurozone States

Dimitrios Kyrkilis, Georgios Makris, and Konstantinos Hazakis

Abstract A widely accepted thesis, especially by international organizations and economic policy practitioners is that national economic competitiveness is determined by the unit labor cost, prescribing a policy of wage reductions, i.e. internal devaluation for improving national economic competitiveness. The current paper disputes this thesis arguing that it is based on theoretical and methodological misconceptions and oversimplifications, misinterpreting the Ricardo's comparative advantage model, especially the source of comparative advantages. The Kaldor's paradox supports in empirical terms the arguments put forward in this paper. Equally important, the paper argues that national economic competitiveness is related to the functional income distribution. It analyses the relationship between gross profits and productive investments, and it applies the conclusions of the analysis to the euro zone southern countries.

1 Introduction

There is a widely spread view among economic theoreticians and policy makers that the unit labour cost best accounts for national economic competitiveness. It is argued that decreasing unit labour costs (ULCs) indicates improving national economic competitiveness. This argument reached momentum soon after the beginning of the euro area debt crisis as many economists argued that workers in Greece, Ireland, Italy, Portugal, and Spain are too expensive, compared to wages in

D. Kyrkilis (✉) • G. Makris
Department of Balkan, Slavic and Oriental Studies, University of Macedonia, 156 Egnatia Str, 540 06 Thessaloniki, Greece
e-mail: kyrkilis@uom.gr; gmakris@uom.gr

K. Hazakis
Department of Economics, Democritus University of Thrace, University Campus, 691 00 Komotini, Greece
e-mail: kmhazaki@otenet.gr

A. Karasavvoglou et al. (eds.), *Economic Crisis, Development and Competitiveness in Southeastern Europe*, Contributions to Economics,
DOI 10.1007/978-3-319-40322-9_2

competitor countries leading to losses of export shares, and deteriorating current account deficits.

The current paper supports the view that the deterioration of current account imbalances, increasing public budget deficits, and mounting public debts for certain euro zone member countries are not mere consequences of the national fiscal policy mismanagement but they reflect low and deteriorating international economic competitiveness. The latter, however, is founded on a number of structural determinants that are favourable to investment activity and technological change that in turn boost productivity and, ultimately competitiveness but not simply on labour cost. Countries of low economic competitiveness suffer from certain structural deficiencies which, in the context of the euro zone are realised as structural divergence vis-à-vis more successful countries. It is these structural divergence which one implicitly refers to when the euro zone is divided into Core and Periphery economies acknowledging that the first group is far more competitive than the second one. Nicholas Kaldor (1978a) was amongst the first to stress the importance of structural factors in determining the competitiveness of a country's performance in international competition highlighting, for example, product quality, technological innovation as well as the geographical orientation of exports affecting the income and price elasticities of demand for imports and exports.

The efficient operation of a common currency area presupposes that adjustments through flexible independent exchange rates are replaced by other adjustment mechanisms. The theory of optimal currency areas (OCA) underlines such mechanisms (a) flexibility in wages so as to align unit labour costs with international competitiveness, (b) significant cross border labour mobility, (c) federal fiscal institutions to provide insurance against asymmetric shocks, and (d) operational fiscal rules to limit negative spillovers of national fiscal policies on other member states.[1]

OCA analysis stresses that there should be a high degree of homogeneity among the states making up a currency area. Since monetary union includes the absence of national autonomy over monetary policy including exchange rates, the homogeneity condition ensures that member states are equally affected by external shocks (including financial shocks) and that none are unduly destabilized by the imposition of centralised monetary area policies as far as it concerns the interest rate, exchange rate and national budgetary balance. Homogeneity requirement is fulfilled by three conditions: symmetry, flexibility and integration.[2] Under the symmetry condition, economies should be roughly similar and synchronized, so that shocks are symmetrical in the sense that if, for example, a negative demand shock takes place, all the member states are affected in the same way—that is, are equally vulnerable—and all are equally affected by any central currency area policies. McKinnon (1963) underlines comparable degrees of "economic openness" (ratio of tradable goods production to non tradable goods production) insisting that if the states making up a

[1]See Mundell (1961), McKinnon (1963) and Kenen (1969).

[2]See De Grauwe (2012).

currency union have similar degrees of openness, shocks will be broadly symmetric. Kenen (1969), argues that homogeneity is attained through 'structural diversity' (diversity of exports) within the states of a single currency area since diversification limits idiosyncratic shocks. Mundell (1961) argues that optimality relates to the state of the labor market. Exchange rates can be fixed between states and regions when labour moves freely between them.

The lack of an automatic fiscal stabilization mechanism as well as limited geographical mobility of factors enforces the asymmetry of demand and supply shocks across the regions making up a currency area. Increased asymmetry in economic shocks across regions means that a common monetary policy is less able to smooth over the shocks across the entire area and it can greatly deteriorate conditions in some regions, given that the latter cannot use independent monetary policies for stabilization. In the absence of OCA fundamental traits (i.e. cross-border labor mobility and the lack of a federal fiscal transfer mechanism), monetary union could increase vulnerability of regions to idiosyncratic shocks through increased regional specialization and agglomeration. According to Krugman (1993) both theory and US historical experience suggest that the EU regions would become increasingly specialized as a result of monetary integration, and that as they became more specialized so they would become more vulnerable to region-specific shocks.

National competitiveness problems within the euro zone and taking into account that currency devaluation, one of the most powerful policies for restoring competitiveness is not feasible because of monetary union terms, it is proposed to be solved through the implementation of an internal devaluation policy. Internal devaluation includes a substantial fall in domestic ULCs relative to those of trading partners through a decline in relative wages or/and rises in labor productivity and other non-price adjustments (i.e. those linked to product quality). More specifically, a state can ameliorate its price competitiveness by reducing real or nominal wages with positive effects on its exports and aggregate demand. This makes easier a reallocation of resources from the production of non-tradable goods to tradable goods, which is needed to achieve full employment within a tighter external funding constraint. With no option of nominal exchange rate adjustment within a currency union, economies need to attain an internal devaluation to fill output gaps and lower unemployment rates through the reinforcement of their tradable sectors, including more exports and fewer imports. This guarantees that once financing constraints are absent, current accounts will not deteriorate again. However, empirical evidence from past policy attempts suggest that attaining internal devaluations can be a long and difficult process in an economy characterized by wage rigidities.[3]

The paper questions the efficiency of this policy option underlining the theoretical misconceptions of the unit labour cost perception as the main determinant of national economic competitiveness. Instead, it argues that the unit labour cost should be related with investment activity taking into consideration the functional

[3]See Alesina and Perotti (1997), and Alesina and Ardagna (1998).

income distribution of the economy. Empirical evidence from the south euro zone countries where internal devaluation was implemented as an antidote to the financial crisis, clearly demonstrate that internal devaluation policies fails to enforce investment flows but it contributes to economic recession, initially triggered by fiscal consolidation policies and it is associated with significant unemployment increases and business shutdown[4] contributing further to economic recession. Overall, such a policy creates a recessionary spiral that leads to deflation and a serious decline of national income both undermining the business and investment climate.

Unit labour cost is estimated by the use of an index constructed on the basis of aggregate data, i.e. the ratio of total in the economy labour remuneration over total domestic output. Such construction is inefficient since aggregate data is not the weighted average of individual company and/or sector unit labour costs. The use of aggregate data conceals structural changes in the economy. Often rising unit labour cost at the firm and/ or sector level reflects labour productivity advances at the respective level or it may be due to shortages in the respective labour and/or labour skill market segment, especially in cases of increasing labour demand as a result of technological change. There is no reason to believe that the rest of the economy follows similar trends. The overall ULC may rise if the sectors and /or firms experiencing such trends weigh overwhelmingly to the total economy or it may decline or stagnate if the remaining sectors weigh more significantly. In any case, asymmetric trends between sectors of an economy are not revealed by a uniform ULC. Besides, a Balassa- Samuelsson effect is a non rarely observed phenomenon. In this case the distinction between tradable and non-tradable sectors is required given that wages in the tradable sectors is more possible to rise due to technological change, therefore they are aligned to the international competitiveness of the economy than in the case of the non-tradable sectors where wages rise due rather to increasing domestic demand triggered by higher incomes in the tradable sectors than to increasing productivity, therefore there are not supposed to adjust according to the economy's external competitiveness.

In addition, aggregate unit labour cost mirrors the distribution of national income between capital and labour. Distribution of income affects aggregate demand and investment functions. Investment in turn affects competitiveness. The paper argues that real unit labor cost (RULC) instead is a more accurate estimator of national income distribution, hence a more relevant indicator of competitiveness However, RULC does not manage to overcome the methodological shortcomings of ULC and it fails to take into account the structure of the economy and its changes limiting its potential as a guideline for macroeconomic policy design.

The paper proceeds as following. Section 2 examines the theoretical roots of the unit labour cost as the competitiveness main determinant and it tries to present the

[4]To the extent that wages are rigid downwards and the labour market is not perfectly flexible wage cuts may be achieved through massive unemployment.

theoretical misconceptions related to the argument. Section 3 analyses the concept of competitiveness and it elaborates methods of measuring it. Section 4 provides a comparative overview of the internal devaluation programs implemented in the south euro zone countries and their outcomes, while Sect. 5 concludes and provides policy implications.

2 Theoretical Roots

A. Marshall (2013) complemented the Ricardian concept of comparative advantages applicable in determining international trade flows with the concept of real cost. In Marshall's view, although prices are determined by demand and supply, labour cost contributes significantly to the supply conditions, therefore it contributes to the determination of prices. To the extent that prices contribute to determining both competitiveness and the terms of trade labour cost is a determinant of them too.

This view suffers from serious misconceptions that exist in two levels. First, in the determinants of comparative advantages. Second, in the definition of economic competitiveness.

In David Ricardo's paradigm the concept of comparative advantages[5] is seen on a bilateral basis. Two commercial partner countries differ in the number of homogeneous physical labour units required for the manufacturing of one physical unit of a product, i.e. labour productivity. Labour productivity differs not only between countries but also between sectors within the same country. A country, although it may supply all goods it specialises in the exporting of goods where it enjoys relatively higher labour productivity compared to the one in the partner country. Accordingly, «The absolute production costs are insignificant internationally, only comparative production costs matter» (Schumacher 2013).

Ricardo grounds his concept of comparative advantages on the classical principle that labour is the only factor that produces value, hence output, labour is an homogeneous production factor, but the opportunity cost of labour differs across sectors and countries. Therefore, labour productivity differs both across sectors within the same country and across countries within the same sector. Different labour productivity means different production functions, therefore different technology inputs across sectors and countries. Finally, different technology inputs means different investment profiles across sectors and countries.

According to Ricardo, production in the two commercial partner countries uses different ratios of labour per unit of output requirements denoted by different labour opportunity costs in each country that reflect different labour productivities which in turn are determined by technological differences in the two countries. Although, the Ricardian analysis underlines the importance of labor requirements per unit of

[5]See Ricardo (1911).

output, hence of unit labour costs as a critical element of comparative advantages and consequently of competitiveness, it is equally true that Ricardo sees the real source of comparative advantages in technological differences which determine labour productivity differentials across countries. Finally, it is labour productivity and its international differentials that determine labour requirements per unit of output, therefore unit labour costs and, ultimately its differences across countries. Consequently, the critical element of comparative advantages, and thus of competitiveness is not labour cost but technology. The latter determines, through labour productivity the per unit of output labour requirements, and it forms the ground on which production capabilities may be build. Furthermore, it is easy to understand that, to the extent that technological change is not frequent and it requires time, in the short and medium term labor productivity is the key term for international trade specialisation and competitiveness; and it imposes the need for labour cost changes to align with labour productivity and its deviations (Felipe 2005). Evidently, if labour costs are connected with labour productivity there is no reason to expect that labor wage reductions would lead to sustainable improvements in the international competitiveness of a country. An exception may be the case where lower wages at given unit of output labour requirements lead to higher profits[6] and through them to higher capital intensive investment activity, thus to higher labour productivity. However, low wages favour *ceteris paribus* the substitution of capital with labour leading to a rather opposite effect.

In the neoclassical tradition value is created by the coordination of labour and capital, and the determination of the production factor prices is considered to be an integral part of the price system within a general equilibrium framework. The production factors remuneration tends to become equal to their respective marginal productivity rates. On the contrary, Ricardo favours the production factors remuneration to be subject to a rather institutional arrangement, such an arrangement could be a system of negotiations between the two factors, but certainly not subject to the neoclassical principle of marginal productivity. In any case, the demand of labour is a function of its real price, i.e. nominal wages in relation to the price level. Therefore, it may be argued that unit labour costs *per se* do not really matter but it is their relation with prices, hence the margin from revenues they allow to be allocated to capital as income, i.e. profits that enters into the function of cost determination and the choice of technology, i.e. labour vs. capital intensive production, ultimately of choosing investment profiles and competitiveness. The simple unit labour cost index is rather inadequate to show any impact the lowering of wages may have on profits.

The dominant international trade neoclassical paradigm is that of Heckscher–Ohlin (H–O), which underlines the abundance of factors of production in a country

[6]Ricardo, perceived profits and labor wages to act complementary to income distribution and suggested that imports of low cost products which are the main consumption of workers will definitely lead to income distribution in favor of capital. However, he didn't link this crucial element with the theory of comparative advantage (Gomes 2003).

relative to another and thus drops out the criterion of relative cost. While many of the Ricardo's statements are used in this approach the fact that two factors of production, i.e. labour and capital are included in the analysis results to a country's trade specialization according to which factor of production is in abundance.[7] Technology used in production is considered to be identical in the countries involved in international trade. More recent approaches tried to extent the H–O paradigm.[8] The Stolper–Samuelson theorem for example, suggests that there will be significant implications on the functional distribution of income under conditions of free trade. More specifically, if a country exports capital intensive goods there will be an income rise for this factor of production relative to prices of goods while labour income will decline, something which does not take place if the basis of analysis is the Ricardian paradigm. Moreover, according to the theorem of factors of production price equalization, in case of small differences between two countries factors of production (focusing on the same product), there will be a trend for complete equalization of factors of production returns (under the condition that free trade takes place with zero transportation cost). As in the Ricardian model, the H–O paradigm considers trade benefits to be more important the greater the two countries differences in factors of production are. However, as the Ricardian model supports, prices are determined in real terms and not in currency units. The main handicap of all versions of H–O is considered to be the elasticity of factors of production substitution within the involved countries (Minhas 1962) and the constant economies of scale.

New theories of international trade after Second World War focused mainly on trade flows between developed countries contradict both the classical and the neo-classical traditions of international trade. It is evident that in many cases there is no rising trade specialization (but reduced trade specialization) as well as that exports are taking place in many sectors often through intra-industry as opposed to inter-industry trade (Ethier 1982). Empirical verifications of these trends are well known and include among others seminal papers those of Smith (1994), Rodriguez and Rodrik (2000) and Rodrik (2001/2).

New trade theory eloquently analyzed by Dixit and Norman (1980), Lancaster (1980), Krugman (1979, 1980, 1981), Helpman (1981) and Ethier (1982) is not based on perfect completion or constant economies of scale and suggests that trade flows take place within an economic environment characterized by economic protection, imperfect market competition, dynamic economies of scale, and product differentiation. Technology and technological change in conjunction with demand patterns return to the analysis as the basis of comparative advantages, trade specializations, and competitiveness undermining the effectiveness of unit labour costs

[7]This conclusion was empirically questioned by V. Leontief and led to a significant refutation of H–O paradigm especially on the hypothesis of identical factors of production intensity between the two countries and consequently in derived relative price differences. For further analysis see Kwok and Yu (2005).

[8]For a critical overview of these theories see Chacholiades (1990).

and prices as determinants of trade flows. However, the question remains. Are the new theories really new attempts to interpret contemporary international trade flows or, as in the H–O paradigm they are an effort to test static theories of perfect resource distribution under free trade terms ignoring unequal development results between countries? (Darity and Davis 2005).

3 The Concept of Competitiveness

There are multiple approaches to the issue of competitiveness that may lead to analytical mistakes and wrong policies (Krugman 1994). A fundamental distinction not taken into account in many analyses is the one between competitiveness at the firm level and competitiveness at the national level. At the firm level competitiveness may be seen as a function of prices, hence of the production factors remuneration.

At the national level the issue of competitiveness takes many different readings. National competitiveness may be analysed under Porter's diamond of national competitive advantages approach (Porter 1990). National competitiveness may be related to national productivity; therefore it may be defined as the aggregation of institutions, policies, practices, and behaviours that determine productivity (World Economic Forum 2010).

National competitiveness may be considered as a function of technology and innovation under the approach of endogenous growth theories.[9] This relation is specified by the notion of "National Systems of Innovation" (NSI) defined as «the network of institutions in the public and private sectors whose activities and interactions initiate, import, modify and diffuse new technologies» (Freeman 1995).

National competitiveness may be approached as a function of institutional arrangements and through the theory of economic convergence, which may be achieved on the basis of "social capability", i.e. the ability of a country to absorb and utilise new technologies that is a function of many structural factors such as education, technological skills and capabilities, and the business organisation culture (Abramovitz 1986).

However, the failure to distinguish national economic competitiveness from that at the firm level has led to the prevalence of the view that national competitiveness is determined by the price level that in turn is determined by the unit labour cost in an effort of the economy to achieve a simultaneous internal and external equilibrium, i.e. an equilibrium between the non-accelerating inflation rate of unemployment (NAIRU) and the desired current account balance. This equilibrium may be mirrored at the real exchange rate of the national currency. International

[9]See papers of Romer (1986, 1987), Lucas (1988) and Frankel and Rose (1998, 2001). For an extensive overview of literature see Mongelli (2002).

commercial partners are compared on the basis of price levels therefore on their relative unit labour cost. That approach fails to take into account that inflation rates are not solely defined by labour cost but by economic and institutional efficiency, market structures, demand patterns, etc. It also fails to understand that labour is not homogeneous, the labour market is highly augmented by labour skills, therefore wages and hence labour cost should be seen as a structure rather as an aggregate number.

Contrary to the predictions of this "macroeconomic" approach to the issue of national economic competitiveness Kaldor (1978b) argued that in the period 1963–1975 countries that have achieved the higher growth rates of both their international trade shares and their national incomes were the countries with the higher growth rates of their unit labour cost. Fagerberg (1996) confirmed Kaldor's paradox for the period 1978–1994.

Felipe (2007) in an effort to see labour cost as a structural variable argues that the latter "... embodies the "social relations" of production that affect the distribution of income between the social classes." If this argument is accepted the ULC index may be replaced by the real unit labour cost index (RULC) which as a matter of fact approaches the income distribution between labour and capital. Indeed, RULC is constructed as the ratio between "...compensation per employee in current prices and labour productivity, i.e. gross domestic product (GDP) per employment in current prices ...(therefore, RULC) shows how the remuneration of employees is related to the productivity of their labour. It is the relationship between how much each "worker" is paid and the value he/she produces by their work. Its growth rate is intended to give an impression of the dynamics of the participation of the production function labour in output value created. Please note that the variables used in the numerator (compensation, employees) refer to employed labour only while those of the denominator (GDP, employment refer to all labour included self employed" (Eurostat 2015). Although RULC measures the labour's GDP share it suffers from the aggregation problems discussed earlier in reference with the unit labour cost. OECD, for overcoming this handicap of RULC approaches the latter by calculating the Annual Income Share.[10]

The adoption of RULC as an indicator of national economic competitiveness leads back to Ricardo's paradigm where labour productivity is positively related to competitiveness, while advances of labour productivity require capital investments. The latter are realised when the GDP share of capital, i.e. profits rises. Nevertheless, increasing capital income shares do not guarantee increasing productive investments for many reasons. In the contemporary economy investments may be diverted to the financial sphere or abroad in the quest of high returns. Investment opportunities may be augmented by stagnated demand, institutional inefficiency, e.g. poorly defined and protected intellectual property rights, high bureaucratic costs, etc. high systemic risks, and many others.

[10]See OECD (2015). System of Unit Labour Cost Indicators, StatExtracts, Paris: OECD.

4 The Case of the South Euro Zone Countries

The case of the euro zone as an optimal currency area has been strongly disputed since the beginning of its establishment (Bukowski 2011). Ignoring significant economic asymmetries within the euro zone, the pendulum of European economic integration swung from Keynesian cognitive framework to monetarism aiming at achieving the nominal convergence criteria of the Maastricht treaty. European policy interests focused on inflation and on natural rate of unemployment (NRU). Price stabilization became the policy priority putting aside all proposals for sustainable employment levels and economic development (Artis 1991).

However, optimum currency areas cognitive power was limited because of the precedence of endogenous growth theory according to which member state convergence is not the rule but rather the exemption and thus, considerable economic divergence will be omnipresent for many years after monetary integration. Empirical evidence support this view demonstrating that absolute convergence is not feasible in the absence of homogeneous economic, especially technological structures. Evidently, traditional optimum currency areas perception on convergence is not applicable in the medium term.[11]

The subprime loans crisis that erupted in the US market in 2007 acted as ignition in the euro zone domino effect that followed, bringing to the surface the fundamental handicaps of the European monetary integration and revealing the inadequacy of monetary criteria for the achievement of smooth macroeconomic stabilization and real economic convergence in the euro zone as a whole. The problems of economic asymmetries between euro zone states have been detected by economists, i.e. Emerson et al. (1992) underlining the negative outcomes on the potential of the monetary zone. Unfortunately, the prescribed policy solution for asymmetric shock control focused on prices adjustment and not on critical issues for an optimal currency area such as labour mobility and competitiveness.[12] Instead of enforcing the fundamentals of symmetric economic development in the euro area so as to achieve real economic convergence, euro zone decision making opted for a short sight vision of macroeconomic stabilization based on wage reduction, deregulation of labour markets and macroeconomic austerity.

However, after 5 years of economic austerity it becomes clear that fiscal primary surpluses are in place not due to real competitiveness improvements but due to wage suppression, tax hikes and general austerity measures, especially in Portugal, Greece and Spain. Export structure differentials between Greece, Portugal, Italy and Germany remain and unit labor cost differentials also insist after 5 years of shock macroeconomic therapy.[13] There is no significant improvement in the international terms of trade for countries in economic turmoil and, especially, for Greece

[11]See Soukiazis and Castro (2005) as well as Christodoulakis (2009).

[12]See also Sachs and Sala-i-Martin (1992), Bini-Smaghi and Vori (1993), Bayoumi and Eichengreen (1993).

[13]See Abdon et al. (2010).

there is no significant shift of export structure from medium and low value added products towards high value added export activity. Consequently, current account balance improvements should be attributed more to the collapse of imports and only marginally to a sustainable improved export performance of the tradable sector.[14]

In addition, the historical low euro zone interest rates after 2001 boosted both euro zone consumption and construction and led to unprecedented levels of private debt. At the same time, huge amounts of capital inflows enforced the euro's exchange value, based on the belief of a strong and optimum European monetary area. The truth was that increased demand and spending was not financed by improved competitiveness performance and when debt started to increase dangerously, external national balances of the fragile states of the south euro zone almost collapsed.

Table 1 shows the RULC growth rates for selected euro zone countries, i.e. Greece, Italy, Portugal, Spain and Cyprus in the 2001–2017 period. In annual average terms for the period 2001–2010, the RULC grew by 1.00 % in Greece, 0.65 % in Italy, −0.60 % in Portugal, and −0.05 % and −0.37 % in Spain and Cyprus respectively, while for the whole euro zone (euro zone 18) it shows a declining trend, i.e. annual average growth rate—0.05 %. The implementation of the internal devaluation policy in the south euro zone countries achieved a reduction of both wages and their GDP share as it is evident by the diminishing RULC growth rate in the consecutive crisis period 2011–2014, i.e. −2.30 % in Greece, −0.12 % in Italy, −1.70 % in Portugal, −1.25 % in Spain, −2.67 % in Cyprus, and −0.07 % in the euro zone 18. However, this policy had some ambiguous effects. In terms of the real exchange effective rate, (see Table 2) as it is measured by the ULC the competitive position of all south euro zone countries with the exception perhaps of Italy was improved as a result of the internal devaluation policy implementation, but in terms of export prices, although labour costs were significantly reduced there is no indication of any improvement but of stability (see Table 3). Therefore, the pass through effect of wage cuts to prices is neutral. Prices are rigid downwards not because of rigid wages but of economic inefficiencies, e.g. market power of firms, willingness to maintain profit rates, and market imperfections in general. In such cases, labour cost is the less significant determinants of prices, and hence of competitiveness. Empirical evidence by Zografakis and Kastelli (2015) reach similar results based on an extensive survey of export performance of euro area states.

Although, internal devaluation had ambiguous, to say the least results on prices and competitiveness, it had devastated effects on investment. Table 4 shows clearly that investment activity recorded negative annual growth rates in all south euro zone countries with Greece, Portugal, and Cyprus to report rates as high as −23.5 %, −16.6 %, and −20.5 % respectively for certain years. At the same time, lower labour income GDP shares and the consequent higher capital income GDP shares in the south euro zone economies failed to trigger investment activity as it

[14]See Athanasoglou et al. (2010).

Table 1 Real Unit Labor Cost (RULC) (percentage annual change), 2001–2014 (Nominal unit labor cost divided by GDP price deflator)

Year	Greece	Italy	Portugal	Spain	Cyprus	Euro area 18
2001–2005 (5 year annual average)	1.8	0.4	−0.5	−0.8	0.3	−0.5
2006–2010 (5 year annual average)	0.2	0.9	−0.7	0.7	−1.0	0.4
2011	−2.2	−0.8	−1.7	−0.9	0.7	−0.5
2012	−1.6	0.5	−2.8	−3.0	−4.6	0.7
2013	−5.0	−0.6	−0.5	−0.6	−4.0	−0.1
2014	−0.4	0.4	−1.8	−0.5	−2.8	0.2

Source: European Commission, European Economic Forecast, Autumn (2015), Institutional Paper 11, November 2015, European Economy, Brussels

Table 2 Real Effective Exchange Rate: ULC relative to rest of a group[a] of industrialized countries (USD) (% change on preceding year), 2001–2014

Year	Greece	Italy	Portugal	Spain	Cyprus	EU	Euro-area
2001–2005 (5 year average)	4.3	3.4	2.0	2.7	3.0	5.5	3.5
2006–2010 (5 year average)	0.9	0.9	−0.7	1.0	−0.4	−0.3	0.3
2011	−0.9	0.4	−2.1	−1.1	2.5	0.5	0.4
2012	−6.1	−2.3	−5.8	−6.6	−5.6	−4.9	−4.1
2013	−6.2	2.4	2.5	1.0	−2.1	7.8	6.2
2014	−2.2	1.2	−1.3	−1.3	−3.9	3.3	1.9

Source: European Commission, European Economic Forecast, Autumn (2015), Institutional Paper 11, November 2015, European Economy, Brussels
[a]37 countries: EU, TR, CH, NO, US, CA, JP, AU, MX and NZ

Table 3 Relative price indicators based on export prices deflator, vs. EU 28, 2005–2014, index 2005 = 100

Year	Greece	Italy	Portugal	Spain	Cyprus	Euro area-18
2005	100.0	100.0	100.0	100.0	100.0	100.0
2006	100.3	99.7	101.7	101.7	100.0	99.1
2007	101.0	100.6	102.2	102.7	101.1	99.4
2008	103.0	101.7	103.1	103.6	102.2	102.6
2009	105.4	104.4	102.0	105.4	106.7	107.8
2010	106.9	102.4	101.4	104.5	103.3	102.3
2011	108.7	102.7	102.6	105.3	100.8	101.4
2012	108.9	102.4	102.1	105.1	99.7	99.2
2013	108.0	103.1	102.5	105.0	101.3	100.8
2014	106.2	103.5	101.5	103.2	99.7	98.4

Source: Price and cost competitiveness, European Commission Directorate—General for Economic and Financial Affairs 2015

Table 4 Gross fixed capital formation, % change on preceding year, 1996–2014

Year	Greece	Italy	Portugal	Spain	Cyprus
% GDP (2014)	11.6	16.6	14.9	19.6	11.5
1996–2011	1.1	1.1	0.6	2.5	1.7
2012	−23.5	−9.3	−16.6	−7.1	−20.5
2013	−9.4	−6.6	−5.1	−2.5	−15.2
2014	−2.8	−3.5	2.8	3.5	−18.0

Source: European Commission, European Economic Forecast, Autumn (2015), Institutional Paper 11, November 2015, European Economy, Brussels

becomes obvious from the part of operational surplus (gross operating profits plus mixed income) channeled to investments (see Table 5). In all countries where internal devaluation was the policy option this percentage fell significantly, more significantly of all in Portugal and Greece but it remained rather steady in the whole euro zone (Eurozone 18). At the same time, Table 6 makes obvious that labour productivity in all south euro zone countries but Spain either fell or remained constant. That implies that the fall of GDP and the disinvestment process that was triggered due to the policies of interval devaluation may have reduced economic inefficiencies but they failed to restore economic efficiency through investments related to reforms and activity modernisation.

5 Conclusion

Economic theory on optimum currency areas anticipates that the European Monetary Union would facilitate economic, financial and labor market integration by converging nominally as a stepping stone towards real economic convergence. In this way, development, regional, technological, productivity and welfare gaps would be gradually reduced and eventually extinguished. Based on the data of the last decade it seems that growth, unemployment, and welfare disparities widened within the euro area, and the same holds true for the fundamental index of RULC. Indeed, differences in production structures, in implemented national economic policies, in consumption patterns, in international trade patterns, and in national financial robustness, gather momentum and created fundamental concerns over the unity and efficiency of the euro zone. Thus, focusing only on nominal convergence criteria for achieving an optimum currency area proved to be a suboptimal both methodology and policy option which enhanced the asymmetries within euro zone, deepening the dichotomy between fragile states of the south and the so called "benevolent" economies of the north. Moreover, deprivation of national monetary autonomy proved to be problematic for the south euro zone states since it was not accompanied by a fiscal union. Although the common monetary policy acted as a straightjacket tool to enforce competitiveness through the real drivers of productivity and export-led tradable sectors, it was inadequate because of inefficient

Table 5 Gross fixed capital formation at current prices, total economy as % of gross operating profits and mixed income at current prices, 2001–13

	2001–8	2009	2010	2011	2012	2013
Greece	46.2	40.1	33.4	28.3	23.6	21.2
Italy	46.3	46.0	43.4	42.7	41.1	39.0
Portugal	63.5	58.3	51.5	47.1	40.2	37.1
Spain	72.2	58.9	53.2	48.6	43.6	39.5
Cyprus	63.5	66.5	60.9	51.7	40.9	34.1
Euro area-18	63.5	66.5	47.8	48.0	47.0	45.0

Source: Eurostat, AMECO and authors' calculation

Table 6 Labor productivity (real GDP per occupied person) % change on preceding year, 2001–2014

Year	Greece	Italy	Portugal	Spain	Cyprus	Euro-area	European Union
2001–2005 (5 year annual average)	2.3	0.2	0.9	0.3	0.5	0.8	1.4
2006–2010 (5 year annual average)	−0.6	0.0	1.3	1.5	1.1	0.6	0.5
2011	−2.4	0.5	0.1	1.6	0.0	1.5	1.7
2012	−1.1	−1.5	0.1	1.9	1.8	−0.2	0.1
2013	0.4	0.7	1.8	1.6	−0.7	0.5	0.6
2014	0.5	−0.7	−0.5	0.2	−0.6	0.3	0.3

Source: European Commission, European Economic Forecast, Autumn (2015), Institutional Paper 11, November 2015, European Economy, Brussels

structures and adjustments for the south euro zone states. Equally important, fiscal policy within the Stability and Growth Pact (SGP), Euro plus Pact, Six pack, Two-Pack and Fiscal Compact do not incorporate sustainable development priorities underling only macroeconomic prudential recipes based on primary surpluses. However, one cannot deny that the long term problem of the fragile economies is not the mounting debt but fragile export structures which perpetuate it, feeding the sustainability of external imbalances, i.e. deficits.

The current paper develops arguments that cast reasonable doubt on the adequacy of the unit labour cost as an estimator of national economic competitiveness. The improvement of the latter is not possible to be caused by wage reductions and labor market deregulation in all tradable and non tradable sectors but it should be linked with labour productivity and investment rates.

Economic policy efforts should turn away from the implementation of internal devaluation policies, which in no way are the substitutes of an external devaluation policy towards upgrading the export potential and improving competitiveness through real structural reforms concerning business environment, entrepreneurial, and market failures and hurdles. Productivity, in its broadest interpretation may include various aspects of economic performance and efficiency, such as improvements in product quality, a firms' capacity to innovate and to adapt to consumer preferences, but also the functioning of the macroeconomic, institutional and policy environment, the quality of financial intermediation and the flexibility of factor markets. While competitive gains are primarily realized at the level of individual firms producing goods and services, governments have an important role to play to facilitate this process. In this context international trade regime policies cannot be isolated of other policy measures, such as labor and product market reforms, education and innovation policies.

Overall, internal devaluation policies lead rather to recession through investment reduction with no real labour productivity gains than to improved competitiveness and ultimately to economic growth as the case of the south euro zone economies indicates. An efficient policy mix should coordinate between structural reforms and economic efficiency measures that would eventually lead to improved competitiveness.

References

Abdon A, Bacate M, Felipe J, Kumar U (2010) Product complexity and economic development. Working paper, Levy Economics Institute, No. 616. www.econstor.eu/bitstream/10419/57018/1/635921618.pdf. Accessed 16 May 2014

Abramovitz M (1986) Catching-up, forging ahead, and falling behind. J Econ Hist 46(2):385–406

Alesina A, Perotti R (1997) The welfare state and competitiveness. Am Econ Rev 87(5):921–939

Alesina A, Ardagna S (1998) Tales of fiscal adjustment. Econ Policy 13(27):487–545

Artis M (1991) One market, one money: an evaluation of the potential benefits and costs of forming an economic and monetary union. Open Econ Rev 2:315–321

Athanasoglou P, Backinezos C, Georgiou E (2010) Export performance, competitiveness and commodity composition. Working Paper, Bank of Greece, No. 114

Bayoumi T, Eichengreen B (1993) Shocking aspects of European monetary integration. In: Torres F, Giavazzi F (eds) Adjustment and growth in the European Monetary Union. Cambridge University Press, New York, NY

Bini-Smaghi L, Vori S (1993) Rating the E.C. as an optimal currency area. Banca d'Italia, Roma, Temi di discussione No. 187

Bukowski S (2011) Economic and Monetary Union—current fiscal disturbances and the future. Int Adv Econ Res. doi:10.1007/s11294-011-9310-7

Chacholiades N (1990) International economics. McGraw-Hill, New York

Christodoulakis N (2009) Ten years of EMU: convergence, divergence and new policy priorities. GreeSE Paper No 22, The Hellenic Observatory, The European Institute. The London School of Economics and Political Science, London. eprints.lse.ac.uk/23192/1/GreeSE_No_22.pdf. Accessed 14 May 2014

Darity W Jr, Davis L (2005) Growth, trade and uneven development. Camb J Econ 29(1):141–170

De Grauwe P (ed) (2012) Economics of Monetary Union. Oxford University Press, Oxford

Dixit A, Norman V (1980) Theory of international trade. Cambridge University Press, Cambridge

Emerson M, Gros D, Italianer A, Pisani-Ferry J, Reichenbach H (1992) One market, one money: an evaluation of the potential benefits and costs of forming an economic and monetary union. Oxford University Press, Oxford

Ethier W (1982) National and international returns to scale in the modern theory of international trade. Am Econ Rev 72:389–405

European Commission Directorate—General for Economic and Financial Affairs (2015) Price and cost competitiveness database, ECFIN/E-4. Brussels

European Commission, European Economic Forecast (Autumn 2015) Institutional Paper 11, November 2015, European economy. Brussels
Eurostat (2015) Unit labor cost growth database. Brussels European Commission, Eurostat
Fagerberg J (1996) Technology and competitiveness. Oxf Rev Econ Policy 12(3):39–51
Felipe J (2005) A note on competitiveness, unit labor costs and growth: Is "Kaldor's paradox" a figment or interpretation? CAMA Working paper series, May, 2005, The Australian National University
Felipe J (2007) A cautionary note on the interpretation of unit labor cost as an indicator of competitiveness, with reference to the Philippines. Philippine J Dev 63(2):1–23
Frankel J, Rose A (1998) The endogeneity of the optimum currency area criteria. Econ J 108 (449):1009–1025
Frankel J, Rose A (2001) An estimate of the effect of currency unions on trade and income. Q J Econ 117:437–466
Freeman C (1995) The national system of innovation in historical perspective. Camb J Econ 19:5–24
Gomes L (2003) The economics and ideology of free trade: a historical review. Edward Elgar, Cheltenham, UK
Helpman E (1981) International trade in the presence of product differentiation, economies of scale and monopolistic competition. J Int Econ 11:305–340
Kaldor N (1978a) The effects of devaluations on trade in manufactures. In: Kaldor N (ed) Further essays on applied economics. Duckworth, London, pp 99–118
Kaldor N (1978b) Causes of the slow rate of economic growth in the United Kingdom. In: Kaldor N (ed) Further essays on economic theory. Holmes & Meyer, New York, NY, pp 100–138
Kenen PB (1969) The theory of optimum currency areas: an eclectic view. In: Mundell RA, Swoboda AK (eds) Monetary problems of the international economy. Chicago University Press, Chicago, IL, pp 41–60
Krugman P (1979) Increasing returns, monopolistic competition and international trade. J Int Econ 9:469–479
Krugman P (1980) Scale economies, product differentiation and the pattern of trade. Am Econ Rev 70:950–959
Krugman P (1981) Intra-industry specialization and the gains from trade. J Polit Econ 89:959–973
Krugman P (1993) Lessons of Massachusetts for EMU. In: Torres F, Giavazzi F (eds) Adjustment and growth in the European Union. Cambridge University Press, Cambridge, pp 241–261
Krugman P (1994) Competitiveness: a dangerous obsession. Foreign Aff 73(2):28–44
Kwok Y, Yu E (2015) Leontief paradox and the role of factor intensity measurement. https://www.iioa.org/conferences/15th/pdf/Kwok_yu.Pdf. Accessed 21 Nov 2015
Lancaster K (1980) Intra industry trade under perfect monopolistic competition. J Int Econ 10:151–175
Lucas R (1988) On the mechanics of economic development. J Monet Econ 22:3–42
Marshall A (2013) Principles of economics. Palgrave Macmillan, London
Mongelli F (2002) "New" views on the optimum currency area theory: what is EMU telling us? Working Paper Series 138, European Central Bank. www.ecb.int/pub/pdf/scpwps/ecbwp138.pdf. Accessed 20 Apr 2014
McKinnon RI (1963) Optimum currency areas. Am Econ Rev 53:717–724
Minhas B (1962) The homo-hypallagic production function, factor-intensity reversals and the Heckscher–Ohlin theorem. J Polit Econ 50:138–156
Mundell RA (1961) A theory of optimum currency areas. Am Econ Rev 51:657–665
OECD (2015) System of unit labor cost indicators, statextracts. OECD, Paris
Porter M (1990) The competitive advantage of nations. Macmillan, London
Ricardo D (1911) Principles of political economy and taxation, with introduction essay, Notes and appendices. Gonner, E.C.K. Bell, London
Rodriguez F, Rodrik D (2000) Trade policy and economic growth: a skeptic's guide to the cross-national evidence. NBER Macroecon Annu 15:261–338

Rodrik D (2001) Les mirages de l'ouverture extérieure. L'Economie Politique 2(10):44–54
Romer P (1986) Increasing returns and long-run growth. J Polit Econ 94(5):1002–1037
Romer P (1987) Growth based on increasing returns due to specialization. Am Econ Rev 77 (2):56–62
Sachs J, Sala-i-Martin X (1992) Fiscal federalism and optimum currency areas: evidence for Europe from the United States. CEPR Discussion Paper No 632. www.nber.org/papers/w3855.pdf. Accessed 14 Apr 2014
Schumacher R (2013) Deconstructing the theory of comparative advantage. World Econ Rev 2:83–105
Smith A (1994) Imperfect competition and international trade. In: Greenaway D, Winters A (eds) Surveys in international trade. Blackwell, Oxford, UK
Soukiazis E, Castro V (2005) How the Maastricht rules affected the convergence process in the European Union. A panel data analysis. J Policy Model 27(3):385–399
World Economic Forum (2010) The global competitiveness report 2010-2011. World Economic Forum, Davos
Zografakis S, Kastelli I (2015) Is it true that the reduction of labor cost suffice to enhance the competitiveness of Greek economy? (in Greek) Crisis Observatory, ELIAMEP. Crisisobs.gr/2015/02/stavros-zografakis/. Accessed 25 Feb 2015

‘Compulsory’ Economic Deflation Turned Political Risk: Effects of Austere Decision-Making on Greece’s ‘True’ Economy (2008–2015) and the ‘Eurozone or Default’ Dilemma

Nikitas-Spiros Koutsoukis and Spyros Roukanas

Abstract The drastic internal deflation approach adopted as a remedy to the Greek government debt problem, gave rise to an unforeseen socio-humanitarian crisis, and increased political populism and polarization. While the macroeconomic merits of this strategy are debatable, politically, Greece seems to have turned into a key political risk, for itself, as well as for the Eurozone, with potentially significant impacts on the world economy. Considering the different perspectives between the current Greek government and EU decision making and stakeholder echelons, we wonder if the ‘true’ value of ‘curing’ the Greek government debt is really equivalent to a rip in the Eurozone, or to Greece’s defaulting, which seems to be the only political dichotomy being considered at present. In this paper, we seek to depict some of the key arguments behind this political economy standoff, by depicting high-level shifts brought about in the Greek economy and its institutions, and the impact of the economic austerity measures on the Greek society.

1 Introduction

The severe economic adjustment of Greece has increased the level of political risk in Greece, with a direct effect on the country’s ability to exit the dire situation it is in. In this paper, elements of political risk and the progression, thus far, of the Greek bailout efforts are used to illustrate how the bailout programme fuels political risk, which in turn affects the ability of Greece to act its way out of the crisis.

N.-S. Koutsoukis (✉)
Department of Political Science & International Relations, University of Peloponnese, 1 Aristotelous Str. & Leof. Athinon, 201 00 Corinth, Greece
e-mail: nkoutsou@uop.gr

S. Roukanas
Department of International & European Studies, University of Piraeus, 126 Gr. Lampraki Str., 185 34 Piraeus, Greece
e-mail: sroukana@unipi.gr

A. Karasavvoglou et al. (eds.), *Economic Crisis, Development and Competitiveness in Southeastern Europe*, Contributions to Economics,
DOI 10.1007/978-3-319-40322-9_3

The rest of this paper is organised in the following way. In Sect. 2 we provide a succinct review of political risk and consider our previous work that led to this paper. In Sect. 3 we provide an overview of the economic adjustment programmes which were adopted as remedies to the problem; in essence, an internal deflation of the Greek economy. In Sect. 3 we review some of the most prominent macroeconomics outputs that seem to be brought about as a result of, and in the context of the economic adjustment programmes. Despite any long term expectations, at present the situation seems to be worsening, putting pressure on an already fragile political system. In Sect. 4 we look at how the pressure has mounted on the political system significantly increasing the associated political risk. In Sect. 5 we conclude.

2 A Review of Political Risk

Political risk may refer to the possibility of relatively abrupt discontinuity in [public] governance due to, and expressed as shifts, interruptions or inconsistency in the implementation and long term coherency of public policy and assorted regulatory environment (McKellar 2010: 11–14; Ramady 2013: 55). While the purist view of political risk tends to relate to expropriation, politically motivated actions and political process-based activity, and currency policy, the notion tends to encompass the majority of risk-factors with a business impact that can be associated with politics, public policy or public governance (Garver 2009; Frei and Ruloff 1988). The reasoning is that such dynamic politically-routed settings affect the stability of the country's market and business environments, and therefore the country's attractiveness for business and other investors (Harms 2000: 72–74).

From this perspective, it seems rather intuitive that the components of stability in public governance and the political domain (e.g. cabinet shifts, partisanship, frequency of opposition-to-government shifts, etc.) define political risk. This intuitive view is also in accordance with Snider' perspective (2005: 205) who sets the yardstick for political risk as the rate for "*which the 'rules of the game' (...) will not change in such a way as to invalidate the original calculation [of risk and return] or the decision to invest*", and suggests that an institutional approach to political risk is more suitable approach for political risk assessment. However, in his review of empirical work on the relationship between political risk and investments, Harms (2000: 74–88) finds that the absence of political risk does not imply higher levels of investment, even though the presence of political risk seems to dissuade investors. Thus political risk as an investment (dis-)incentive should only be considered in tandem to other factors.

An illustration of political risk elements, in the contexts reviewed above can be seen in Fig. 1.

It is noteworthy that 'political risk' is typically used as an aggregate of other factors, that collectively signify the [absence] of politically-motivated dynamic setting in the country of interest. In this context the term 'country risk' is often used to signify a comprehensive aggregate that combines political, economic and

Fig. 1 Elements of political risk

financial perspectives (Ramady 2013; Kosmidou et al. 2008: 1–2; Frei and Ruloff 1988: 3). However, political risk may also include economic policy outlooks (for instance, Coplin and O'Leary 1983; Stoychev 2013).

The authors have previously approached country risk and, within it, political risk using a reputation risk framework as a proxy measure (Koutsoukis et al. 2012). In the context of the reputation risk framework, political risk in particular, was decomposed along the following reputation risk dimensions:

- *Governance and leadership*, measured through the following indicators: government term duration, party successions to power, and election system modifications.
- *Regulatory compliance*, measured as the number of Greece' infringement cases of EU regulations and the level of Transposition of community law within the Greek regulatory system
- *Corporate responsibility*, measured the level of Transposition of community law within the Greek regulatory system in particular for the environment, health and consumer protection.
- *Communication and crisis management*, measured by the repeated and deliberate inconsistency of the Greek authorities to accept and report to its partners regarding the looming economic situation.
- *Workplace talent and culture*, measured as Greece's rating corruption perceptions index steadily dropping over the course of a decade, signifying that transparency was neither an asset nor a forthcoming goal of the Greek economic environment.

We note that these are five out of seven [reputation risk] dimensions all of which are driven by or require the involvement of the political system (executive, legislative and judicial branch). The other two dimensions are only relevant in an economic/business analysis context (financial performance and long-term investment value, and delivering customer promise).

Although the study was developed in hindsight during the peak of the Greek crisis, our findings suggest that reputation risk as an analytical framework may offer advanced warnings in similar situations.

3 Overview of the Economic Adjustment Programmes

Greece entered a severe sovereign debt crisis in 2010, following suit on the world economic crisis events of 2007 and 2008, with a debt that was over 129.7 % of the country's GDP concurrently with a deficit for 2009 that run to 15.7 % of its GDP significantly over the Eurozone limit of 3 %, (Eurostat 2015a, b). This fiscal problem was amplified and thus received world-wide attention because of Greece's full-fledged Eurozone membership. Greece's fiscal problems had an immediate effect on the Eurozone and therefore the rest of the European Union (Kotios and Roukanas 2013). Following the general elections in the fall of 2009 Greece's position in the financial markets began to worsen rapidly, with consecutive degradations from Rating Agencies, and repetitive negative performance in the stock markets. The cost of Government lending sky-rocketed as can be seen in Fig. 2 for the Greek 10-year Government Bond (Tradingeconomics 2014).

The debate was on, as to whether Greece could default, or not, and whether it should exit the Eurozone, willingly or not, to minimize collaterals. A '*Grexit*' i.e. an exit of Greece from the Eurozone could prove to be disastrous to the Eurozone and the world economy (Koutsoukis and Roukanas 2014). The relevant arguments also took into consideration the fact that Portugal, Ireland, Italy and Spain (at the time coined as "PIIGS"; Greece being the 'G') had equally large sovereign debts and deficit problems, again severely amplified by the economic events of 2007–2008. If Greece failed, many assumed, profiteers could use this as a paradigm to bring down any one of the other countries, most notably those in southern Europe.

At the heart of this debate the dilemma is whether the remedy for sovereign debt symptoms should be composed of more austerity reforms, or more economic development push. The dilemma in turn has brought forward the 'Grexit' paradox; Recession is worsening Greece's finances so that Greece may remain in the Euro, at the same time when Greece's poor-and getting-worst finances suggest that it is probably better if Greece left the Euro (Koutsoukis and Roukanas 2014). While we are waiting for Greece and Europe to figure out the answer(s) in top-down, institutional style, we think it is equally important to consider the effects that strategic politics have on the 'true' stakeholders, the people, or the 'true' economy as it is variably known. In doing so we aim to outline some of the thresholds between optimal and satisficing fiscal performance for the decision makers

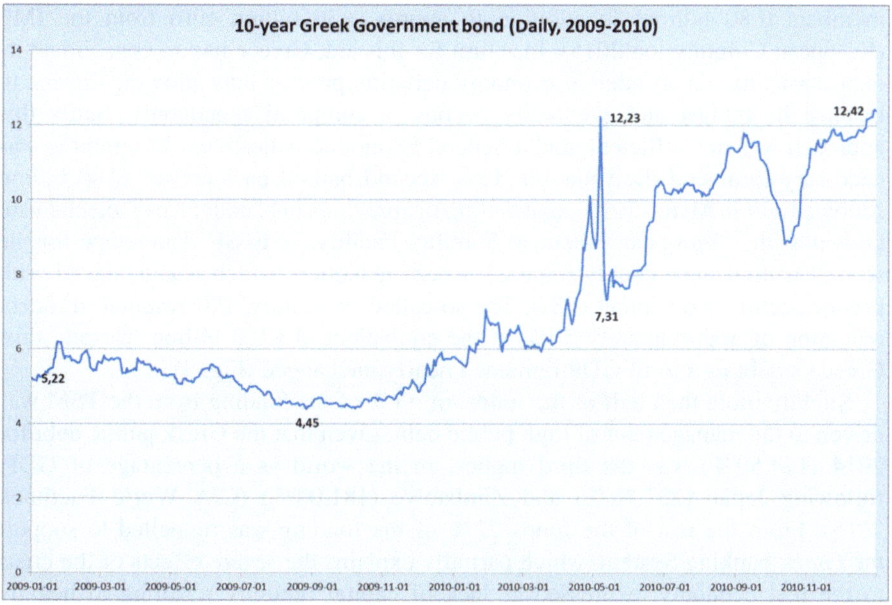

Fig. 2 10-year Greek government bond yield (*Source*: Tradingeconomics 2014)

involved in these decisions, in accordance with Herbert Simon's well-known thesis (1956: 136).

Hence, in this paper, we seek to gauge some of the lesser known the effects of this fiscal discipline that are frequently overlooked in favor of the larger fiscal, and admittedly strategic, picture. We start by looking at the 'big' picture and using it as a backdrop for looking at the recession picture. In particular, for this macro-perspective, we contrast Greece's performance 5 years on its remedy, by comparing the 'before' and 'after' snapshots of Greece's reputation risk, a framework that we previously used to gauge some of the root causes of the crisis (Koutsoukis et al. 2012). In this way, we try to establish if the 'big' picture of Greece has, ultimately, shifted, or adjusted, as a result of the bail-out program. We then proceed to focus on the implication of the observed shifts (or lack thereof). In particular, we outline the high-level 'demands' of the bail-out programs and subsequently snapshot the achievement in the fiscal indicators and contrast them to their corresponding indicators in the 'true' economy as it were.

So, the bets were on, whether the prospect of Greece's default could 'bring down' the Euro, or whether some, until then unknown, *deus-ex-machina* would be able to save Greece from default and therefore the Euro currency. To this end, Greece enter its First economic adjustment programme" in May 2010, a.k.a. the 'first bailout package'. This was set by a Trilateral Support Mechanism (TSM) comprising of the European Commission (representing the Eurogroup), the European Central Bank (ECB) and the International Monetary Fund (IMF). This first rescue package totalled €107.3 billion in the form of bilateral loans from EU members (€80 billion) in addition to approx. €30 billion euro from the IMF (European Commission 2015). In return for this aid, Greece had to consolidate its debt, basically via an internal economy deflation process thus allowing Greece to balance its budget and eventually become a competitive economy. Sadly this approach was not sufficient, and a Second Economic Adjustment Programme was necessary to amend the situation. This 'second bailout package' of €100 billion followed suit in March 2012, superseding the previous one, under a new mechanism known as the "European Financial Stability Facility, or EFSF. The recipe for the second bailout unavoidably required a debt reduction, which was achieved with private sector involvement (PSI). The so called 'voluntary' PSI resulted in a debt reduction of approximately 50 % or the equivalent of €100 billion. Despite this, Greece's debt as a % of GDP remained nearly unchanged (Fig. 3).

Slightly more than half of the funds, or 53 % of the funding from the TSM was driven to the management of high public debt, given that the Greek public debt for 2014 (174.50 %) was the third highest in the world as a percentage of GDP, following Japan (227.70 %) and Zimbabwe (181.00 %) (CIA World Factbook 2015). From the rest of the funds 22 % of the funding was tunnelled to support the Greek banking System, which partially explains the severe effects of the crisis to the real economy, expressed as lack of capital liquidity resulting in heavily reduced investment activity (illustrated in Fig. 4).

The TSM appointed a technical executive group to monitor progress, and advise the Greek government, soon to be referred to as the 'troika.' All the same, Greece had no choice but to enter a period of austere fiscal discipline, in exchange for the

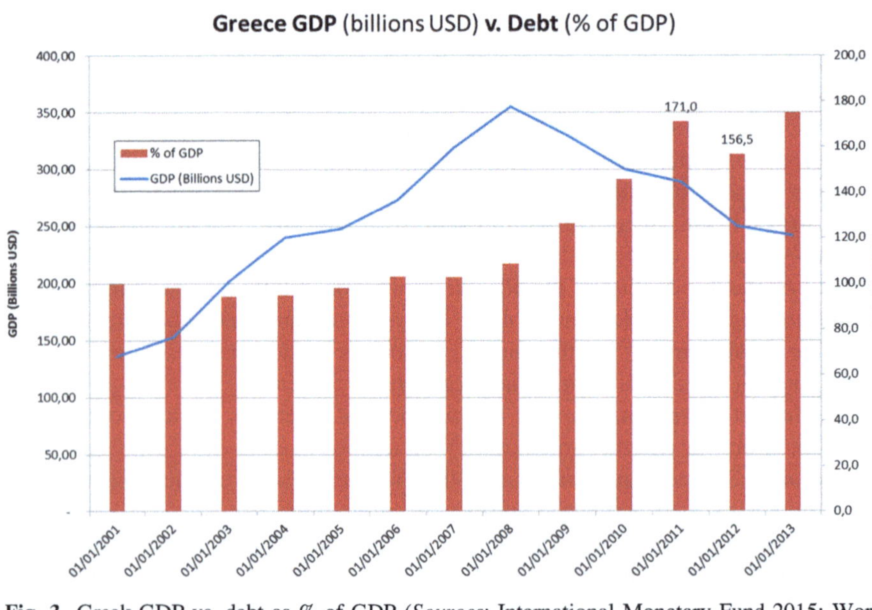

Fig. 3 Greek GDP vs. debt as % of GDP (*Sources*: International Monetary Fund 2015; World Bank 2015a)

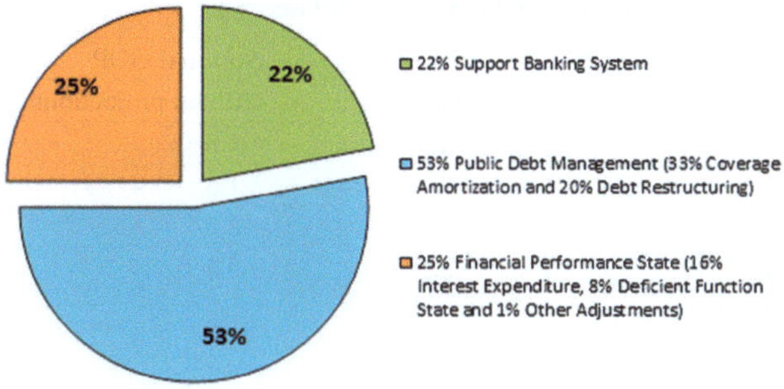

Fig. 4 Allocation of funds from TSM, 2010–2014 (*Source*: Triantopoulos 2015: 12)

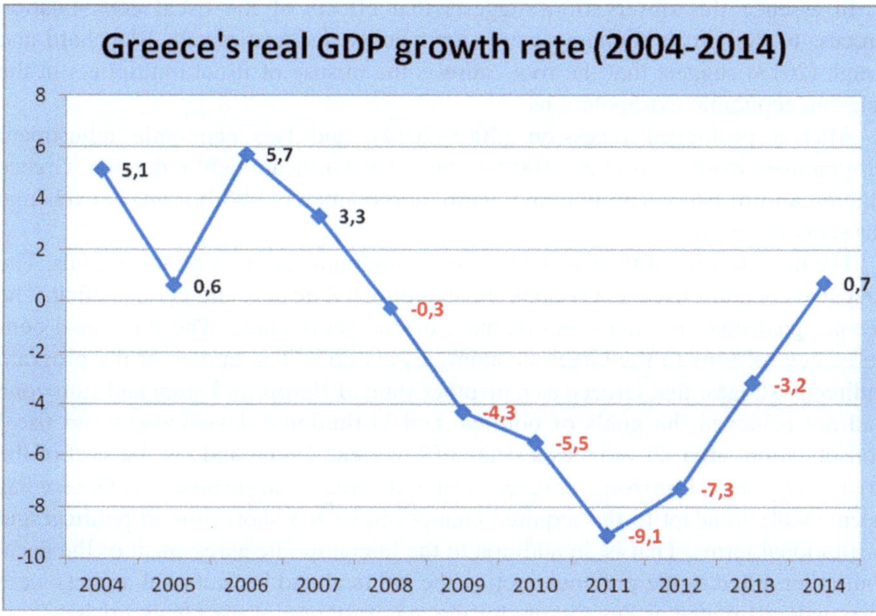

Fig. 5 Real GDP growth rate of Greece, 2004–2014 (*Source*: Eurostat 2015c)

economic assistance and in order to get out of this dire situation. Technically this resulted in an unprecedented domestic deflation of the Greek economy (a paradigm that was adopted and adapted accordingly by the other countries in sovereign debt troubles, namely Portugal, Ireland, Italy and Spain). Greece's therapy, as expected, brought about an unprecedented recession that is depicted in Fig. 5.

Following an economic slowdown, Greece entered recession in 2008 which peaked in 2011 at a rate of approximately 9 %; a hint of growth reappeared in 2014, nearly 6 years later. As can be seen in Table 1, the negative effects to the real GDP growth were severe, in essence over the estimates by international economic

Table 1 OECD's GDP projections and outcomes for Greece

	Real GDP		Nominal GDP	
Years	Official projections	Outcomes	Official projections	Outcomes
2010	−4.0	−4.9	−2.8	−3.9
2011	−3.0	−7.1	−1.5	−6.1
2012	−3.0	−6.4	−2.8	−7.2
2013	−4.2	−3.5[a]	−5.4	−5.9[a]

Source: OECD (2013: 17)
[a]*OECD Projections*

organizations, including the International Monetary Fund and the Organization for Economic Cooperation and Development.

In essence this observation suggests that effects of the fiscal consolidation process to the Greek economy were significantly underestimated. Blanchard and Leigh (2013) suggest that the root cause is the misuse of fiscal multipliers in the relevant economic extrapolations.

After a prolonged recession (2008–2014), and two economic adjustment programmes worth well over €100 billion and a significant debt reduction, Greece entered a third bailout programme, worth approximately €86 billion, in exchange for economic reforms.

The main targets of the fiscal adjustment programmes focus on three goals. The first goal concerns fiscal consolidation, regarding public debt and public deficit. The second goal concerns the reinforcement of competitiveness. The third goal concerns key reforms to the Greek economy as a whole. The targets of the program indirectly suggest that Greece as a member state of European Union and Eurozone had not achieved the goals of political and institutional development and fiscal consolidation, after 29 years as a -state of European Union and –at the start of the crisis– n9 years a Eurozone member. It should come as no surprise that Greece has been unable to adapt to the required changes in such a short time in political and institutional terms. That is, in addition to the inappropriate assessment of the fiscal multiplier noted in the previous section the political and institutional aspects were also underestimated as key factors for the manifestation of the Greek crisis.

Taking the above discussion into consideration, is seems that Greece's woes are far from over, and as we discuss below, the situation has a direct impact on the political environment in Greece, which in turn affects the effectiveness of the bailout programs, and the negative spiral of the Greek crisis seems never ending.

4 Economic Adjustments Fuelling Political Risk

We focus momentarily on the macroeconomic outputs of economic adjustment programmes, depicted in Table 2.

Table 2 Macroeconomic outputs of the economic adjustment programmes

Years	General government gross debt (% GDP)	General government deficit/surplus (% GDP)	Real GDP growth rate	Inflation	GDP at market prices (Millions of euro)
2008	112.9	−9.8	−0.4	4.2	242,096.1
2009	129.7	−15.7	−4.4	1.3	237,431.0
2010	148.3	−10.9	−5.4	4.7	226,209.6
2011	171.3	−10.2	−8.9	3.1	207,751.9
2012	156.9	−8.7	−6.6	1.0	194,203.7
2013	175.0	−12.3	−3.9	−0.9	182,438.3
2014	177.1	−3.5	0.8	−1.4	179,080.6

Sources: Eurostat (2015a, b, c, d, h)

Table 3 Balance of Payments (million euro)

	Current account balance	Trade balance	Exports of goods	Imports of goods	Direct investment (+) Net inflow (−) Net outflow
2008	−34.797,6	−44.048,8	19.812,9	63.861,7	1.420,7
2009	−25.818,7	−30.767,3	15.318,0	46.085,3	274,5
2010	−22.975,6	−28.279,6	17.081,5	45.361,0	−927,0
2011	−20.633,5	−27.229,1	20.230,6	47.459,6	−452,6
2012	−4.615,0	−19.619,0	22.020,6	41.639,7	827,1
2013	1.088,5	−17.229,4	22.534,8	39.764,2	2.713,6
2014	1.656,7	−17.976,1	23.647,5	41.623,6	991,8

Source: Bank of Greece (2015a)

Succinctly put, the debt is at an all-time high, the deficit has been significantly reduced trending at 3.5 % but is still over the Eurozone required limit. After 6 years of recession, there I a hint of growth at 0.8 % in tandem with a negative inflation, typically associated with recession, suggesting that the growth needs to analysed further, whereas the actual GDP is still dropping.

From another perspective, the crisis situation and the fiscal adjustment programmes further impacted the prospect of economic development: Greece is unable to resort to international lending, it cannot afford to make public investments necessary to spark economic development, and domestic private investments are victims of the overall situation. Hence, the only viable option for Greece is to attract Foreign Direct Investments (FDI), that may fuel the economy with the necessary capital to spark economic growth. Sadly, this was not the case (Table 3).

In view of this downturn, the anticipated economic recovery stabled upon another hurdle. The fear of an exit from the Eurozone resulted in an outflow of bank deposits and resulted in a liquidity problem (Table 4).

One way to interpret this is to presume that the fiscal adjustment program caused a crisis to the Greek banking system. Notice that even after the debt reduction of 2012, the deposits' outflow continued.

Table 4 Analysis of deposits and repos at Greek banking system of domestic enterprises and households (Millions of euros)

Period	Deposits
June 2008	218,843
December 2008	235,878
June 2009	245,590
December 2009	245,470
June 2010	228,826
December 2010	222,874
June 2011	197,281
December 2011	182,790
June 2012	158,580
December 2012	173,347
June 2013	175,889
December 2013	177,018
June 2014	177,634
December 2014	173,220
March 2015	149,035

Source: Bank of Greece (2015b)

Table 5 Bank nonperforming loans to total gross loans (%)—2008–2014

Years	World	Greece
2008	3.0	4.7
2009	4.2	7.0
2010	4.0	9.1
2011	3.9	14.4
2012	3.7	23.3
2013	4.3	31.9
2014	–	33.5

Source: World Bank (2015b)

Inadvertently this economic setting got hold of the persons behind the numbers (Table 5). Private investment came to a halt as the Greek banks strived to protect capital adequacy.

Drilling down further, this prolonged economic adjustment period we note that productivity has dropped, unemployment has tripled and the ration of the population at risk of poverty has steadily increased (Table 6).

Thus within the 5 years of economic adjustment, the Greek economy steadfastly progressed to a standstill. The government is unable to spend; the banks are unable to lend; the people are unable to consume. The social unrest continues and pressure on the political system is hardening, fuelling political risk and it is very likely that the economic crisis will soon be in tandem to a political crisis. In support of the last observation we summarise the political system dynamics in Table 7.

Drilling down into the political dynamics of the period, the data is quite clear: in a succession of almost exactly 8 years to the day (19 Sept 2007–21 Sept 2015) the country has seen eight Prime Ministers (PMs), two of which were interim, and one

Table 6 Outputs of the economic adjustment programmes at the person level

Years	GDP per capita in PPS (EU-27 = 100)	Unemployment (%)	People at risk of poverty (% of total population)
2008	93	7.8	28.1
2009	94	9.6	27.6
2010	87	12.7	27.7
2011	77	17.9	31.0
2012	74	24.5	34.6
2013	73	27.5	35.7
2014	–	26.5	–

Sources: Eurostat (Eurostat 2015e, f, g)

Table 7 Political system dynamics in Greece, 2008-present

Start	Finish	Prime Minister	Years	Cabinet shuffles	Ministerial changes	Total
19/09/2007	06/10/2009	K. Karamanlis	2.05	1	6	7
06/10/2009	11/11/2011	G. Papandreou	2.10	2	6	8
11/11/2011	16/05/2012	L. Papadimos[a]	0.51	0	4	4
16/05/2012	21/06/2012	P. Pikrammenos[b]	0.10	NA	NA	NA
21/06/2012	26/01/2015	A. Samaras	2.60	2	11	13
26/01/2015	27/08/2015	A. Tsipras	0.59	1	4	5
27/08/2015	21/09/2015	V. Thanou[b]	0.07	NA	NA	NA
21/09/2015	*present*	A. Tsipras	0.19	0	2	5
Period average 2009-present[c]			*1.6*			*7*
Historical average 1974–2009			*2.2*			*10*
Historical average 1909–2009			*0.9*			*6*

[a]Not elected to parliament
[b]Interim Prime minister/Government
[c]The calculation excludes the interims. With the interims the average duration is 1.14 years

was a non-parliamentary person (i.e. not elected), but selected and appointed by the parties that formed a coalition government at the time. It is easily seen that the statistical trend is long-lasting and seems to be worsening due to the crisis: Prime ministers change on average every 1.6 years, significantly lower than the average of 2.2 years of the 40+ years of the "3rd Hellenic Republic" (i.e. the period after the abolition of monarchy and the fall of the military junta). We inform out reader that the Greek constitution anticipates a period of no more than 4 years between successive elections. In addition to the PM changes, we notice that the cabinet structure also undergoes frequent changes. In Table 7 we consider as cabinet shuffles the events whenever more than half of the cabinet ministers were changed (i.e. replaced, shuffled, resigned, or their ministry was cancelled). The rest of the changes are identified as 'simple' minister changes. The trend here is on par with the longer terms, which in effect implies a minister change on average every 3 months or so. We purposely left out the statistics regarding the cabinet structure (i.e. hierarchy and ministerial portfolio) which, unfortunately, tends to change in every cabinet reshuffle (for a discussion, see for instance Koutsoukis 2013).

In parallel to this dynamic situation in the executive branch, parliament entry has also been more dynamic (Table 8).

During the crisis the crisis has been through six general elections, and one referendum. The six elections resulted in four coalition governments, and one interim government. This is important considering that in the previous 35 years out of there had only coalition governments twice before (in two elections held during 1989). It is also important to notice that during the crisis the number of parties entering parliament seems to have been stabilised to seven parties or more. Contrast this in long trend of four or five parties with the odd exception here and there (Fig. 6). Admittedly party entry to parliament is often the outcome of the election law, which is changes every other election or so.

When considering the rather simple political statistics presented above it appears that Greece seems to be in a period where the executive branch/political system

Table 8 Parliamentary election dynamics 2008-present

National elections of	Parliament parties	New in parliament	Not re-elected	Coalition
16/09/2007	4	1		No
04/10/2009	5	0		Yes[a]
06/05/2012	7	3	1	Interim
17/06/2012	7	0		Yes
25/01/2015	7	1	1	Yes
20/09/2015	8	1		Yes

[a]The majority single-party government resigned mid-term to give place to a coalition government

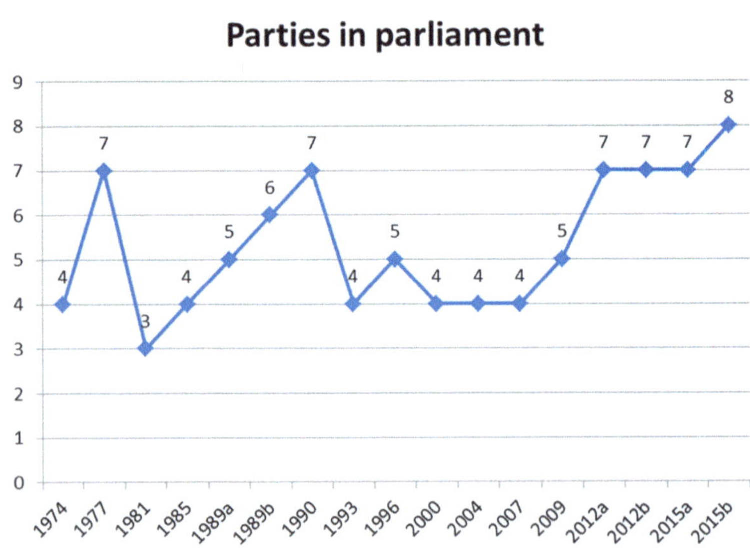

Fig. 6 Number of parties in parliament 1974-present

seems to be rather fluid. An analysis of voter preferences is beyond the scope of this paper but voter preferences have also changed dramatically during this period in comparison to the pre-2009 era. The increased fluidity of the executive branch implies increased political risk. When these trends are viewed in tandem with the economic adjustment programmes and outcomes, it is easy to identify an interrelationship between political risk and the compulsory economic deflation brought about by the economic adjustment programmes and Greece's place in the euro, in support of our thesis.

5 Conclusions

Our study of Greece's 'compulsory' economic deflation in tandem with key characteristics of its political system suggests that the economic adjustment programmes have increased the level of political risk in Greece. In our previous work we have argued how political factors, political risk included have in addition to poor economic and fiscal policy, brought Greece to the difficult situation it is still facing. Despite the general expectation that the economic adjustment programmes and an unprecedented financial aid of over €280 billion would allow Greece to improve on its fiscal and economic practices, it appears that the austerity assorted to the aid, has also given rise to a severe spiral of political risk that threatens to blow apart Greece and potentially crack the much valued solidarity of the Eurozone and perhaps the European Union. We sincerely hope that this will not be the case, for Greece, but especially Europe.

Acknowledgements This paper has been partly supported by the University of Piraeus Research Center.

References

Bank of Greece (2015a) Annual report of the Bank of Greece. http://www.bankofgreece.gr/Pages/el/Publications/GovReport.aspx?Filter_By=8. Accessed 25 Apr 2015

Bank of Greece (2015b) Deposits of credit institutions. http://www.bankofgreece.gr/Pages/el/Statistics/monetary/deposits.aspx. Accessed 25 Apr 2015

Blanchard O, Leigh D (2013) Growth forecast errors and fiscal multipliers. IMF Work Pap 13 (1):1–43

CIA The World Factbook (2015) Country comparison public debt. https://www.cia.gov/library/publications/the-world-factbook/rankorder/2186rank.html#gr. Accessed 30 Apr 2015

Coplin WD, O'Leary MK (1983) Systematic political risk analysis for planners. Plan Rev 11 (1):14–17, 10.1108/eb054010

European Commission (2015) Financial assistance to Greece. http://ec.europa.eu/economy_finance/assistance_eu_ms/greek_loan_facility/index_en.htm. Accessed 25 Apr 2015

Eurostat (2015a) General government gross debt. http://epp.eurostat.ec.europa.eu/tgm/table.do?tab=table&init=1&plugin=1&language=en&pcode=tsdde410. Accessed 25 Apr 2015

Eurostat (2015b) General government deficit/surplus. http://epp.eurostat.ec.europa.eu/tgm/table.do?tab=table&init=1&plugin=1&language=en&pcode=tec00127. Accessed 25 Apr 2015
Eurostat (2015c) Real GDP growth rate—volume. http://epp.eurostat.ec.europa.eu/tgm/table.do?tab=table&init=1&plugin=1&language=en&pcode=tec00115. Accessed 25 Apr 2015
Eurostat (2015d) HICP—inflation rate annual average rate of change (%). http://ec.europa.eu/eurostat/tgm/table.do?tab=table&init=1&language=en&pcode=tec00118&plugin=1. Accessed 25 Apr 2015
Eurostat (2015e) GDP per capita in PPS. http://epp.eurostat.ec.europa.eu/tgm/table.do?tab=table&init=1&plugin=1&language=en&pcode=tec00114. Accessed 25 Apr 2015
Eurostat (2015f) Unemployment rate, by sex. http://epp.eurostat.ec.europa.eu/tgm/table.do?tab=table&init=1&plugin=1&language=en&pcode=tsdec450. Access date. 25 Apr 2015
Eurostat (2015g) People at risk of poverty or social exclusion. http://epp.eurostat.ec.europa.eu/tgm/table.do?tab=table&init=1&plugin=1&language=en&pcode=t2020_50. Accessed 25 Apr 2015
Eurostat (2015h) Gross domestic product at market prices. http://epp.eurostat.ec.europa.eu/tgm/table.do?tab=table&init=1&plugin=1&language=en&pcode=tec00001. Accessed 25 Apr 2015
Frei D, Ruloff D (1988) The methodology of political risk assessment: an overview. World Futures 25(1):1–24. doi:10.1080/02604027.1988.9972072
Garver P (2009) The changing face of political risk. In: Lu KW, Verheyen G, Perera SM (eds) Investing with confidence: understanding political risk management in the 21st century. World Bank, Washington, DC
Harms P (2000) International investment, political risk, and growth. Springer, Boston, MA, 10.1007/978-1-4615-4521-7
International Monetary Fund (2015) General government gross debt for Greece© [GGGDTAGRC188N]. Retrieved from FRED, Federal Reserve Bank of St. Louis https://research.stlouisfed.org/fred2/series/GGGDTAGRC188N/. Accessed 28 Nov 2015
Kosmidou K, Doumpos M, Zopounidis C (eds) (2008) Country risk evaluation: methods and applications. Springer, New York, NY
Kotios A, Roukanas S (2013) The Greek crisis and the crisis in Eurozone's governance. In: Sklias P, Tzifakis N (eds) Greece's horizons: reflecting on the country's assets and capabilities. Springer, London, pp 91–105
Koutsoukis NS (2013) Ekato eti Ellinikis Diakivernises: 1909-2009 (Εκατό έτη Ελληνικής Διακυβέρνησης: 1909-2009) Working paper, PT-GOVERN-01-102013. Research Group 'Political Technology,' Department of Political Science and International Relations, University of Peloponnisos, Korinth, Greece. http://politech.uop.gr/?ddownload=339. Accessed 1 Mar 2015
Koutsoukis NS, Roukanas S (2014) The GrExit paradox. Procedia Econ Financ 9:24–31
Koutsoukis NS, Roukanas S, Sklias P (2012) A reputation risk perspective on the Greek crisis. Int J Decis Sci Risk and Manage 4(1–2):38–57
McKellar R (2010) A short guide to political risk. Gower, Burlington, VT
OECD (2013) OECD economic surveys Greece, November 2013. http://www.keepeek.com/Digital-Asset-Management/oecd/economics/oecd-economic-surveys-greece-2013_eco_surveys-grc-2013-en#page3. Accessed 25 Apr 2015
Ramady MA (2013) Political, economic and financial country risk. Springer, New York, NY
Simon HA (1956) Rational choice and the structure of the environment. Psychol Rev 63(2):129–138
Snider LW (2005) Political risk: the institutional dimension. Int Interactions 31(3):203–222, 10.1080/03050620500294176
Stoychev SP (2013) Political risk in Europe: a quantitative index based on measures of corruption, market distortion, and the shadow economy. J Polit Risk 1(5). Available at https://www.jpolrisk.com/political-risk-in-europe-a-quantitative-index-based-on-measures-of-corruption-market-distortion-and-the-shadow-economy/

Tradingeconomics (2014) Greece Government Bond 10Y. http://www.tradingeconomics.com/greece/government-bond-yield. Accessed 30 Apr 2015

Triantopoulos Ch. (2015) It is true that money borrowed by Greece intended solely to repay previous debts and bank bailouts? (In Greek). Understanding the Greek crisis, March 2015, No 3, ELIAMEP

World Bank (2015a) Bank nonperforming loans to total gross loans (%). http://data.worldbank.org/indicator/FB.AST.NPER.ZS/countries?page=1. Accessed 25 Apr 2015

World Bank (2015b) Gross Domestic Product for Greece [MKTGDPGRA646NWDB]. Retrieved from FRED, Federal Reserve Bank of St. Louis. https://research.stlouisfed.org/fred2/series/MKTGDPGRA646NWDB/. Accessed 29 Nov 2015

Theory of Optimum Currency Areas and the Balkans

Edgar Juan Saucedo Acosta and Jesus Diaz Pedroza

Abstract The theory of optimum currency areas show which are the optimal conditions for a group of countries sharing the same currency, such theory also points out the costs and benefits of giving up a national currency. There are costs and benefits for countries that decide to use the currency of another country or if they choose to belong to a monetary union. The main cost for a country when it is part of a monetary union is the loss of monetary policy, however if such country has credibility problems in monetary policy (high inflation in the past), this cost is significantly reduced or even it can become a benefit. Countries may choose to use another currency to import credibility (Dollarization or Euroisation), belonging to a monetary union or to create central banks with credibility. There are economies with anchors currencies, that is, economies with credible central banks (with inflation controlled for several years), while on the other hand there are economies that have no anchor currencies and therefore can choose to import credibility from economies with anchor currencies. The aim of this paper is to apply some theoretical elements of the theory of optimum currency areas to Balkans countries. We start to consider the idea that there are anchor currencies and non-anchor currencies on the economies of the world. Starting from the above, it is considered that the anchor currency for the countries of the Balkans is the euro, due to the credibility that the European Central Bank has acquired since its creation to the present. Furthermore, we propose to evaluate the relevance for Balkan countries choose one of the following three options: keep their national currencies, create a new regional currency or to use the euro (Euroisation or to be part of the euro area). To assess the relevance of any of the three options above, we estimate the co-movement of the economies of the Balkans with the eurozone and with themselves, besides we analyse the credibility of central banks in the region (the record

E.J. Saucedo Acosta (✉)
University of Veracruz, AV. Luis Castelazo s/n, C.P. 91190 Xalapa, Mexico
e-mail: esaucedo@uv.mx

J. Diaz Pedroza
Autonomous Metropolitan University- Iztapalapa, Av. San Rafael Atlixco No. 186, C.P. 09340 Mexico City, Mexico
e-mail: jdp@xanum.uam.mx

A. Karasavvoglou et al. (eds.), *Economic Crisis, Development and Competitiveness in Southeastern Europe*, Contributions to Economics,
DOI 10.1007/978-3-319-40322-9_4

in the inflation in the countries of the region), trade flows of the countries of the region with the euro-zone and among themselves, and finally we estimate a political proximity variable (coincidence of voting in the UN General Assembly).

1 Introduction

The Balkan region is formed by countries that have different types of relationships with the European Union (EU). Greece, Bulgaria and Croatia are already members of the EU, while Albania, FYROM, Montenegro and Serbia are official candidates and Bosnia & Herzegovina is a potential candidate, officially recognized by the European Commission. On the other hand, from a monetary point of view, the countries of the region are linked to the euro zone and the euro, because Greece is a member of such zone, Montenegro uses the euro (Euroisation), Croatia and Bulgaria will have to use such currency and all other countries of the Balkans have to do the same once they enter the EU.

In the medium and long term, the Balkans will be linked to the euro zone, so it is relevant to analyse how convenient it is for these countries to use the euro. We will use the Optimum Currency Areas (OCA) theory which analyses what are the ideal conditions for a group of countries sharing a common currency and what are the costs and benefits of using a single currency.

In the Balkan region is interesting to apply the OCA theory, because in that region Greece already share the same currency with its partners in the euro area, so that such country can be used as parameter to analyse the pertinence of the other countries in the region to enter in the euro zone. Although Greece has its own characteristics, especially after the European financial crisis, we believe it can serve as parameter.

There are papers that have studied whether the region is an OCA with the euro zone. The results are mixed, because some studies show that for the Balkans is optimal use the euro (Sideris 2009), while other studies show that only some Balkan countries should use the euro (Gouveia 2014; Broz 2007) and others show that is not optimal use of the euro to the region (Belke and Zenkić 2007; Gockov and Jovanovski 2013; Gligorov et al. 2008). The methodology of previous studies uses some of the following criteria for OCA: trade integration, synchronization of business cycles, labour mobility and the exchange rate indicator.

The originality of the paper is based on the analysis of the feasibility of the Balkans use a regional currency or the euro. To do this, we use innovative criteria, including the criterion of co-movement of the product (which differs from the synchronization of business cycles), and a criterion of political proximity. On the other hand, we use the criteria of trade integration and inflation (used in most previous studies).

2 Theories of Optimum Currency Areas

There is a wide range of exchange rate regimes (ERR). At one extreme is the ERR free floating and the other is Monetary Union (MU). Frankel (1999) found nine ERR that vary according to the degree of monetary flexibility. The ERR of free floating and MU are known as corner solutions, because they are at the extremes of the range of the ERR. In recent years several countries have chosen one of the corner solutions.

In the ERR free floating, governments do not aim its exchange rate, it is the market that determines it. The free-floating ERR must be supported by an independent Central Bank to better results.

MU occurs when two or more countries use the same currency and may be considered in two ways. In the first case, called Dollarization (or Euroisation), a country adopts the currency of another country. Montenegro has used the euro (previously the German mark). The second case, called MU, a group of countries creates a new currency, as the euro zone when a group of European countries began to use the euro since 1999.

The OCA theory studies when it is best to have a MU, in other words, the benefits of using the fixed ERR. The choice of corner solutions will be focused using the OCA theory.

An OCA can be defined as a geographic area where it is optimal to use a single currency and one Central Bank. This area may include two or more countries. The OCA theory studies the disadvantages and advantages of MU's. According to Dellas and Tavlas (2001), there are two types of approaches in the literature that evaluated when it is optimal form a MU. The first considers the conditions that countries must meet to adopt a common currency, while the second shows the costs and benefits of forming a MU.

According to the first approach, countries must meet the following conditions to form an OCA (Table 1).

Mundell (1961) states that if there is free movement of workers between two countries, it is optimal sharing a single currency. Mckinnon (1963) was the first to show that when two or more countries trade a lot the benefits of sharing the same

Table 1 Criteria of OCA and authors

	Criteria	Authors
1	Labour mobility and flexibility of wages and prices	Mundell (1961)
2	Trade openness	Mckinnon (1963)
3	Diversification of consumption and production	Kenen (1969)
4	Political integration	De Grauwe (2006), Lee and Barro (2006)
5	Financial integration	Mundell (1973a, b)
6	History of high inflation	Alesina and Barro (2002)

Source: own elaboration

currency are high. Kenen (1969) showed that the diversification of production becomes more viable monetary integration.

De Grauwe (2006) shows that political integration among countries is a determining factor for share the same currency. Mundell (1973a, b) indicated the importance of financial integration in the decision of monetary integration. Alesina and Barro (2002) showed the role that the inflation record of a country in its decision to share the same currency.

The main problem with using this method is that there are several conditions that may result conflicting results. For example, two countries can trade a lot between them. However, these countries may have low labour mobility. If we consider the first condition, such countries should share the same currency, while the second condition it would not be desirable for these countries share the same currency.

The second approach shows the costs and benefits of forming a monetary union (Table 2 below):

The Table 2 above shows the main costs and benefits of sharing a single currency. When a currency is shared, the costs of foreign exchange are eliminated (De Grauwe (2007)); this reduces uncertainty about possible appreciations and depreciations of the exchange rate (Dellas and Tavlas (2001)). When the new MU has a credible monetary policy (McCallum (1995)), there is a benefit of having a commitment to fight inflation (Alesina and Barro (2002)).

Benefits: The main benefit of being part of a MU is the reduction of transaction costs.

Costs: the main cost being part of a MU is the loss of the exchange rate and monetary policy (Mundell (1961)) to face an external imbalance.

Another benefit of being part of a MU is based on the "hypothesis of credibility". According to such hypothesis, the stronger the commitment to have a fixed exchange rate, credibility is greater. The "hypothesis of credibility" is based on the notion that a MU implies a stronger commitment by having a fixed exchange rate. A MU with a strong commitment to price stability will increase the credibility of the members of the MU, so the result is that new entrant imports credibility of the MU.

New trends in the OCA theory include new costs and benefits of forming a monetary union. For example, Alesina and Barro (2002) showed that the benefits and costs of forming a monetary union are:

Table 2 Benefits and costs of sharing a currency

Benefits and costs	Authors
Benefits	
Elimination of transaction costs	De Grauwe (2007)
Reducing uncertainty	Dellas and Tavlas (2001)
A more credible monetary agreement	McCallum (1995)
Commitment to maintain low inflation	Alesina and Barro (2002)
Costs	
Loss of monetary policy (Traditional consideration)	Mundell (1961)

Source: own elaboration

Benefits of Trade: two countries trade more with a single currency than with two currencies, therefore, a MU would increase trade.

The benefit of commitment: inflation bias is reduced when a country adopts the currency of a country with credibility in monetary policy.

Asymmetric shocks: the main cost is the effect of monetary policy in the presence of asymmetric shocks, because in the MU, monetary policy is implemented throughout the Union and not just for an individual country, so that if a country receives a shock that does not affect the Union, there is no way for this country to react to the shock.

From the new perspective of the costs and benefits of forming a MU, potential candidates are countries ("clients") with long periods of high inflation. The "clients" should choose countries with low inflation ("anchors"), i.e. countries with high credibility in monetary policy. Additionally, an important element is that the "clients" and "anchors" have symmetric shocks, to reduce the costs of forming a monetary union.

Sometimes there are MU's with several "clients" and only one "anchor", as in the case of the euro area. It may happen that a "client" unilaterally adopts the currency of an "anchor", as in the case of Montenegro with the euro. In both cases the "client" ("clients") gets more credibility, therefore, the "client" import monetary stability from the "anchor".

In the euro area the "anchor" is Germany, because the Bundesbank has had a record of low inflation and a high degree of independence. Therefore, inflation bias has been declining for Germany since the end of World War II.

Before the launch of the euro, there were two monetary systems in Europe, where Germany was the "anchor". The first was the snake in the tunnel, where European countries in the early seventies coordinated their monetary policies to keep their exchange rates linked to the US dollar. The second occurred in the late seventies, the European Monetary System (EMS), which was created to import stability of an "anchor" in this case the Bundesbank.

Capital mobility has increased since the eighties, so it was very difficult to maintain the credibility of EMS members. One solution to this problem was the creation of the Economic and Monetary Union (EMU) with only one currency and a Central Bank for Europe. McCallum (1995) points out that the stronger is the commitment largest is credibility, so that EMU was the solution to maintain the credibility of the euro zone.

Table 3 EU membership and the Balkans

Country	EU		
	Member	Candidate	Potential
Albania		2014	
Bosnia and Herzegovina			2003
Bulgaria	2007		
Croatia	2013		
Greece	1981		
FYROM		2004	
Montenegro		2010	
Serbia		2012	

Source: own elaboration

3 Exchange Rate Regimens and Monetary Unions in the Balkans

3.1 The Balkans and the European Union

We have considered for this text the following countries: Albania, Bosnia and Herzegovina, Bulgaria, Croatia, Greece, FYROM, Montenegro and Serbia.

The Balkan countries have different types of relationships with the EU, because they have the following statuses: members, candidates and potential candidates.

Table 3 shows the relationship of the Balkan countries and their status with the European Union. There are three groups of countries according their status in the EU:

Group 1: EU Member States

Greece joined 1981 to the EU and the euro area in 2001, Bulgaria is a member of the EU since 2007 and is not a member of the eurozone and Croatia joined to the EU in 2013 and is not part of the eurozone.

Group 2: EU candidates

These countries are considered candidates who have acquired this status from 2004 to 2014. In this group are included Albania, FYROM, Montenegro and Serbia. Montenegro uses the euro since 2002 (before the German mark).

Group 3: EU potential candidates

Bosnia Herzegovina is considered by the European Commission as a potential candidate for the EU.

Table 4 Monetary policy framework and exchange rate arrangement in Balkans

Exchange rate arrangement	Monetary policy framework		
	Exchange rate anchor	Inflation targeting framework	Other
	Euro		
No separate legal tender	Montenegro		
Currency Board	Bosnia and Herzegovina, Bulgaria		
Stabilized arrangement	FYROM		
Crawl-like arrangement	Croatia		
Floating		Albania, Serbia	
Free floating			Greece (in the euro zone)

Source: International Monetary Fund (2013)

3.2 Exchange Rate Regimes and O Monetary Policy in the Balkans

The exchange rate regimes and monetary policy differ in the Balkans. Table 4 shows the types of monetary policy and ERR. The region has a wide range of ERR, from unilateral dollarization to floating.

3.2.1 Greece

Greece has no longer a monetary policy and national currency. Since 2001, such country is a member of the eurozone and uses the euro and the European Central Bank determines monetary policy in this area. The European Central Bank manages monetary policy that is based on two pillars, one economic and the other monetary (Saucedo 2009), that is why the IMF classifies the Monetary Policy of such Central Bank as "other" (International Monetary Fund 2013). Exchange rate policy in the euro area is free floating (International Monetary Fund 2013), i.e. is the supply and demand for that currency determines its price.

3.2.2 Albania

Albania applies a monetary policy classified as inflation targeting. The Central Bank of Albania has the aim of achieving price stability, and for such the Central Bank has set a target of an annual increase in the consumer price index of 3 %. The policy exchange rate in Albania is free floating, although the International Monetary Fund (IMF) considers the regime as floating because sometimes there are interventions by the Central Bank in the foreign exchange market (International Monetary Fund 2013).

3.2.3 Serbia

Serbia applies an inflation targeting monetary policy. The Central Bank of Serbia aims price and financial stability, and has set a target by inflation, in the medium term, of 2–4 %. The exchange rate policy is managed float, because it's Central Bank intervenes when there is a lot of variability in the exchange rate. The IMF points out that Serbia has an exchange rate regime classified as floating.

3.2.4 Croatia

The Central Bank of Croatia applies a monetary policy that is anchored to the exchange rate (International Monetary Fund 2013). The IMF classifies exchange rate regime in Croatia as crawl-like arrangement, where the Central Bank of that country intervenes to achieve a controlled depreciation of its national currency (kuna) with the euro, which is not greater than 2 %, otherwise would be considered as floating (International Monetary Fund 2013).

3.2.5 FYROM

The Central Bank of FYROM applies a Monetary Policy that is anchored to the exchange rate, because its intermediate target is a certain value of its currency (Denar) in relation to the euro. The IMF classifies exchange rate regime of FYROM as Stabilized arrangement (International Monetary Fund 2013), where the Central Bank intervenes in the foreign exchange market to avoid abrupt depreciation (appreciation).

3.2.6 Bulgaria

The Central Bank of Bulgaria applies a Monetary Policy that is anchored at the exchange rate at a fixed level 1.9558: 1 EURO. The exchange rate regime in Bulgaria is an Currency Board (International Monetary Fund 2013), which consists of keeping fixed the value of its currency (lev) relative to the euro, and the rule followed is that the money supply grows (decreases) as international reserves grow (decrease).

3.2.7 Bosnia and Herzegovina

The Central Bank of Bosnia and Herzegovina applies a monetary policy that is anchored at the exchange rate at a fixed level 1.9558: 1 EURO. The rate of exchange rate of Bosnia and Herzegovina is Currency Board (International Monetary Fund 2013), which is to keep fixed the value of its national currency (mark) relative to the euro (it was linked to the German mark before), and the rule followed is that the money supply grows (decreases) as international reserves grow (decrease).

3.2.8 Montenegro

Montenegro has no own currency, uses the euro (previously used the German mark). This country uses the euro unilaterally and the main objective of the Central Bank is to achieve and maintain financial stability. The IMF classifies its exchange rate policy as "no separate legal tender" (International Monetary Fund 2013).

3.3 Monetary Options for Balkan Region

In the Balkans can be considered three options:

(1) To continue using their national currencies, although Montenegro and Greece use the euro, and Bulgaria, Croatia will have to use it in the medium and long term, because they are members of the EU.
(2) Creation of a regional currency, although in the case of Greece and Montenegro already use the euro, which would complicate this option.
(3) Using the euro as the national currency, and there are two choices: which countries become members of the euro zone (Greece) or if they decide to do so unilaterally (Montenegro).

4 Methodology

4.1 Databases, Sources and Indicators

4.1.1 Price Stability

Inflation data come from the World Development Indicators 2014 (World Bank), and we use the variable Consumer Price Index for the period 1990–2012. Not all countries have data for the entire period, because several countries acquired their independence recently, for those countries the annual average inflation data of short periods was taken into account.

Information of inflation in the euro zone come from the IMF, World Economic Outlook Database, October 2014, and we use the variable Consumer Price Index for the period 1990–2012.

$$\pi = \frac{CPI_t - CPI_{t-1}}{CPI_{t-1}}$$

Where:

CPI Consumer Price Index

4.1.2 Trade Openness

The bilateral trade data come from the Department of Trade Statistics of the IMF. Imports and exports are in US dollars for the period 1980–2013. For the calculation of trade opening we needed the Gross Domestic Product (GDP) of each of the countries, so it used the IMF, World Economic Outlook Database, October 2014. The GDP used was in billions of US dollars.

To compute the Trade Openness (TO) the following formula is used:

$$TO = \frac{M's + X's}{GDP}$$

Where:

M's imports;
X's exports;
GDP Gross Domestic Product

4.1.3 Co-Movement of GDP

The methodology used in this paper is based on the proposal of Alesina et al. (2003) in which co-movements are calculated in economies that should form a MU. Based on the results the convenience of belonging or not to an OCA (if you consider the Euro as such) is inferred.

The IMF contains all the information needed for this document. Eurostat has information for all countries in Europe, but there are some missing years for countries that are candidates to join the euro zone. The OECD database has conversions PPP exchange rates. Finally, the database of the World Bank is one of the sources used. With all these information bases we will be able to integrate a panel covering a time period of at least fifteen years for each of the countries analysed.

The model that we propose allows observe how co-movement the variable GDP per capita of a set of economies in the Balkans. The Y_{jt}/Y_{it} variable measures the ratio of GDP of the j-th country in terms of the ith country. Eight countries were used with an annual time period ranging from 2000 to 2014, homogenizing the series at PPP prices to compare these economies. An autoregressive second order process was used to estimate model parameters, such as indicated Alesina, Barro and Tenreyro:

$$ln\frac{y_{jt}}{y_{it}} = C_0 + C_1 ln\frac{y_{jt-1}}{y_{it-1}} + C_2 ln\frac{y_{jt-2}}{y_{it-2}} + u_{ijt} \tag{1}$$

With $\widehat{u_{ijt}}$ which measures the relative product that is not predictable from the previous two periods. Then a measure of co-movement would be given by the root mean square of error:

$$VY \equiv \sqrt{\frac{1}{T-3}\sum\nolimits_{t=1}^{T} u_{tij}^{\hat{2}}} \tag{2}$$

The above expression shows that for small values VY indicates a higher co-movement of products between countries i and j, and that most of the explanation (between products) is given by the expression (1).

The econometric technique for estimating parameters and root mean square consisted of a 2nd order autoregressive panel was developed by Arellano and Bond (AB) (1991) and Arellano (2003), due to the dynamic nature of the autoregressive process. Thus AB estimator is performed by the Generalized of Method of Moments (GMM) and to estimate a dynamic model is not required to include external instruments. Cannot be used the usual technique Pooled OLS estimator by the presence of autocorrelation of unobserved individual effect and lagged variables. The same problem would be using the methodology of the estimates of fixed effects and random effects.

Estimation by dynamic methods poses a relationship that is characterized by the presence of lags of the dependent variable in the regressors. In addition, it is assumed that the error terms follow a model with a single error component with the property that are independent and identically distributed (IID).

4.1.4 Political Proximity

The information on the resolutions of the General Assembly of the United Nations (UN) comes the Official Document System of the UN (http://www.un.org/es/documents/ag/resga.shtml) for the 2014. The degree of coincidence in the voting at the General Assembly of the UN was compute, and the options are for, against, abstentions and no vote. The option did not vote was taken as a fourth option, so that if a country did not vote and the other yes, it was considered that there was no coincidence in the resolution.

We followed Lee and Barro (2006) on the degree of coincidence of countries in the General Assembly of the UN. We used the latest available year (2014), for political proximity to the countries of the Balkans. FYROM does not belong to the UN, for reason we do not include in this analysis. For each of the Balkan countries the degree of coincidence was calculated (each resolution 2014) regarding themselves and the countries of the euro zone, and then we obtained an average of the degree of coincidence.

5 Results

5.1 Price Stability

Table 5 shows the average inflation, using the consumer price index, for the Balkans. We divide the information into two sub-periods, 1990–2000 and 2000–2012. Nevertheless, there are countries for which there were not data for the first period (Bosnia and Herzegovina and Montenegro) because they became independent at later dates. In the nineties was a period of low inflation in Europe, because several countries had to fulfil the Maastricht criteria, in order to enter the euro zone, but the countries of the Balkans did not have to meet these criteria (with the exception of Greece).

In the period 1990–2000, the countries of the Balkans had a double-digit inflation (excluding Greece with high inflation, but with one digit), due to the instability that occurred in this period in the region. It is noteworthy Bulgaria with an average annual inflation 117.5 %, Croatia (86.2 %) and Serbia (50.2 %). On average the Balkan region had an inflation rate of 50.22 %, very high when is compared to the euro area (2.21 %).

In the period 2000–2012, the countries of the Balkan region had lower inflation than the previous period. Inflation in the Balkans was only one digit, except Serbia having a price increase annual average of 12.9 %. Albania, Bosnia and Herzegovina, Croatia, Greece, FYROM and Montenegro had inflations very close to 3 %. The Balkans region had an average inflation 4.64 %, while in this period the euro zone had an inflation rate of 2.17 %.

The euro area seems to be an anchor in the region, because the inflation in that region is low compared with that of the Balkans. Many Balkan countries have low inflation due to: they have linked their currencies to the euro (Bulgaria and Bosnia and Herzegovina have a Currency Board) or they use the euro (Greece and Montenegro) and as a result of the process of transitional evolution of their economies. The euro is now an anchor currency for the region, so it would be very likely for countries

Table 5 Mean of annual inflation rates for Balkans region (%)

Country	1990–2000	2000–2012
Albania	27.8	2.9
Bosnia and Herzegovina		3
Bulgaria	117.5	5.9
Croatia	86.2	2.9
Greece	9	3.2
FYROM	10.6	2.4
Montenegro		3.9
Serbia	50.2	12.9
Average	50.22	4.64
Euro zone	2.21	2.17

Source: own elaboration with data from The World Bank

of the Balkans to use it in the future as a means to import stability. Greece and Montenegro uses the euro, Bulgaria and Croatia will eventually use that currency (once they pass a series of tests) because they are part of the EU, while other countries are candidates (with the exception of Bosnia and Herzegovina), so that when they become member of the EU will have to use the euro.

5.2 Bilateral Trade

Table 6 shows the bilateral trade (% GDP) of the countries of the Balkans with respect to the euro zone and among themselves. In general, countries in the Balkans are more integrated with the euro area (15.88 %) than among themselves (7.80 %), so it would be more likely to share a currency with the euro area than among themselves. Montenegro is the only country in the region with greater regional integration with the Balkans (15.10 %) compared with the euro area (12.36 %), while other countries in the region have greater trade integration with the euro zone. Croatia, Albania, Bosnia and Herzegovina, Bulgaria and FYROM are more integrated with the euro area than Greece, even that the latter is already using the euro. Although Montenegro already uses the euro, it is the most integrated, in terms of trade, with the Balkan region.

Overall, if we use the criterion of trade integration, the countries of the Balkans would be ideal candidates to use the euro, because their level of trade integration with the euro area is larger than themselves. The alternative of a regional currency is not feasible if we use the criterion of trade integration.

Table 6 Bilateral Trade (% GDP) for Balkans region, 2005–2013

Country	Trade partners	
	Euro zone (%)	Balkans (%)
Albania	13.73	4.32
Bosnia and Herzegovina	17.56	13.98
Bulgaria	19.98	4.80
Croatia	20.77	4.41
Greece	13.58	1.85
FYROM	16.70	11.97
Montenegro	12.36	15.10
Serbia	12.38	5.97
Average	15.88	7.80

Source: own elaboration with data from the IMF

5.3 Co-Movement of Product

To estimate Eq. (1) a transformation of the variable in logarithm is performed and the results are presented in Table 7.

However, the interest of our empirical analysis focuses on the residuals of the regression, because they represent the co-movements or interdependence of all countries in this panel.

Table 8 shows the co-movement of GDP per capita between the countries of the Balkans and the euro zone and among the countries of the Balkans (lower values means higher co-movements). On average, countries in the Balkans have higher co-movement among themselves (regarding the euro area). Therefore would not be optimal for those countries using the euro as a whole, while a regional currency would be more justified if we use the criterion of co-movement of products. However Greece and Montenegro, which already use the euro, have the lowest co-movement with the euro zone, which would be a contradiction if we rely on the criterion of co-movement of products. The above indicates that the decision to use the euro by Greece, and to a lesser extent Montenegro (by the size of its economy), was based more on political criteria. The low co-movement of the Greek economy with the euro zone is not new, there are studies (Lee and Barro 2006; Saucedo 2009) showing that the synchronization of its economy is low relative to the area euro.

5.4 Political Proximity

The Table 9 shows the political proximity (degree of coincidence in voting of the resolutions of the General Assembly of the UN) of the countries of the Balkans with the euro area and among themselves.

The Balkan countries have more political proximity to the members of the euro area than themselves, because the level of political proximity to the euro area (0.9013) is higher than among themselves (0.8820), therefore, would be more

Table 7 Results of estimation of Eq. (1)

Dependent variable	Coefficient
$ln(y_{jt}/y_{it})$	
Independent variables	
$\ln\left(y_{jt-1}/y_{it-1}\right)$	1.2524
	(0.1037)
$\ln\left(y_{jt-2}/y_{it-2}\right)$	−0.3619
	(0.1040)
c_0	−0.7446
	(0.1767)

Source: own estimation
Note: The standard error is shown in parentheses below the coefficient
All coefficients are significant at the 5 % statistical significance

Table 8 Co-movement of GDP per capita, 2000–2014

Country	VY Euro zone	VY Balkans (average)
Albania	0.0202	0.0103
Bosnia and Herzegovina	0.0222	0.0113
Bulgaria	0.0208	0.0119
Croatia	0.0246	0.0127
FYROM	0.0225	0.0121
Greece	0.0272	0.0147
Montenegro	0.0292	0.0163
Serbia	0.0259	0.0138
Average	**0.0241**	**0.0129**

Source: own estimation

Table 9 Political proximity for Balkan countries, 2007–2014

Country	Euro zone	Balkans (average)
Albania	0.9116	0.8869
Bosnia and Herzegovina	0.8543	0.8523
Montenegro	0.9341	0.9114
Serbia	0.8166	0.8119
Bulgaria	0.9213	0.8939
Croatia	0.9240	0.9013
Greece	0.9472	0.9162
Average	**0.9013**	**0.8820**

Source: own estimation with data from UN

appropriate that the euro will be used in the region regarding a the creation of a new regional currency. At the country level, Croatia, Greece, Bulgaria, Montenegro and Albania are more integrated with the euro zone.

We will use Greece as a parameter, in this section, because is already member of the euro zone and we suppose that such country has a high level of political proximity with their partners due to negotiations before and during the euro zone creation. So, using Greece as a parameter, only Bosnia and Herzegovina and Serbia would not be politically very close to the euro zone, so it would not be desirable for these countries to use the euro.

6 Conclusion

The countries of the Balkan region are linked to the euro zone in different ways. In the future the region will be further linking with countries that share the euro, so it is relevant to investigate whether it is optimal for that region using the euro, or if a better scenario to create a new regional currency or to continue using their national currencies.

The paper shows that for the countries of the region the benefits of using the euro are large, so that the option of a regional currency would not be a good choice. The use of the euro is a feasible option once these countries have joined the EU. The option to continue using their national currencies is not viable in the long term, because there are countries that already are using the euro in the region (Greece and Montenegro), while other countries have linked their currencies to the euro. Only Serbia and Albania have implemented monetary and exchange rate policies that are not linked to the euro, because these countries have monetary policies of inflation targeting and a flexible exchange rate.

If we use as a criterion to price stability, although the countries of the Balkan region have reduced inflation, the price increase in this region is almost double that in the euro area in the period 2000–2012 while in the previous period (1990–2000), the average annual inflation Balkan region was 50 %, while in the euro area was only 2 %. The euro is an anchor currency that would serve the region to import price stability.

The criterion of bilateral trade shows that on average the Balkan countries trade more with the euro area with such region, so that the best option would be to utilize the euro instead of creating a new regional currency. Most countries in the region have greater bilateral trade with the eurozone than Greece with its euro zone partners.

The criteria of co-movement of the product shows that for Balkan countries is beneficial to use a regional currency, because their economies are more synchronized with themselves than with the euro zone. Nevertheless if we use Greece as a parameter, for the rest of Balkans countries would be optimal to use the euro, because those countries have higher co-movement than Greece (regarding euro zone).

The criterion of proximity policy shows that in general the countries of the region are more politically closer to the euro area than among themselves, so the best option is to use the euro instead of a regional currency.

The paper has the advantage that from a set of criteria is possible to determine whether it is optimal for the Balkan countries to be integrated monetarily with the euro zone. Thus, it was concluded that the best option for the region is to use the euro in relation to launch a new regional currency. However, from the case of Greece is possible to note that monetary integration responds to political factors rather than the criteria of OCA, because that country have lower values on several criteria than other countries of the Balkans. In this sense, one of the limitations of the text is that political factors that influence share a single currency are not included, although a political proximity indicator was used. It possible to apply the same methodology to other regions that are involved in economic integration processes to analyse the feasibility of monetary integration.

When a country is a member of a monetary union loses control of its monetary policy to address economic national shocks. In the case of the eurozone, decisions of the Governing Council of the ECB are based on macroeconomic variables in such area and not a particular country, however, as a country is larger, such as Germany, its macroeconomic variables affects more the euro zone, unlike a small country (Greece). If the business cycle of a small country is synchronized with the cycle of the eurozone, a single monetary policy is optimal, but if the cycles are not synchronized a single monetary policy is not optimal. When members of a monetary union have different economic paths, the costs of belonging to a monetary union increase, because a single monetary policy is not optimal for a group of countries with different economic cycles.

References

Alesina A, Barro RJ (2002) Currency unions. Q J Econ 117(2):409–436

Alesina A, Barro RJ, Tenreyro S (2003) Optimal currency areas. In: Gertler M, Rogoff K (eds) NBER Macroeconomics annual 2002. The MIT Press, Cambridge, MA, pp 301–356

Arellano M (2003) Panel data econometrics. Oxford University Press, Oxford

Arellano M, Bond S (1991) Some tests of specification for panel data: Monte Carlo evidence and an application to employment equations. Rev Econ Stud 58:277–297

Belke A, Zenkić A (2007) Exchange-rate regimes and the transition process in the Western Balkans. Intereconomics 42(5):267–280

Broz T (2007) The application of optimum currency area criteria to Croatia. Revistatineriloreconomisti 1(9):7–19

De Grauwe P (2006) What have we learnt about monetary integration since the Maastricht treaty? J Common Mark Stud 44:711–730

De Grauwe P (2007) The economics of monetary integration. Oxford University Press, New York, NY

Dellas H, Tavlas GS (2001) Lessons of the euro for dollarization: analytic and political economy perspectives. J Policy Model 23(3):333–345

Frankel JA (1999) No single currency regime is right for all countries or at all times. NBER Working papers 7338

Gligorov V, Iara A, Landesmann M, Stehrer R (2008) Western Balkan countries: adjustment capacity to external shocks, with a focus on labour markets. "Wiener Inst. für Internat. Wirtschaftsvergleiche" (WIIW)

Gockov G, Jovanovski K (2013) Macroeconomic shocks asymmetry: see as an optimal currency area. Review-Časopiszaekonomiju-APEIRON 6(2)

Gouveia S (2014) Business cycle correlation between the Euro area and the Balkan countries. Int J Econ Sci Appl Res 1:33–49

International Monetary Fund (2013) Annual report on exchange arrangements and exchange restrictions 2013. International Monetary Fund, Washington, DC
Kenen PB (1969) The optimum currency area: an eclectic view. In: Mundell RA, Swoboda AK (eds) Monetary problems of the international economy. University of Chicago Press, Chicago, IL, pp 41–60
Lee JW, Barro RJ (2006) East Asian currency union. Harvard University Working paper
McCallum BT (1995) Two fallacies concerning Central-Bank independence. Am Econ Rev 85 (2):207–211
McKinnon RI (1963) Optimum currency areas. Am Econ Rev 53(4):717–725
Mundell RA (1961) A theory of optimum currency areas. Am Econ Rev 51(4):657–665
Mundell RA (1973a) A plan for a European currency. In: Johnson HG, Swoboda AK (eds) The economics of common currencies. Harvard University Press, Cambridge, MA, pp 143–173
Mundell RA (1973b) Uncommon arguments for common currencies. In: Johnson HG, Swoboda AK (eds) The economics of common currencies. Harvard University Press, Cambridge, MA, pp 114–132
Saucedo EJ (2009) Essays on the European Central Bank: Ensayos sobre el Banco Central Europeo. University of Veracruz, Xalapa, Mexico
Sideris D (2009) Do the new EU member states form an optimum currency area with the eurozone? Evidence from six Central and Eastern European countries (No. 15), National Bank of Serbia

The Balance-of-Payments Constrained Growth Model in Transitional Economy: The Case of Bulgaria

Elena Spasova

Abstract This paper examines the growth dynamics of the Bulgarian economy in the last 20 years in the light of the concept of balance-of-payments (BOP) constrained growth developed by Anthony Thirlwall (Thirlwall's Law).

Thirlwall's Law aims at evaluating a country's growth rate consistent with internal and external economic equilibrium. It states that BOP equilibrium requires a rate of economic growth not exceeding the ratio of the income elasticity of a country's exports to the income elasticity of its imports—giving focus on price and non-price competitiveness.

The study aims to verify whether the balance-of-payments constrained growth approach is suitable for explaining the Bulgarian growth performance in the last two decades.

To this end, an econometric analysis of the equilibrium (sustainable) growth rate of the Bulgarian economy according to the concept of the BOP constraint on growth is made and compared to the actual registered levels of growth. The analysis clearly demonstrates that the characteristics of Bulgarian external trade represent a constraint on the country's growth dynamics and hinder the process of sustainable economic convergence with the developed world.

1 Introduction

The debate between supply-constrained and demand-constrained growth remains at the core of the discussion on the factors for economic growth. Anthony Thirlwall (1979) contributes to the debate in favour of demand-constrained growth through the model of the balance-of-payments constraint to growth, known as Thirlwall's Law. The basic assumption of the law is that no country can grow faster than what is consistent with the balance-of-payments equilibrium because it would face ever increasing trade deficits and external debt. As a result, an economy facing such a situation reduces the national income which leads to unemployment. For that

E. Spasova
New Bulgarian University, 21 Montevideo Str, 1618 Sofia, Bulgaria
e-mail: elenaspasova@nbu.bg

A. Karasavvoglou et al. (eds.), *Economic Crisis, Development and Competitiveness in Southeastern Europe*, Contributions to Economics,
DOI 10.1007/978-3-319-40322-9_5

reason, Thirlwall reaches the conclusion that the balance-of-payments equilibrium growth rate equals the ratio between the growth of exports and the income elasticity of the demand of imports. This perspective focuses on the non-price competitiveness of the economy on the external markets and allows further analysis of the tools and methods for sustainable long-term growth.

The aim of this paper is to analyse whether "Thirlwall's Law" is suitable for explaining the actual growth of the Bulgarian economy over the 1994–2013 period. Although this methodology is not new, it is still widely used in the empirical growth literature to predict actual growth. The elasticities of demand are estimated via OLS and 2SLS regressions. The results strongly confirm the validity of the Thirlwall's Law for the Bulgarian economy and the estimated coefficients of demand elasticity of exports and imports show problems with Bulgarian external competitiveness. This results in relatively lower sustainable levels of economic growth of the country and lack of capacity for catching-up strategy.

The paper is structured as follows: In Sect. 2 the model and its theoretical explanation are presented. In Sect. 3, initial descriptive analysis of the data is made and additional information of the Bulgarian economy is provided. The estimations results are demonstrated in Sect. 4 together with the analysis of the main findings of the regression outcomes and the test of the validity of Thirlwall's law for the Bulgarian economy. The final section concludes on the relevance of Thirlwall's Law as a method of predicting the actual growth rate of the Bulgarian economy and poses basic recommendations for improving the external competitiveness of the economy.

2 Theoretical Framework and Empirical Background

In traditional growth theories the equilibrium (natural) level of growth has two main functions. First, the natural growth rate provides a ceiling for the sustainable development of an economy and determines the cyclical fluctuations—the difference between the natural level and the actual level, which indicates the presence of an economic boom or decline. Second, it determines the long-term growth rates around which the economy gravitates. According to these theories, the natural rate of growth is presented as strictly exogenous, determined by the growth of employment and productivity, without considering the dependence or endogeneity of the two factors on demand. Therefore, different economic schools (mostly the Neoclassical vs. the Keynesian school) explore ways of bringing the actual level of growth to its natural level. Whilst the neoclassical theory sees this adjustment through substitution between capital and labour with the aim to change the resource productivity per unit, Keynesians argue that the equilibrium level is achieved through a change in the income distribution. Both schools, however, accept the natural rate of growth as a constant, not as a subject to change—the adaptation of the actual growth of the economy to its natural levels is carried out in terms of constancy of the predetermined equilibrium level (at full employment). The natural level can be changed only under the influence of exogenous factors—technological changes or changes in labour productivity.

Anthony Thirlwall develops a model that proves that the abovementioned growth factors are endogenous to demand, i.e. he makes the assumption that as a result of a demand change (internal and external demand) the natural level of national production may also change through accumulation of resources (capital and labour). His conclusions are empirically proven for a number of countries (see Dixon and Thirlwall 1975; Thirlwall 1969; Thirlwall 1987) and are based on the Verdoorn law, which states that "long-term change in production volume by about 10 % is related to change in labour productivity by about 4.5 %." Kaldor proves a factor change of 0.484 and confirms the findings of Verdoorn (1993).

Provided that the natural rate of growth is endogenous to demand or to the actual level of growth, we could draw two main conclusions. Firstly, theoretically the presence of such a correlation has an impact on the efficiency and the speed of convergence between the actual and natural growth rates. Secondly, it has an effect on the manner in which the growth process should be analysed and gives clarity to the question why different economies grow at different rates: whether growth is determined by aggregate supply or is determined by demand restrictions before the supply capacity is fully reached (León-Ledesma and Thirlwall 2002).

The neoclassical growth paradigm focuses on the supply-side of the economy and explains economic growth as a function of the rate of growth of capital and labour and, in general, the growth of production factors and their efficiency. However, it does not explain why growth rates are different for different countries or why production factors in one economy are more effective than those in another. An answer to this question can be given, only if demand is taken into consideration; namely the growth rates are different, because internal and external demand is different. Therefore, the question that should be answered regards the constraints facing demand. In this sense, in contemporary open economies a major obstacle to growth is balance-of-payments constraint on demand. The meaning of this constraint is defined by Anthony Thirlwall. He claims that an economy's growth could not be indefinite, if it is due to the rising levels of external indebtedness of the economy.

However, Thirlwall model does not ignore the impact of aggregate supply (which is a function of technology, the structural characteristics of the economy and specialization), but rather assumes that the macro-level effects of aggregate supply on economic growth are reflected in the coefficients of income elasticity of imports and exports, which characterize the non-price competitiveness of domestic production.

The model is generated from the initial condition for balanced BOP:

$$P_dX = P_fME, \tag{1}$$

where P_d and P_f are the prices of exports and imports, E is the exchange rate, and M and X are the imports and exports volumes. Thirlwall describes the import and export functions as:

$$M = b(P_fE/P_d)^{\psi}Y^{\pi},\ \psi < 0,\ \pi > 0 \tag{2}$$

$$X = a(P_d/P_fE)^{\eta}Z^{\varepsilon}, \eta < 0,\ \varepsilon > 0 \tag{3}$$

where Y and Z are respectively domestic and world income, ψ and η are price elasticities of demand of imports and exports; π and ε are income elasticities of demand of imports and exports.

After substitution and transformation, we get the formula for the balance-of-payments equilibrium growth rate (small letters indicate growth rates):

$$y_b = \left[(1 + \eta + \psi))(p_d - p_f - e) + \varepsilon z\right]/\pi \tag{4}$$

Analysing this formula, we can outline several conclusions about the dynamics of the equilibrium growth rate. First, it can be concluded what the effect of higher inflation in the local economy and abroad would be.

If there is a rise in inflation in the local economy, the prices of domestic products (p_d) will rise. Whether this will have a lowering effect on the equilibrium growth rate depends on the sum of the indices of the price elasticity of demand for exports (η) and price elasticity of demand for imports (ψ). If this amount is greater than 1, then the equilibrium growth rate will decrease.

If there is a rise in inflation abroad (growth of p_f) and the amount of the price elasticity of demand for imports (ψ) and price elasticity of demand for exports (η) is greater than 1, it will lead to an increase in the equilibrium rate of growth.

The effect of a possible devaluation (e) also depends on the price elasticity of domestic demand for imported goods and foreign demand for exported goods. This pattern is known as the Marshall–Lerner condition. The coefficients of both price elasticities should be more than 1 in order to have a positive effect on the sustainable rate of growth.

Furthermore, growth of world income (z) would increase y_b, considering that the income elasticity of demand of imports is negatively related to the y_b—the higher the elasticity, the lower the sustainable growth rate.

It can be said that the higher growth of an economy must be aligned with the balance-of-payments constraint in order for this growth to be sustainable and to pose no threat of future destabilization. If the equilibrium rate of growth in a balanced balance of payments environment rises as a result of the increase of attractiveness of exports or reduction of income elasticity of demand for imports, this growth would not pose a threat of future imbalances. On the other hand, if we just observe an increase in the economy's production capacity without any change in the nature of the demand for these goods, this would be a precondition for unemployment.

This observation raises the issue of different levels of sustainable growth in the balance-of-payments constrained growth (BPCG) model. It could be stated that these differences are due to the characteristics of import and export goods reflected in their price and income elasticities. For example, countries with low levels of sustainable growth rates are characterized by low income elasticity of demand for exports and high income elasticity of imports. This means that goods produced in this economy are attractive neither to foreign markets, nor to local consumers. In practice, this model places the export growth and the improvement of its competitiveness as the key strategy for sustainable growth. The nature of exports is of particular importance, since due to the different characteristics of demand for these goods abroad and domestically, identical rates of growth of exports would lead to different levels of steady economic growth. It is important not only to answer the question "how much is produced and exported", but also "what is produced and what is its demand", i.e. the essential characteristic of exports that could determine the ability of an economy to develop and implement a successful export-based growth strategy, is its non-price competitiveness.

Thirlwall (1979) and McCombie (1985) argue that in the long term the rates of change in the relative prices of imports and exports play a small role in determining the level of exports and imports. Taking into consideration their observations and after a simplification of the above mentioned formula, we get the so called weak version of Thirlwall's Law:

$$y_b = x/\pi \tag{5}$$

The law states that the long-run equilibrium growth rate in the BPCG framework is determined by the ratio between the long-run export growth and the income elasticity of import. McCombie adds that differences in growth rates across economies are determined by the discrepancies between the values of the income elasticity of demand for their exports and the income elasticity of demand for the imports in the economy (respectively, ε and π).

It is important to note that the proposed model is valid only in the long term as in the short term countries can register balance-of-payments deficits covered by capital inflows. The situation changes in the long term as deficits cannot grow indefinitely and be covered at the cost of increasing foreign indebtedness, i.e., according to Thirlwall, in the long term the role of capital inflows is negligible.

Bértola et al. (2002) reformulates the law of Thirlwall as follows:

$$y_b/z = \varepsilon/\pi, \tag{6}$$

where y_b is the level of sustainable growth in the BPCG model, π and ε are the coefficients of income elasticity, and z is the level of world income. This equation shows that an economy can achieve a greater equilibrium growth rate if its non-price competitiveness (ε / π) is above 1. If $y_b/z = \varepsilon/\pi = 1$, the rate of growth of an economy to the world rates will be maintained. These observations confirm the usefulness of the model in explaining the international differences in economic growth rates.

A number of economists apply the Thirlwall model to individual economies and to whole regions regardless their level of development. However, it is noteworthy the amount of literature on the application of the model for developing countries, primarily in the Latin American region. One of the reasons for the interest is the fact that this theory is not entirely new to the region because it shares common grounds with the work of Raul Prebisch and his center-periphery model, which interprets the high income elasticity of exports and low income elasticity of imports as factors for sustainable external imbalances and modest growth.

Although it is relatively unknown (compared with its application in Latin America), the BPCG model is empirically tested to some European economies. Two major studies focus on economic growth and balance-of-payments imbalances of Spain. León-Ledesma (1999) examines the validity of the Thirlwall law for Spain in the period of 1964–1994. In order to estimate the coefficients of demand elasticity for imports and exports, Leon-Ledesma used functions of exports and imports. The results confirm the validity of the model for that period—estimated growth rates are close to the real ones. Bajo-Rubio (2010) also makes long-term analysis of the balance-of-payments constrained growth of Spain for the period 1850–2000. The analysis is done by dividing the period into several stages, allowing assessment of BPCG in different historical periods and in different environments. Other studies focusing on European countries are the works of Soukiazis et al. (2013a) and Kvedaras (2012) on Portugal; Garcimartín et al. (2012) on sample of OECD countries.

In recent years, the BPCG model is applied also for some of the transition economies of Central and Eastern Europe. An interesting example in this regard is the study of Bekö (2003) for a small economy in transition—Slovenia. The period under consideration is short—from 1992 to 2002, which is one of the main weaknesses of the study. However, the study shows that the Slovenian economy grows above its equilibrium level which corresponds with the increasing negative net exports. Cointegration analysis shows a clear long-term relationship between real GDP and real exports. Beko uses the data to analyze the structural problems of the Slovenian economy. The author concludes that economic growth consistent with the long-term equilibrium level requires either a change in the terms of trade and increased capital inflows, or change in the elasticity of exports and imports. The later requires a relatively long period and targeted policies. Furthermore, according to the author, it cannot be expected a substantial decrease in the income elasticity of imports due to the consumer preferences and the dependency of exports on imported raw materials. He suggests that it is appropriate to focus on exports. Exports could be driven in two main ways: (1) exchange rate changes and (2) policies to stimulate export production. According to Beko, the exchange rate changes would be ineffective because of the low price elasticity of exports and the risk of inflation and increased interest rates. The recommendations are for changes in the structure of export production through investments in new technologies and human capital.

Hansen and Kvedaras (2004) tested the model for the three Baltic countries—Estonia, Lithuania and Latvia for the period 1995–2003. They modify the model in order to come closer to the specifics of the region. The Balassa–Samuelson effect is included in the import function to allow estimation of the effect of long-term real appreciation of the national currency. Their results are alarming. Firstly, the estimated sustainable levels of growth are low and cannot provide catching-up of

Western economies. Furthermore, the authors indicate that economic growth is not significantly affected by changes in exports due to the relatively high demand elasticity of import and the dependence of exports on imported raw materials.

One of the latest studies on the subject in the region of Central and Eastern Europe is the study of Soukiazis et al. (2013b) focusing on Slovakia. The BPCG model turns out to be valid in explaining the growth dynamics in Slovakia after 1993. The main recommendation for raising the sustainable growth rate of the country is stimulating the production of higher-quality tradable goods.

The conclusion that may be derived from the theoretical and empirical studies applying the BPCG model is that it is not appropriate to think of growth only as a function of production factors after, to some extent, demand can create its own supply. The growth rates of certain economies, as well as economic divergence between countries could be explained only if restrictions on demand (internal and external) are taken into account. This is particularly true for developing countries where restrictions on demand are present before potential output is reached. This fact dooms them to modest growth.

3 Economic Growth and International Competitiveness of Bulgaria: Descriptive Analysis

Before proceeding to the econometric test of Thirlwall's Law applied to the Bulgarian economy, it would be useful to take a look at the dynamics and long-term trends in the export and import flows of Bulgaria, as well as its growth rate. The period of interest is 1994–2013 which is found to be appropriate in evaluating the character of transition to market economy and allows long-term estimation of the appropriateness of the BPCG model in estimating the sustainable growth rate of the Bulgarian economy.

Table 1 illustrates the main indicators that characterize the external trade relations of Bulgaria in the period of 1994–2013. As can be observed, both exports and imports in the analysed period are increasing, which is not surprising considering the intensive process of trade liberalization. What is more interesting is the accelerated rate of growth of imports compared to exports. Another important factor is the higher volatility of exports compared to imports. Both of these tendencies are worrying and could be a basis for further analysis.

A closer look at the historical dynamics of exports and imports shows that the negative tendencies develop after year 2000 (Fig. 1). The period of 2002–2008 (the period of economic boom) is characterized by increasing external deficit. During the crisis period a certain adjustment takes place, however the imports are constantly exceeding the levels of exports. As can be expected, the mean value of current account balance and of the external trade balance of Bulgaria are both negative.

Table 1 Summary statistics of main indicators, Bulgaria, 1994–2013

Variable	Mean	Standard deviation	Minimum	Maximum
Exports, annual % change, base: previous year	5.861051	13.77357	−17.72319	30
Imports, annual % change, base: previous year	6.681754	12.57156	−21.5083	26.24329
GDP growth, annual % change, Bulgaria base: previous year	2.675573	3.610211	−5.646222	6.907381
GDP growth, annual % change, developed countries	2.805597	2.215915	−4.593135	4.963135
Final consumption, annual % change	2.173989	6.736841	−15.34359	10.80616
Gross Capital formation, annual % change	147.5501	633.7145	−75.1252	2836.958
External balance on goods and services, current US$	−2,060,000,000	3,240,000,000	−10,800,000,000	1,440,000,000
Current account balance, % of GDP	−5.52795	7.830871	−24.323	3.886
Price index, imports of goods and services	3.194444	7.71038	−12.9	14.9
Price index, exports of goods and services	4.033333	8.796791	−17.8	21.1
Terms of trade	92.44	18.50	72.67	134.40

Sources: see Appendix

The GDP statistics also show negative comparative trends. During the 20-year period the national income grows at 2.68 % on average while the group of developed countries (used as a reference for the rest of the world because the Bulgarian exports are mainly oriented towards their territories) grows on average by 2.81 %. It turns out that the catching-up growth process did not happen in Bulgaria, what is more—Bulgaria has lagged even further behind the developed world.

A more detailed overview of the national income growth rates shows that the negative difference between Bulgaria's GDP and developed countries' GDP is due to the 90s when Bulgaria goes through a severe crisis. The growth rates after year 2000 are visibly higher. However, it became clear that the increased growth was at the cost of rising external indebtedness (Fig. 2).

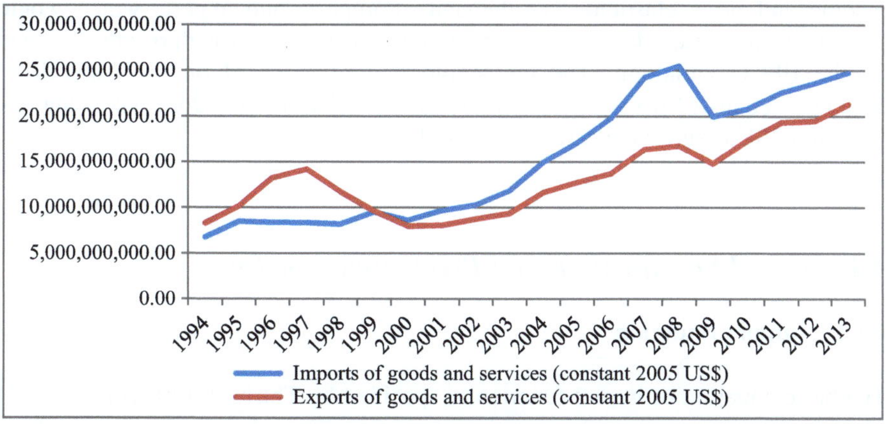

Source: World Bank, World Development Indicators, 2015

Fig. 1 Exports and imports volumes, constant 2005 US$

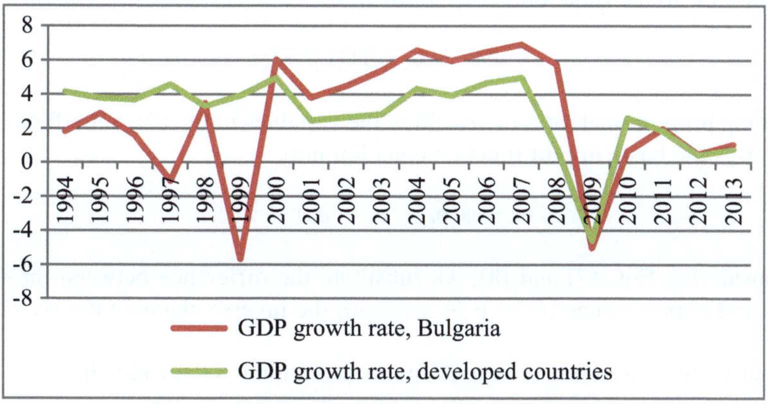

Source: World Bank, World Development Indicators, 2015

Fig. 2 GDP growth, Bulgaria and developed world, % change, 1994–2013

4 Thirlwall's Law: Methodology and Application for the Bulgarian Case

Thirlwall's Law, as has been defined in Eqs. (5) and (6), will be tested empirically for the Bulgarian economy over the 1994–2013 period. The aim is to test whether the balance-of-payments constrained growth model is able to explain the performance of the Bulgarian economy over this period. In order to conduct that experiment, import and export functions are specified in order to receive estimates of the income and price elasticities of demand of imports and exports which would provide the necessary data for estimation of the sustainable growth rate provisioned by the BPCG paradigm. The methodology used is based on the research of Soukiazis et al. (2013b). The econometric calculations are done via Stata 13. OLS and 2SLS regressions are used as tools.

4.1 Model Specification and Pre-Estimation Tests

4.1.1 Import Function

The basic equation of import function as specified by Thirlwall (2012) is:

$$M = b(P_f E/P_d)^{\Psi} Y^{\pi}$$

The ratio of the import prices to export prices is basically the inverse terms of trade (TOT), so the function is transformed to:

$$M = b(1/TOT)^{\Psi} Y^{\pi} \tag{7}$$

Taking proportional rates of growth of the variables in Eq. (2), Setterfield (2011) transforms the basic import function equation into:

$$m = \psi(p_f + e - p_d) + \pi y \tag{8}$$

Considering Eqs. (7) and (8), we substitute the difference between the import prices and export prices ($p_f + e - p_d$) with the inverse change rates of terms of trade.

Finally, the import equation used in this estimation is the following:

$$m = \pi y_t - \psi tot_t \tag{9}$$

Small letters indicate growth rates of the variables. The expected value of the income elasticity of demand of imports (π) is positive, while the price elasticity of imports (ψ) is expected to be negative.

4.1.2 Export Function

The basic equation of the export function as specified by Thirlwall is:

$$X = a(P_d/P_f E)^{\eta} Z^{\varepsilon}$$

After substituting P_d/P_fE with TOT (terms of trade), the function is transformed to:

$$X = a(TOT)^{\eta}Z^{\varepsilon} \tag{10}$$

Taking growth levels of the equation variables results in:

$$x_t = \eta tot_t + \varepsilon z_t \tag{11}$$

The expected value of the income elasticity of demand of exports (ε) is positive, while the price elasticity of exports (η) is expected to be negative.

4.1.3 Pre-Estimation Tests

Before proceeding further, all the data to be used in the regression estimations is taken in levels on annual basis. Annual values of the variables are used due to the fact that quarterly data for some variables is not available. In order to ensure the validity of the regression results, the variables are checked for non-stationarity. Two tests are applied—Augmented Dickey-Fuller test and the test of Elliott et al. (1996). The optimal lag order (Elliott-Rothenberg-Stock test) is calculated by the Ng and Perron (1995) sequential *t* test on the highest order lag coefficient, stopping when that coefficient's p-value is less than 0.10.

Both tests show similar results. The tests fail to reject the null hypothesis of unit roots for the data on final consumption and external balance of goods and services. However, taking the first differences of the variables provides satisfactory results (Table 2).

4.2 *Regression Results and Conclusions*

4.2.1 Empirical Test

The first step is to estimate separately each equation (of imports and of exports) using OLS. The results of the regression model are shown in Table 3. The results for the import and export functions reveal positive and statistically significant income elasticities of demand. The estimated coefficient of the export income elasticity (ε) is 1.95 significant at 1 % level, while the import income elasticity (π) is estimated to 1.88 significant at 1 % level. Interestingly, the income elasticity of exports is higher than the income elasticity of imports, which could be interpreted as a sign for a gradual catching-up process characterizing the Bulgarian economy.

The estimated coefficients of price elasticities are also statistically significant. Expectedly, the price elasticity of imports is negative. However, the export price

Table 2 Unit root test

Variable	Augmented Dickey–Fuller test for unit roots	Elliott-Rothenberg-Stock test (1996)
GDP growth, annual % change, Bulgaria base: previous year	−3.486*** (0.0083)	−3.585**
Imports, annual % change, base: previous year	−4.629*** (0.0001)	−4.513***
Exports, annual % change, base: previous year	−2.663* (0.0807)	−3.586**
GDP growth, annual % change, developed countries	−2.740* (0.0674)	−3.723***
Gross Capital formation, annual % change	−2.212* (0.0674)	−3.685**
Final consumption, annual % change	−2.212 (0.2018)	−2.206
Final consumption, annual % change, first difference	−4.224*** (0.0006)	−4.479***
External balance on goods and services, % change, previous year	−1.424 (0.5706)	−1.393
External balance on goods and services, % change, previous year, first difference	−3.170** (0.0218)	−3.389***
Terms of trade, annual % change	−3.068** (0.0290)	−3.219*

Note: Listed test statistics and p-values in brackets; *, ** and ***—levels of rejection of the hull hypothesis of unit root at 10 %, 5 % and 1 % levels of significance, respectively

elasticity has a positive sign. The paradoxical shift in sign of the export price elasticity deserves more attention.

On one hand, a positive relation between the price index of exports and export volumes could be an indication of nominal convergence as a result of the trade liberalization process in Bulgaria and the intensification of international relations. Another point raised by Benáček et al. (2003) is the trade-off between quality and price competitiveness. If the coefficient is statistically significant and negative, than we could expect that decrease in export prices results in more purchases of exported goods. The price fall would not be explained by decrease in quality, because it would not result in more intensive exports. So, the export price change could be due to increased cost competitiveness of the economy. On the other hand, a statistically significant and positive coefficient of price elasticity would find an explanation in the supply side—the positive correlation could be due to improvement in quality of exports resulting in higher prices, but also higher volumes. If we analyse aggregated data (as in the case of Bulgaria) the surprising positive sign could be explained by a gradual transformation of the export structure towards higher added value productions or by a process of convergence. However, detailed analysis and estimation of the price elasticities of demand of exports according to sectors is needed to identify the factors at play.

Table 3 Estimation results, export and import demand functions, Bulgaria 1994–2013

	OLS		2SLS
Variable	Exports	Imports	Imports
GDP growth, annual % change, developed countries	1.949584*** (0.009)		
Terms of trade, annual % change	0.7514564*** (0.003)	−.4075758* (0.085)	−.3818717* (0.074)
GDP growth, annual % change, Bulgaria		1.883809*** (0.003)	2.242322*** (0.000)
Observations	20	20	18
Adjusted R-squared	0.4736	0.3854	
F(2,18)	10.00	7.27	
Tests for autocorrelation			
Durbin's alternative test for autocorrelation (H0:no serial correlation)	Chi2 = 0.255 (0.6138)	Chi2 = 2.3471 (0.1255)	
Breusch-Godfrey LM test for autocorrelation, lags(1) (H0:no serial correlation)	Chi2 = 0.2951 (0.5870)	Chi2 = 2.427 (0.1193)	
Breusch-Pagan/Cook-Weisberg test for heteroscedasticity	chi2(2) = 1.65 (0.4374)	Chi2(2) = 0.49 (0.7833)	
Tests of overidentifying restrictions			
Sargan statistic			Chi2 = 1.83257 (0.40)
Basmann statistic			Chi2 = 1.58689 (0.45)
#Weak instruments			$F_{(2,14)} = 12.4081$

Note: Listed estimated coefficients and p-values in brackets; *, ** and ***—levels of statistical significance: 10 %, 5 % and 1 % levels of significance, respectively

The estimation of the import demand function gives statistically significant coefficients of the expected sign. However, the import equation includes the growth of domestic GDP which raises the question of possible endogeneity of national income. The problem is addressed by Soukiazis et al. (2013a, b). In the first place, if the import growth is higher than the export growth, this would create balance of payments imbalances, which would result in lower economic growth. In this case, growing imports would impact national income negatively. On the other hand, if national imports consist of primary or investment goods, initial economic growth could result in increased imports, but, at a second stage, these imports would contribute to the further growing of the economy. In order to overcome the potential threat of endogeneity, which would affect the consistency of the estimates, a second regression technique is used for the import function. Using 2SLS model allows inclusion of instrumental variables of national income. As instruments of GDP we will use the growth rates of national consumption, of gross capital formation and the second differenced change rates of external balance.

The 2SLS regression outcomes can be seen in Table 3. The estimates remain significant and the reported p-values are better. Several post-estimation tests are run

Table 4 Evaluation of the validity of Thirlwall's Law for Bulgaria

	Estimation
GDP growth, annual % change, Bulgaria average 1994–2013	2.68
Imports, annual % change, Bulgaria average 1994–2013	6.68
Exports, annual % change, Bulgaria average 1994–2013	5.86
GDP growth, annual % change, developed countries, average 1994–2013	2.81
Income elasticity of imports, Bulgaria, π (2SLS estimation)	2.24
Income elasticity of exports, Bulgaria, ε (OLS estimation)	1.95
Price elasticity of imports, Bulgaria, ψ (2SLS estimation)	−0.38
Price elasticity of exports, Bulgaria, η (OLS estimation)	0.75
Thirlwall's Law (weak): $y_b = x/\pi$	2.62
Thirlwall's Law (Bertola formulation): $y_b = z\varepsilon/\pi$	2.44

to check the validity of the instruments. Both Sargan and Basmann statistics confirm their validity. The Wald F-statistic indicates that the instruments are strong enough.

4.2.2 Application of Thirlwall's Law to the Bulgarian Economy

The main results of the regression analysis are presented below in Table 4 together with the calculation of Thirlwall's Law according to formulas (5) and (6). Additionally, several averaged estimations of variables are presented in order to facilitate the comparative analysis.

The results clearly demonstrate that the actual growth rate of the Bulgarian economy in the period of 1994–2013 is very close to the average level predicted by Thirlwall's Law regardless of its formulation. The actual rate of growth is 2.68 % on average, while the sustainable level of economic growth predicted by the BPCG model is, respectively, 2.62 % ("weak" Thirlwall's Law) and 2.44 % (Bertola's formulation).

Considering that $y_b/z = \varepsilon/\pi$, it is interesting to see if the structure of Bulgarian exports and imports allows levels of economic growth consistent with catching-up and convergence. The ratio between the income elasticities of exports and imports is 1.95/2.24; a coefficient smaller than unity. It can be concluded that the current structure of imported and exported goods and services does not allow accelerated growth rates above the global level. On the contrary, with the present characteristics of Bulgarian national production, the sustainable growth path of the economy is further lagging behind the developed world.

These disappointing findings should be further analysed through a more detailed overview of the structure of Bulgarian imports and exports. Traditionally the exports of Bulgaria are concentrated in raw materials and primary products. According to the statistics of the Bulgarian National Bank, in the 1995–2013 period the raw materials account for nearly 45 % of total exports (53.10 % in 1995, 43.46 % in 2013). The share of consumer goods in total exports is between

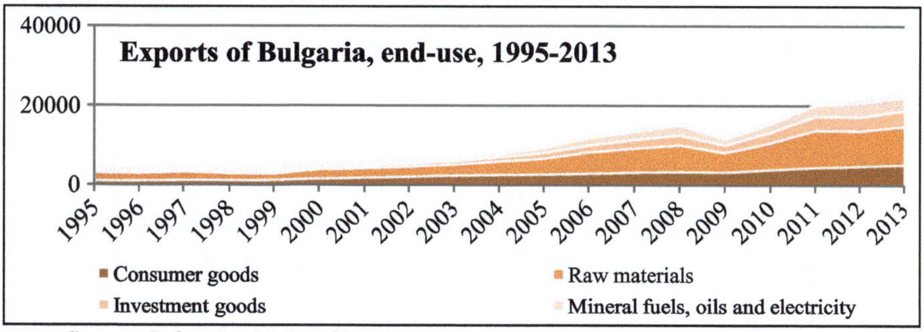

Source: Bulgarian National Bank

Fig. 3 Bulgarian exports, end-use classification, 1995–2013, in million euros

26.11 % (in 1995) and 23.40 % (in 2013). The average share of consumer goods for the whole period is 28.27 %. The share of exported investment goods and energy resources is considerably smaller (Fig. 3).

This information can be supplemented with data from the Ministry of Economy and Energy of Bulgaria, according to which high-tech exports to other countries represent only 6 % of total exports. Only 4 % of them are a result of production and export specialization and have competitive advantage in international markets. The export of medium- and low-technology products predominates (almost 70 %), 64 % of them are a result of production and export specialization and have competitive advantage on international markets. In short, although there are some trends of restructuring of Bulgarian exports, these changes are very slow and the overall profile of Bulgarian exports continues to be oriented towards low added value products and low-tech industries. Transition from low to medium industries and high-tech production would result in an increase in the income elasticity of exports which would create preconditions for a more sustainable catching-up process and export-led development.

Imports are mainly concentrated in raw materials, investment and energy resources. This fact is easily explained considering the lack of considerable conventional energy resources and the profile of Bulgarian industry oriented towards services and the light industry sector. More interestingly, the share of imported consumer goods constantly increases: in the years before the crisis, the share of consumer goods ranges between 15 % and 16 %, while in the years after 2009 the share increased to levels 20 % of total imports, which signals the reluctance to replace imported consumer goods with local substitutes (Fig. 4).

Except through structural changes affecting the export competitiveness of Bulgaria, another opportunity for increasing the sustainable growth rate of an economy is the devaluation of the national currency. The estimates on price elasticities of imports and exports demonstrate that the Marshal–Lerner condition is met. However, the sum of the absolute values of the elasticities is 1.13 which is very close to unity. Possible devaluation of the Bulgarian lev probably won't affect

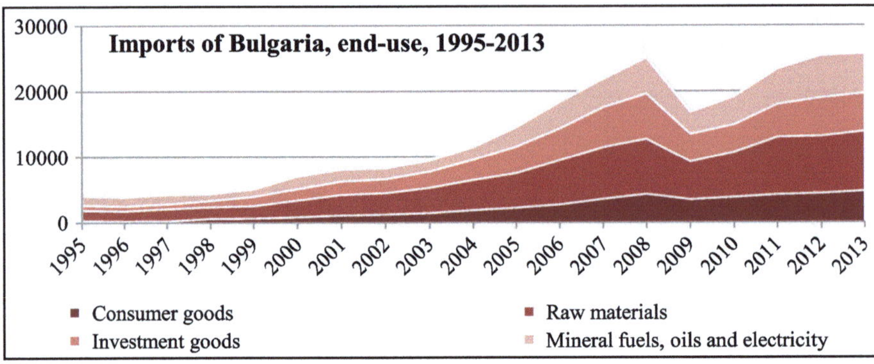

Source: Bulgarian National Bank

Fig. 4 Bulgarian imports, end-use classification, 1995–2013, in million euros

the external positions of the country considerably and its effect would be limited and short-lived.

5 Conclusion

The aim of the paper was to estimate the relevance of Thirwall's Law for the Bulgarian economy. The results indicate that the estimated average growth rate of the economy is consistent with the actual registered level. However, several worrying trends on Bulgarian economic growth were identified. In the first place, it can be concluded that the negative difference between the average developed world GDP and the Bulgarian GDP over the period is proof of the lagging behind of the economy instead of convergence. This conclusion poses serious questions to the eventual success of the so called transition period to market economy in Bulgaria. This inference is confirmed via the tests of Thirlwall's Law.

Additionally, the estimates of the income elasticities of imports and exports indicate structural problems of the national production which are factors for a lower sustainable level of growth and reduced external competitiveness. Overview of the historical data on the imports and exports structures shows certain progress in overcoming the deficiencies, but the problems remain unsolved.

Though the balance-of-payments constraint to growth theory is part of the new Keynesian paradigm, and, in this sense, it is demand-oriented; in fact this model demonstrates the importance of the structure and efficiency of production of an economy. The basic principles of the model clearly state that the productive efficiency of exported goods ultimately determines the level of sustainable economic development. In this sense, Thirlwall's law reflects the opportunities for export-oriented growth.

The opportunities for export promotion facing an economy are as follows:

(1) Devaluation: considering that a currency board system has operated in Bulgaria since 1997, the question of the level of the real exchange rate of the Bulgarian lev to foreign currencies is a subject of conjecture. However, if we consider devaluation as a tool for expenditure-switching policy, the Marshal–Lerner condition should be implemented. Moreover, a number of economists have pointed out that this step has a temporary effect and no long-term impact on the current account. Also, a significant feature of the Bulgarian export is its low level of technology and added value. This implies serious structural problems, which would not be solved by devaluation—a step to improve only the price competitiveness of exports.
(2) More capital flows: attracting foreign investments in the economy. Bulgaria has experience in this direction and it is clear that the flow of investment may provide only temporary coverage of current account deficits, if not concentrated in the generation and development of productive capacity.
(3) Structural changes: Blecker (1998) defines three types of structural changes that may increase the rate of growth of the economy without causing a deterioration of the balance of payments: (1) an increase of production; (2) change in the income elasticity of demand for imports; (3) change in the income elasticity of demand for exports. Each of these changes requires a change of local production towards sectors which are characterized by higher income elasticity; improved non-price competitiveness of local production; industries oriented to import-substitution. In short, economic policy must be directed towards a gradual restructuring of the economy and promotion of sustainable growth based on increased productivity and competitive exports by stimulating the development of medium- and high-tech industries with high added value.

Appendix

Data	Source of the data
GDP growth, annual % change, Bulgaria base: previous year	International Monetary Fund, World Economic Outlook Database, 2015
Imports, annual % change, base: previous year	World Bank, World Development Indicators, 2015
Exports, annual % change, base: previous year	World Bank, World Development Indicators, 2015
GDP growth, annual % change, developed countries	International Monetary Fund, World Economic Outlook Database, 2015, sample of 37 developed countries
Gross Capital formation, annual % change	World Bank, World Development Indicators, 2015
Final consumption, annual % change	World Bank, World Development Indicators, 2015
External balance on goods and services, % change, previous year	World Bank, World Development Indicators, 2015
Terms of trade, annual % change	World Bank, World Development Indicators, 2015, own calculations

References

Bajo-Rubio O (2010) The balance-of-payments constraint on economic growth in a long-term perspective: Spain, 1850-2000. Working papers on International Economics and Finance DEFI 10-10, Diciembre 2010

Bekö J (2003) The validity of the balance-of-payments—constrained growth model for a small economy in transition: The case of Slovenia. J Post Keynesian Econ 26(1):69–93

Benáček VL, Prokop L, Víšek JÁ (2003) Determining factors of the Czech foreign trade balance: structural issues in trade creation. Working paper series No. 3/2003, Czech National Bank

Bértola L, Higachi H, Porcile G (2002) Balance-of-payments-constrained growth in Brazil: a test of Thirlwall's Law, 1890-1973. J Post Keynesian Econ 25(1):123–140

Blecker R (1998) International competitiveness, relative wages and balance of payment constraint. J Post Keynesian Econ 20(4):495–526

Dixon RJ, Thirlwall AP (1975) A model of regional growth rates differences on Kaldorian lines. Oxford Econ Pap 27:201–213

Elliott G, Rothenberg TJ, Stock J (1996) Efficient tests for an autoregressive unit root. Econometrica 64:813–836

Hansen J, Kvedaras V (2004) Balance of payments constrained economic growth in the Baltics. Ekonomika 65:82–91

Garcimartín C, Alonso JA, Rivas L (2012) Convergence and balance of payments constrained growth: is there a puzzle? In: Soukiazis E, Cerqueira P (eds) Models of balance of payments constrained growth: history, theory and empirical evidence. Palgrave Macmillan, Basingstoke, pp 189–216

Kvedaras V (2012) Empirical testing of export-led and balance of payments constrained growth: the case of Portugal. In: Soukiazis E, Cerqueira P (eds) Models of balance of payments constrained growth. History, theory, evidence. Palgrave Macmillan, Basingstoke, pp 168–186

León-Ledesma MA (1999) An application of Thirlwall's law to the Spanish economy. J Post Keynesian Econ 21(3):431–439, M.E. Sharpe

León-Ledesma MA, Thirlwall AP (2002) The endogeneity of the natural rate of growth. Camb J Econ 26(4):441–459, Oxford University Press

McCombie JSL (1985) Economic growth, the Harrod foreign trade multiplier and the Hicks super-multiplier. Appl Econ 17(1):55–72

Ng S, Perron P (1995) Unit root tests in ARMA models with data-dependent methods for the selection of the truncation lag. J Am Stat Assoc 90:268–281

Setterfield M (2011) The remarkable durability of Thirlwall's law. PSL Q Rev Economia civile 64(259):393–427

Soukiazis E, Cerqueira PA, Antunes M (2013a) Growth rates constrained by internal and external imbalances and the role of relative prices: empirical evidence from Portugal. J Post Keynesian Econ 36(2):275–298, M.E. Sharpe

Soukiazis E, Muchova E, Lisy E (2013b) Slovak economic growth and the consistency of the balance-of-payments constraint approach. J Econ Slovak Acad Sci 61(9):879–896

Thirlwall AP (1969) Okun's law and the natural rate of growth. South Econ J 36(1):87–89

Thirlwall AP (1979) The balance of payments constraint as an explanation of international growth rate differences. Banca Nazionale del Lavoro Q Rev 32:45–53

Thirlwall AP (1987) Keynes, economic development and the developing countries. In: Thirlwall AP (ed) Keynes and economic development. Macmillan, London

Thirlwall AP (2012) Balance of payments constrained growth models: history and overview. In: Soukiazis E, Cerqueira P (eds) Models of balance of payments constrained growth. History, theory, evidence. Palgrave Macmillan, Basingstroke, pp 11–50

Verdoorn JP (1993) On the factors determining the growth of labor productivity. In: Pasinetti L (ed) Italian economic papers, vol II. Oxford University Press, Oxford

The Nexus Between Imports and National Income in Turkey

Özcan Karahan and Olcay Çolak

Abstract Nowadays the investigation of the relationship between import and national income has been the major issue of many empirical studies in literature. Keynesian Models traditionally argue that a rise in import decrease the net export and hence aggregate demand as a basic source of economic growth, which implies a negative causal relationship from import to national income. Contrarily, Endogenous Growth Models put forward that imports play a positive and promoting role in a rise in real national income via technology transfer. Accordingly, imports transfer new technologies embodied in capital and intermediate goods and thus spur production productivity especially in developing countries. Consequently, Endogenous Growth Models advocate the import-led economic growth while Keynesian Models assert import-led economic shrinkage. The aim of this paper is to test these arguments concerning with the impacts of import on Turkish economy. We use time series techniques based on Johansen co-integration and Granger causality tests and Innovation Accounting Techniques for the quarterly data from 2002 to 2014. Empirical findings indicate that there is a strong causality relationship from the imports towards economic growth, supporting the argument of Endogenous Growth Models. Thus, sustainable growth rates in Turkey need outward-looking policy including not only exports but also import and policy covering the measures supporting steadily financing of imports.

Ö. Karahan
Bandırma Faculty of Economics and Administrative Sciences, Balıkesir University, 10200 Bandırma, Turkey
e-mail: okarahan@balikesir.edu.tr

O. Çolak (✉)
Faculty of Economics and Administrative Sciences, Department of Economics, Uşak University, Uşak, Turkey
e-mail: olcay.colak@usak.edu.tr

A. Karasavvoglou et al. (eds.), *Economic Crisis, Development and Competitiveness in Southeastern Europe*, Contributions to Economics,
DOI 10.1007/978-3-319-40322-9_6

1 Introduction

Economic growth is one of the most important economic indicators and the goal of policy makers in any economy. Therefore, the sources of economic growth have been a very popular subject in the economics literature at all times. Recently, deep attention has been given to the link between foreign trade and economic growth. Accordingly, the positive impact of international trade on economic growth has been widely investigated empirically in different ways. It seems that most previous investigation have mostly focused on the effect of the export expansion on economic growth while little attention has been paid to identifying the impact of imports on economic growth. However, some recent studies have shown that there is a strong causal link between imports and economic growth especially in developing countries. Thus, most of the studies now indicate that both the export and import sectors can contribute to economic growth, which are called as "export-led growth" and "import-led growth", respectively.

Concerning with the link between foreign trade and economic growth, well-known Keynesian multiplier model advocates the export-led growth as opposed to import-led growth. Keynesian macroeconomic theory, paying detailed attention to the demand side of the economy, suggests that increases in aggregate demand boosts economic growth towards full employment level of output. Thus, any increase in the components of aggregate demand like consumption, investment, government expenditure and net export results in economic growth as much as the increase in aggregate expenditure multiplied by the related expenditure multiplier. It is clear from the Keynesian point of view that net exports, which equal exports minus imports, positively affect the level of national income. An increase in exports over imports will raise aggregate demand and economic growth while an increase in imports over exports will reduce aggregate demand and economic growth. Accordingly, there is a negative causal relationship from import to economic growth since import decreases the total demand that is the basic sources of economic growth. In other words, imports have a negative multiplier effect on output since imports like saving represent a leakage from the aggregate demand. Thus, according to Keynesian approach, import is often recognized as a leakage of total demand of which lead to economic downturn while exports as an injection to total demand lead to economic growth (Chen 2009, p. 128).

In line with the above thinking, mainstream studies have tended to rely on econometric analysis focusing particularly on the correlation between exports and economic growth. Indeed, based on this approach, the researches on relationship between foreign trade and economic growth mostly focused on export-led growth. There exist a vast literature on the relationship between foreign trade and economic growth by focusing especially on export-led growth hypothesis. However, in recent years, it seems that there has been much attention devoted to the role of import in analyzing the link between foreign trade and economic growth. Researchers show that expanded imports have also the potential to play a complementary role in stimulating overall economic performance. Especially, Endogenous Growth

Models has paid intensive attention to imports as a channel of technological diffusion (Grossman and Helpman 1991; Coe and Helpman 1995) and hence a significant source of economic growth. They have emphasized that imports has a significant role as a channel for transferring of high production technology from developed to developing countries.

Of course, import has a positive impact on productivity growth in developing countries since firms can get the much more inputs like capital and intermediate goods in order to produce much more. Thus, imports work for creating the appropriate conditions for growth through providing production requirements and equipment. But, more importantly than this, imports has a vital role as a medium of technology transfer on economic growth. Developing economies with limited technological endowment can benefit from access to foreign technology via imports. Accordingly, technological knowledge can be transmitted to developing countries by being embodied in imported capital or intermediated goods. To this respect, imports play crucial role in the process of international technological spillovers (Keller 2002, 2004). It can be argued that the greater import volume enhances the accumulation of more new production knowledge in a developing country. Thus, by enhancing the technology spillovers, imported intermediate and capital goods generate a trade benefit much more than only having access to more input. In other words, increased imports have the potential to play a complementary role in promoting economic development by increasing productive growth via technology transfer (Lee 1995; Mazumdar 2002). Therefore, consistent with the endogenous-growth literature, imports can be treated as a medium of technology transfer which play significant role on long run economic growth.

In summary, Keynesian Theory asserts that imports as leakage of total demand inversely affect to national income while Endogenous Growth Theory argues that increased imports have the potential to play a significant role in promoting economic growth via transfer of technology. From this point of views, the purpose of this paper is to provide empirical tests of the hypothesis of Keynesian and Endogenous Growth Models concerning with the relationship between import and economic growth. The rest of this article is organized as follows. Section 2 provides a brief overview of literature on the link between import and economic growth. Section 3 presents the data, methodology and empirical results. Section 4 concludes and makes some policy implications.

2 Previous Literature

There are so many studies available investigating the relationship between foreign trade and economic growth in literature. However, most of the previous studies have focused on the effect of export expansion on economic growth while ignoring the effect of imports on economic growth. Consequently, export-led growth hypothesis has been widely documented from both a theoretical and empirical point of view. Nonetheless, researchers recently start to concern with imports as a significant dynamic of economic growth like export in analysing the link between foreign trade and growth. Thus, while examining the trade-growth nexus, more recent studies have focused on testing both the export-led and import-led growth hypothesis jointly. In conclusion, there has been an increase in country-specific studies focusing on the relationship among exports, imports and economic growth. Concerning with developing Asian countries, Thangavelu and Rajaguru (2004) investigated the relationship between foreign trade and productivity growth focusing by using the multivariate co-integration test based on the Johansen-Juselius method for annual data covering period from 1960 to 1996. They found significant causal effects from import to productivity growth and hence presence of import-led productivity growth in India, Indonesia, Malaysia, Philippines, Singapore and Taiwan.

For the case of Malaysian Economy, Baharumshah and Rashid (1999) explored the links among export, import and economic growth from 1974 to 1994 in the Johansen Procedure and vector-error correction (VEC) model. They detected the presence of a stationary long-run relationship between exports, imports and growth. Thus they concluded that an important determinant of long-run growth in Malaysian Economy is outward-oriented development strategies which result in imports of foreign technology. With regard to the case of The Republic of Korea, Kim et al. (2010) investigated the relationship between exports, imports, and economic growth in the framework of Johansen Cointegration and Granger causality tests and impulse response functions by using quarterly data from 1980 to 2003. Results indicated that imports have a significant positive effect on productivity growth while disproving the export-led growth hypothesis. He argued that the notion of desirable exports and undesirable imports may be misguided and counterproductive. He also made significant implications for policymakers that import liberalization will bring about substantial benefits in the form of higher productivity and economic growth.

In connection with transition economies in Europe, Awokuse (2007) analysed the relationship between exports, imports and economic growth by employing Johansen Cointegration Test and Granger Causality Test for different monthly data set between 1993 and 2004. The results showed that import-led hypothesis is valid for both Czech Republic and Poland. Furthermore, Awouke concluded that the singular focus of many past studies on just the role of exports as the engine of growth may be misleading or at best incomplete. Awokuse (2008) also tested the import-led growth hypothesis for Latin American Economies in the framework of Johansen Cointegration and Granger causality tests and impulse response functions by using different quarterly data set between 1990 and 2002. Empirical results confirm the significant role of imports in stimulating the economic growth of Argentina, Colombia and Peru. Moreover, Awouke indicated that the strength of imports on growth is relatively stronger than the effects of exports.

More recently, besides the studies testing the export-led and import-led growth hypothesis jointly, researchers have focused on testing import-led growth hypothesis separately and elaborately. Kogid et al. (2011) used the bivariate cointegration and causality analysis based on the Engle–Granger two steps, Johansen and Toda-

Yomamoto procedures to analyze the economic growth and the imports in Malaysia from 1970 to 2007. The findings of this study showed that import has a paramount important role in spurring the growth of the economy. Mishra (2010) attempted to investigate the dynamics of the relationship between imports and economic growth in India for the period 1970–2010 by using Johansen co-integration and Granger causality tests. The study indicated the existence of long-run equilibrium relationship between imports and real economic growth in India. Rahman and Shahbaz (2013) investigated the impacts of imports on economic growth of Pakistan over the period 1990 to 2010. They applied the structural break autoregressive distributed lag (ARDL) bounds testing approach to examine the long-run relationship between the growth and imports. Empirical results confirmed the import-led growth hypothesis for Pakistan by indicating a strong causality running from imports to economic growth.

Concerning with the studies specially focusing on Turkey, Ugur (2008) provided an empirical test of the causal relationship between economic growth and imports by using the Granger causality test and Impulse Response and Variance Decompositions Models for the monthly data set between 1994 and 2005. Evidence presented in this study is clear that economic growth is significantly influenced by import. Azgun and Servinc (2010) also analyzed effects of export and import on economic growth in Turkey by using Engle Granger Causality Test for the period between 1998 and 2008. The findings obtained from this research shows that economic growth in Turkey is more dependent on importing rather than exporting. Conclusively, no findings could be reached as to support the export-led hypothesis while import-led growth hypothesis is valid for Turkey. Moreover, it is concluded that exporting itself grows based on importing. Uçak and Arısoy (2011) lastly attempted to investigate the link between foreign trade and productivity growth for Turkish Economy in the period of 1980–2007. Accordingly, they examined the relations among exports, imports and the index of productivity per worker in manufacturing. The findings suggested that both export and import growth contributes to productivity growth and thus the expansion of trade is an integral part of productivity growth. Thus, besides export-led growth, significant causal effects were also found from imports to productivity growth, suggesting import-led productivity growth. Finally, they interpreted these results as strongly supportive of the role of endogenous growth models in explaining continuous growth in Turkey.

3 Data, Methodology and Empirical Results

In our complete econometric analysis, we try to examine the impact of imports on Turkish Economy. Firstly, we check whether time series of national income and imports are stationary or not. Then, long run relationship between imports and economic growth is analysed by using Johansen Cointegration Test. Later, we explore the causality from import to economic growth by operating Granger Causality Test. Finally, Standard Innovation Accounting Techniques including

Table 1 Summary statistics

	M	GDP
Number of observation	51	51
Mean	6839022.31	25008019.15
Median	6954589	25105839
Maximum	9261805	31546290
Minimum	3480947	17582703
Standard deviation	1539199	4089489.76
Skewness	−0.4830	−0.1168
Kurtosis	2.3511	1.9957
Jarque-Bera (Prob.)	2.8782 (0.2371)	2.2593 (0.3231)

Source: Authors' estimations

Impulse-Response Functions (IRFs) and Variance Decomposition (VDCs) is used to produce the time path of the variables for presenting the relationship between them.

Data set used in this paper cover the quarterly series of seasonally and calendar adjusted imports (M) and Gross Domestic Product (GDP) of Turkey for 2002:1–2014:3 in Turkish Lira. The data set for both variables obtained by main statistics of the Turkish Statistical Office (TURKSTAT) under National Accounts. On the other hand each variable logarithmically transformed and summary statistics for the series displayed in Table 1. According to Jarque-Bera statistics both series normally distributed as the null hypothesis concerning the normal distribution of the series could not be rejected. Standard deviations of both series are high as the difference between their maximum and minimum values get larger.

3.1 Unit Root Test

Before proceed to the main analysis, stationary of the series are checked by the unit root tests. In this context, Augmented Dickey-Fuller (ADF), and Phillips-Perron (PP) unit root tests performed. Table 2 exhibits the results of the unit root tests. The results of unit root tests do indicate that both variables are stationary when their first differences are taken either with intercept or with intercept and deterministic trend. Absolute values of ADF-test and PP-test are greater than MacKinnon critical values at 1 % significance level which means that null hypothesis of the non-stationary of the series are rejected. It means that series are integrated at I (1) which indicates the existence of long-run relationship or cointegration between the variables in consideration.

Table 2 Results of unit root tests

	ADF (Intercept)		ADF (Trend + Intercept)		PP (Intercept)		PP (Trend + Intercept)	
Variable	Level	1st Dif.	Level	1st Dif.	Level	1st Dif.	Level	1st Dif.
M	−2.3276	−5.6914[a]	−3.0654	−5.9949[a]	−2.2713	−5.6914[a]	−2.2035	−6.0097[a]
GDP	−1.6153	−5.3975[a]	−2.2946	−5.4318[a]	−1.5334	−5.3975[a]	−2.0805	−5.4069[a]

[a]indicates the significance level at 1 %. Maximum lag length is specified by considering Akaike Information Criterion (AIC)

Table 3 Johansen cointegration test results

Null hypothesis	Eigenvalue	Trace statistics	0.05 Critical value	Probability
$r = 0$	0.2976	17.7350	15.4947	0.0226
$r \leq 1$	0.0086	0.4252	3.8414	0.5143
		Maximum Eigenvalue Statistics		
$r = 0$	0.2976	17.3097	14.2646	0.0160
$r \leq 1$	0.0086	0.4252	3.8414	0.5143

Optimum lag length is determined as 1 by using the minimum values of Likelihood Ratio (LR), Final Prediction Error (FPE), Akaike Information Criterion (AIC), Schwarz Information Criterion (SIC), and Hannan-Quinn Information Criterion (HQ). r indicates the number of ranks or cointegrated vectors

3.2 *Johansen Cointegration Test*

In this section, presence of long-run relationship between import and gross domestic product is checked by the methodology proposed by Johansen (1988) and Johansen and Juselius (1990) that is based on system equation rather than single equation co integration relationship. This methodology is based on maximum likelihood estimation in which it allows for testing the long-run relationship between the variables by using the maximum eigenvalue and trace statistics. Table 3 shows the Johansen cointegration test results by including linear trend. The null hypothesis examines the cointegrating vector number which is stated by the rank (r) equals zero of equal less than one. The null hypothesis of no cointegrating relationship or no long-run relationship between import and gross domestic product ($r = 0$) is rejected by the trace statistics and maximum eigenvalue statistics. The critical values of these statistics are significant at 5 % significance level which in turn indicates that at least there is one cointegration or long-run relationship between economic growth and imports do exist.

Table 4 Lag length selection

Lag	LR	FPE	AIC	SIC	HQ
0	NA	0.00000675	−8.5330	−8.4502[a]	−8.5026
1	13.5228[a]	0.00000578[a]	−8.6892[a]	−8.4410	−8.5982[a]
2	1.3603	0.00000675	−8.5355	−8.1218	−8.3839
3	5.7044	0.00000696	−8.5080	−7.9288	−8.2957
4	1.9309	0.00000800	−8.3760	−7.6313	−8.1031
5	2.9022	0.00000892	−8.2792	−7.3690	−7.9456
6	5.9530	0.00000894	−8.2940	−7.2183	−7.8997
7	1.2284	0.0000106	−8.1490	−6.9078	−7.6941
8	2.6678	0.0000119	−8.0653	−6.6586	−7.5496

[a]indicates lag order selected by the criterion

Table 5 Granger causality/Block exogeneity Wald test results

Dependent variable	Excluded variable	Null hypothesis	χ^2 (Prob.)	Decision	Result
M	GDP	GDP doesn't Granger cause of M	0.2223 (0.6373)	Accepted	GDP doesn't Granger cause of M
GDP	M	M doesn't Granger cause of GDP	6.6444 (0.0099)[a]	Rejected	M Granger causes of GDP

[a]indicates the significance at 1 %. Lag order selected to be 1 according to minimum values of LR, AIC, SIC, FPE, and HQ

3.3 Granger Causality Test

After indicating the presence of cointegration or long run relationship among the variables, in this part of study we test the causality link between imports (M) and growth (GDP). Granger causality test is carried out using block exogeneity Wald tests (that use Chi-square test, X^2) under VAR mechanism since Johansen cointegration test indicates there is a long run relationship between imports and economic growth. In estimating the VAR Model, variables of national income and imports are added with their first differences. Estimation of proper lag length of each endogenous variable are selected by lag length criterion like Likelihood Ratio (LR), Final Prediction Error (FPE), Akaike Information Criterion (AIC), Schwarz Information Criterion (SIC), and Hannan-Quinn Information Criterion (HQ). Table 4 shows the results of lag length selection of VAR Model.

Since we deal with quarterly data set maximum lag length is chosen as eight. Subsequently, lag order is selected to be 1 that satisfies the necessary minimum value conditions by the four of five criterions. Then based on specified VAR model, the VAR Granger Causality Test/Block Exogeneity Wald Test is operated. The results of the test are exhibited in Table 5. Accordingly, the null hypothesis arguing that imports (M) don't Granger cause of income (GDP) is clearly rejected. On the other hand, the null hypothesis asserting that income (GDP) doesn't Granger cause of import (M) is accepted. As a result import (M) is decided to be the exogenous

Table 6 Residual and stability check

LM-Test	Jarque-Bera normality test (Prob.)	White test (χ^2)		VAR Stability condition	
		No cross terms	Cross terms	Root	Modulus
LM (1) = 4.6741 (0.3224)	$\chi^2(4) = 7.7507$ (0.1207)	12.8665 (0.1289)	13.7914 (0.1687)	0.2564	0.2564
LM (2) = 1.7473 (0.7821)				−0.2192	0.2192

Note: p-values are given in brackets

part of the estimated VAR Model while income (GDP) is accepted as the endogenous part. In conclusion, the hypothesis arguing that of imports does not Granger Cause economic growth is rejected at 1 per cent level of significance while the hypothesis asserting that economic growth does not Granger cause imports is accepted. In short, Granger Causality Test supports the import-led growth in Turkey.

We also test whether the estimated VAR Model violates serial correlation, constant variance and normality assumptions. According to LM-Test results shown in Table 6, there is no serial correlation of the residuals of the VAR Model up to lag 2 which yields the acceptance of null hypothesis of no serial correlation among the residuals. The result of Jarque-Bera Normality Test indicates that the residuals of the VAR Model are normally distributed. Heteroskedasticity of the residuals are checked by the White Test by including cross-terms and without cross terms. Results show that there is no heteroskedasticity among the residuals of the VAR Model in terms of cross terms and without cross terms. Finally, stability condition of the VAR Model is checked by autoregressive roots (AR). Accordingly, there are two real roots; one is positive and the other one is negative with two modulus. The results indicate that both roots do not lie outside the unit circle which in turn satisfies the stability condition of the VAR Model.

3.4 *Impulse-Response Function and Variance Decomposition Analysis*

In this section, the relationship between import (M) and gross domestic product (GDP) will also be examined by using the Innovation Accounting Techniques proposed by Litterman (1979). Accordingly, based on the estimated VAR models, Impulse-Response Functions (IRFs) and Variance Decompositions (VDCs) analyses are computed to indicate the causality relationship from import to economic growth.

The results of Impulse-Response Functions for GDP are displayed in Fig. 1. Vertical axis of each graph represents the direction of the response function and

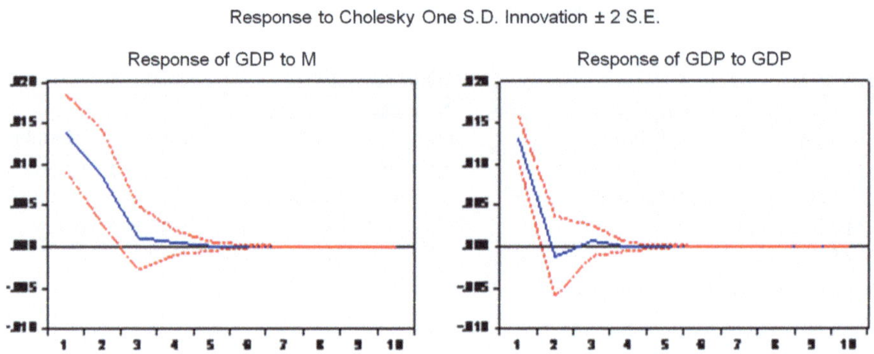

Fig. 1 Impulse-response functions

Table 7 Variance decompositions results

Variance Decompositions of GDP			
Periods	S.E.	M	GDP
1	0.019114	52.54937	47.45063
2	0.020937	60.12193	39.87807
3	0.020977	60.16422	39.83578
4	0.020984	60.18809	39.81191
5	0.020984	60.18849	39.81151
6	0.020984	60.18858	39.81142
7	0.020984	60.18858	39.81142
8	0.020984	60.18859	39.81141
9	0.020984	60.18859	39.81141
10	0.020984	60.18859	39.81141

Cholesky Ordering: M, GDP

magnitude in percentage term while horizontal axis shows the number of periods. The dashed lines display the confidence interval by ± 2 standard deviations. Left panel of Fig. 1 shows the response of GDP to the one standard deviation shocks that come from M. This graph indicates that there is significant response by GDP to the shock comes from M. The positive effect or response of GDP to M remains until second quarter and after second quarter the effect of shock disappears. Thus, it can be concluded that import positively affects GDP and hence economic growth rate.

The findings for Variance Decomposition of GDP are given in Table 7. By performing VDCs variables are ordered according to Cholesky ordering and the maximum length of the period is taken to be ten. Almost 60 % of shocks that come to M would explain the error variance of GDP by the second period which in turn indicates that import affects significantly GDP. These results of Variance Decomposition of GDP are consistent with the causality from import to GDP. Overall, the findings derived from Innovation Accounting Techniques including both Impulse-

Response Functions and Variance Decompositions analyses suggest that a shock in import (M) has significant effect on economic growth (GDP), supporting to import-led growth.

4 Conclusion

It has been long argued in the literature that international trade promotes economic growth. Relating this link between trade and economic growth, Keynesian Multiplier Theory argued that imports as a leakage from total demand lead to economic shrinkage while exports as an injection to total demand lead to economic growth. Thus, Keynesian approach has supported to export-led hypothesis while completely rejecting the import-led hypothesis. On the contrary, Endogenous Growth Theory has argued that economic growth can be driven by imports since imports have a significant potential to be a channel for foreign technology to flow into the domestic economy. Thus increased imports play a complementary role, besides increasing the amount of input, in promoting economic growth. Accordingly, new technologies embodied in imports of capital and intermediate goods can increase the productivity growth over time.

In the line with these arguments, we tested the relationship between import and economic growth in Turkey using Johansen co-integration and Granger causality tests and Innovation Accounting Techniques for the quarterly data from 2002 to 2014. Empirical results assert that Turkish experience does give support to the import-led growth hypothesis in both short-run and long-run. In other words, the findings of this study show that in the case of Turkey, import has a paramount important role in spurring the growth of the economy. Thus, our findings bear out the implications of Endogenous Growth Theory with relate to link between import and economic growth. The results, hence, indicated imports as a medium of technology transfer which play more significant role on long term economic growth. Accordingly, this study also shows that import will be able to an important mean to break the bottleneck of technological development for developing countries. Therefore, outward-looking policy including not only export but also import is essential for effective growth policies. Furthermore, the policy adjustments to promote economic growth should also include the measures supporting permanent finance of import.

References

Awokuse TO (2007) Causality between exports, imports and economic growth: evidence from transition economies. Econ Lett 94:389–395

Awokuse TO (2008) Trade openness and economic growth: is growth export-led or import-led? Appl Econ 40:161–173

Azgun S, Servinc H (2010) Are imports a reason of growth? Evidence from Turkey. Soc Sci 5(2): 60–69

Baharumshah AZ, Rashid S (1999) Exports, imports and economic growth in Malaysia: empirical evidence based on multivariate time series. Asian Econ J 13(4):389–406

Chen H (2009) A literature review on the relationship between foreign trade and economic growth. Int J Econ Financ 1(1):127–130

Coe T, Helpman E (1995) International R&D slipovers. Eur Econ Rev 39:859–887

Grossman G, Helpman E (1991) Innovation and growth in global economy. MIT Press, Cambridge, MA

Johansen S (1988) Statistical analysis of cointegration vectors. J Econ Dyn Control 12:231–254

Johansen S, Juselius K (1990) Maximum likelihood estimation and inferences on cointegration-with applications to the demand for money. Oxf Bull Econ Stat 52:169–210

Keller W (2002) Trade and the transmission of technology. J Econ Growth 7:5–24

Keller W (2004) International technology diffusion. J Econ Lit XLII:752–782

Kim S, Lim H, Park D (2010) Could imports be beneficial for economic growth: some evidence from Republic of Korea? ERD Working paper series, No. 13

Kogid M, Mulok D, Ching KS, Lily J (2011) Does import affect economic growth in Malaysia. Empir Econ Lett 10(3):297–307

Lee W-J (1995) Capital goods imports and long-run growth. J Dev Econ 48:91–110

Litterman RB (1979) Techniques of forecasting using vector autoregressions. Federal Reserve Bank of Minnepolis, Working paper No. 115

Mazumdar J (2002) Imported machinery and growth in LDCs. J Dev Econ 65:209–224

Mishra PK (2010) The dynamics of the relationship between imports and economic growth in India. South Asian J Macroecon Public Financ 1(1):57–79

Rahman MM, Shahbaz M (2013) Do imports and foreign capital inflows lead economic growth? Cointegration and causality analysis in Pakistan. South Asia Econ J 14(1):59–81

Thangavelu SM, Rajaguru G (2004) Is there an export or import-led productivity growth in rapidly developing Asian Countries? A multivariate VAR analysis'. Appl Econ 36:1083–1093

Uçak H, Arısoy İ (2011) An analysis of causality among productivity, export and import in Turkish economy. Ege Acad Rev 11(4):639–651

Ugur A (2008) Import and economic growth in Turkey: evidence from multivariate VAR analysis. J Econ Bus IX(1–2):54–74

Part II

Interaction Between Competitiveness and Innovation: Evidence from South-Eastern European Countries

Jelena Stankovic, Vesna Jankovic-Milic, and Marija Dzunic

Abstract The traditional doctrine of classical economic theory mostly considers economic growth and competitiveness at the level of the national economy. The problem of competitiveness within this stream of economic theory is mainly approached as the need to find the answers why some countries develop faster and become richer than others, i.e. how an economy gains the ability of sustainable growth, which makes it more competitive than others. In contrast to this point of view, the neoclassical economic theory shifts the focus of the research of growth and competitiveness from the national economy to the field of resource allocation and enterprise efficiency. The logic is simple—competitive enterprises make competitive economy and vice versa, competitive economy creates an environment that encourages the competitiveness of enterprises. The research concept of this paper is based on the synthesis of these two approaches.

The aim of the paper is to evaluate the importance of innovative activity in improving competitiveness. The paper provides a comparative analysis of the competitiveness of the Balkan countries, with special attention to determining the correlation between the indicators of innovative activities and the competitiveness of the observed countries. For the purpose of this analysis, a method of dependency analysis has been applied, as well as correlation analysis. Then, the analysis of the results of empirical survey on innovation activities of enterprises in Serbia is performed. It is pointed out to the lack of innovation activities in enterprises in Serbia as one of the main causes of their low competitiveness.

1 Introduction

In terms of globalization and the increasing integration of markets, competitiveness is a prerequisite of success in the global market. However, the assessment of competitiveness is a complex process. As it requires a vast amount of

J. Stankovic (✉) • V. Jankovic-Milic • M. Dzunic
Faculty of Economics, University of Nis, Nis, Serbia
e-mail: jelena.stankovic@eknfak.ni.ac.rs; vesna.jankovic@eknfak.ni.ac.rs; marija_dzunic@ni.ac.rs

A. Karasavvoglou et al. (eds.), *Economic Crisis, Development and Competitiveness in Southeastern Europe*, Contributions to Economics,
DOI 10.1007/978-3-319-40322-9_7

macroeconomic and microeconomic knowledge, different approaches in defining the concept of competitiveness have appeared in the literature. Some authors identify competitiveness with comparative advantages, while others insist on wider framework for determining the level of competitiveness. Most authors regard competitiveness as a multidimensional and dynamic concept, considering that the attributes of competitiveness are subject to change in different periods and conditions (Spence and Hazard 1988). Finally, the concept of competitiveness can be discussed at the level of products, enterprises, industries, clusters, regions, and national economies, unions of countries or even continents.

The most common approach to competitiveness assessment is based on traditional doctrine of classical economic theory and analyses competitiveness and economic growth at the national economy level. The aim of such analysis is to explain why some countries gain competitive advantage, develop faster and become richer compared to others. In other words, the focus is on identifying the determinants of growth and competitiveness, as well as on their measurability. The Gross Domestic Product (GDP) is the most commonly used indicator of growth. The main reason for prevalence and acceptance of GDP as an indicator of growth and competitiveness is the existence of an operational definition and methodology for measuring the GDP uniformly accepted all over the world. However, current literature points out that the GDP is a necessary, but not sufficient indicator in evaluating successes and failures of the development process. There are opinions that too much attention is paid to GDP growth rates, while other indicators are underrepresented: inflation, fiscal balance, the current account, measures of inequality, etc. For example, some authors analyze the relationship between level of development and foreign direct investments (Lankauskiene and Tvaronaviciene 2011). There are no widely accepted and regularly observed indicators of measuring the development process through acceleration or slow-down of technical progress (Kornai 2010). Based on the fact that GDP is not always the most relevant indicator of the competitiveness of a country, the paper aims to demonstrate that, in the case of the South-Eastern European countries (SEE), there is no correlation between GDP and GCI (Global Competitiveness Index), which implies the need to include additional indicators into the analysis of the competitiveness of these countries.

Since there is a real need for complementing GDP as a measure of growth with indicators that reflect other aspects of welfare and development, scientific and professional efforts of economists and economic statisticians are aimed at complementing the data on aggregate output with various indicators of health, education, income distribution, etc. (Kornai 2010). Such example is the invitation of the President of the French Republic addressed to a group of economists and statisticians, chaired by Joseph Stiglitz, Amartya Sen and Jean-Paul Fitoussi, to work on new proposals for improving the measurement of growth and development (see Stiglitz et al. 2009). It is evident that institutional and structural changes as well as technological progress and innovation are unambiguously relevant for improving competitiveness. Special attention in recent literature is paid to analysis of innovative activities and the innovation process, i.e. the problems of diffusion and leaders and followers in the innovation process (Davila et al. 2006). Neo-Schumpeterian approach to international competitiveness focuses on the process of creating technological competitiveness, which implies a sustainable increase in the share of world trade for those whose innovative efforts are most successful (Cantwell 2003).

The importance of competitiveness at the macro level stems from the fact that stable institutional framework and adequate macroeconomic policy creates a solid foundation for economic progress. However, wealth is created at the micro level, i.e. the level of enterprises, which produce goods and services that consumers value, using efficient production methods (Golubovic and Dzunic 2012). In this framework the factors that influence competitiveness may be grouped into several categories: resources or capabilities, institutions, markets or demand conditions, and inter-company networks (Mowery and Nelson 1999). Enterprises have to fortify their competitive strategy, in terms of the transition from competition based on comparative advantages (low wages and cheap natural resources) to the competition based on competitive advantages, arising from the uniqueness of the product and the production process. This competitive advantage is obtained through continuous improvement of products and processes, which stems from a well-designed and properly conducted innovation activities.

Through a synthesis of different approaches to the analysis of the competitiveness of Serbian economy, as well as the competitiveness of Serbian enterprises, the paper evaluates the importance of innovative activity in improving competitiveness. The paper provides a comparative analysis of the competitiveness of the Balkan countries, with special attention to determining the correlation between the indicators of innovative activities and the competitiveness of the observed countries. It is pointed out to the lack of innovation activities in enterprises in Serbia as one of the main causes of their low level of competitiveness.

2 Theoretical Background of Competitiveness Assessment

Measuring national competitiveness has been a controversial issue from the very beginning, ever since the first composite indices have been constructed for this purpose. As a response to the increasing interest of policy makers, numerous research institutions, analysts and consultants have taken on to the task of providing solutions for benchmarking competitive performance of different countries.

The main problem of measuring national competitiveness stems from the fact there is no widely accepted definition of this concept and no consensus about whether improving competitiveness is the right strategy. According to Krugman (1994), not only there is no sense in the meaning of the word *competitiveness*, when applied to national economy, but it is "a dangerous and wrong obsession". He explains that leading countries of the world do not compete with each other and that most economic difficulties do not come from foreign competition, but are home-made. However, this "growing obsession with competitiveness" could easily be responsible for trade wars, protectionism and wasting taxpayers' money for enhancing competitiveness. Opposing scholars claim that countries do compete against each other (Dunn 1994) and that country's economy is the source of economic means they need to achieve political interests, as well as a source of attractiveness as a location for international business, the strength of national currency, and in the end—economic and political power and influence.

This debate is of major importance for measuring competitiveness. Countries are bound to compare themselves in achieving the mentioned goals. The indicators used need to correspond to the underlying economic features. It is very difficult to measure competitiveness using only one indicator, since it cannot be determined by one isolated factor. Instead, there are many factors that affect macroeconomic performance—productivity, innovation, political stability, education, etc. This is the main reason for constructing composite indices, as complex measures that include several groups of indicators. The main advantage of such indicators is that they can summarize multi-dimensional process into single number, which enables comparison between countries and measuring progress over time. However, summarizing complex and often elusive processes into a single measure used for benchmarking countries' performance, if poorly constructed, can be misleading (OECD 2008). Also, there are many moments in the process of constructing such indices where subjective judgments are in place, the results may be misused, or subject to political interpretations.

Beside acknowledged analytical, methodological and quantitative weaknesses, the most widely used index of competitiveness is the World Economic Forum's (WEF) Global Competitiveness Index (GCI). Since 2005, WEF constructs the Global Competitiveness Index (GCI) as a "measure of competitiveness and a tool for evaluating the microeconomic and macroeconomic foundation of national competitiveness". In accordance with the requirements contained in the GCI, the term competitiveness itself is defined "as the set of institutions, policies, and factors that determine the level of productivity of a country" (Schwab 2012).

GCI takes into account the large number of different components of competitiveness, which are grouped into 12 pillars of competitiveness. These pillars are grouped into the tree sub-indexes, which are organized as follows (Schwab 2012):

1. Sub-index—*Basic requirements* that involves the following pillars: (1) Institutions, (2) Infrastructure, (3) Macroeconomic stability and (4) Health and primary education;
2. Sub-index—*Improving efficiency* which includes pillars such as: (5) Higher education and training, (6) Goods market efficiency, (7) Labour market efficiency, (8) Financial market sophistication, (9) Technological readiness and (10) Market size;
3. Sub-index—Innovative *and sophisticated factors*, which include pillars: (11) Business sophistication and (12) Innovation.

The significance of each sub-index in the GCI is defined by a certain weight, which varies depending on the stage of development of the economy of the country observed. The stage of development is determined by the level of the GDP per capita.

Table 1 Income thresholds for stages of development of SEE countries

	Stage of development				
	Stage 1: Factor-driven	Transition from stage 1 to stage 2	Stage 2: Efficiency-driven	Transition from stage 2 to stage 3	Stage 3: Innovation-driven
GDP per capita in US$	<2000	2000–2999	3000–8999	9000–17,000	>17,000
SEE countries included in sample	–	–	Albania Bosnia and Herzegovina Bulgaria FYROM Montenegro Romania Serbia	Croatia Hungary Turkey	Greece Slovenia
Total in the sample (12 countries)	0 (0.00 %)	0 (0.00 %)	7 (58.33 %)	3 (25.00 %)	2 (16.67 %)

Source: World Economic Forum, The Global Competitiveness Report (2012–2013)

The Global Competitiveness Report 2012–2013 (World Economic Forum) includes a total of 144 countries in the analysis. All countries have been categorised into five groups, according to GDP per capita. The sample used in the paper includes 12 countries of South-Eastern Europe: Albania, Bosnia and Herzegovina, Bulgaria, Croatia, Greece, Hungary, FYROM, Montenegro, Romania, Serbia, Slovenia and Turkey (Table 1).

The data from Table 1 clearly indicate that countries that achieve the highest GDP pc belong to the group of countries whose key factor in the development is innovation. Economists specializing in comparative economics draw the attention to the strong causal relationship between the specific properties of a system, as well as stage of development and the characteristics of technical progress (Balcerowicz 1995). The countries in the lower stages of development may rely to a greater extent on increasing productivity through the adoption of modern technologies from the high-developed countries. On the other hand, in high-income countries, this approach is not sufficient and can not provide the expected increase in productivity. Companies in high-income countries need to design and develop cutting-edge products and processes in order to maintain a competitive advantage and achieve greater added value. This kind of progress requires an environment that largely supports innovation activities, which involves continuous investment in research and development, primarily in the private sector, the existence of high-quality scientific research institutions that are able to generate the necessary knowledge to develop new technology, intensive cooperation in research and technological development between universities and industry, as well as the protection of intellectual property.

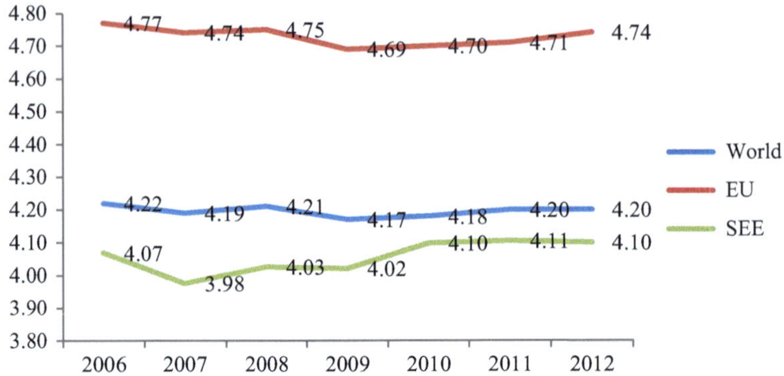

Fig. 1 Average score of GCI for period 2006–2012

3 Statistical Analysis of the Indicators Within the Global Competitiveness Index of Serbia and the SEE Countries

Looking at the period after 2006, it can be concluded that most of the SEE countries increased their competitiveness in terms of increasing the score of the GCI. At the same time, the SEE region did not achieve exceptional results in improving competitiveness.

Despite the fact that the scores of GCI of these countries recorded an increase, these countries are still below the EU average and the world average (Fig. 1). Statistical analysis of the indicators of the competitiveness of the SEE countries is aimed at identifying the main areas for improvement. Special attention will be paid to the analysis of innovative activities.

Table 2 shows the scores of GCI and their sub-indices for observed countries in 2012. It can be seen that Turkey has the highest score of GCI in 2012 (4.45). The competitiveness of this country is above the EU average for 2012. The least competitive country in this sample is Greece (3.86).

During the period 2006–2012, Serbia recorded an increase in its score by almost 0.5, from 3.38 to 3.87. However, this increase was not sufficient to improve Serbia's ranking, which shows that other countries were more successful. This faces Serbia with the task of strengthening the efforts towards improving competitiveness (Savic 2012).

Descriptive statistics of GCI score and his sub-indices is presented in the Table 3. According to the results presented in this table, it can be concluded that the lowest average score for SEE countries belongs to the sub-index *Innovative and sophisticated factors* (3.4). This supports the fact that components of this pillar need to be better managed in order to improve competiveness (Table 4).

Reason for attributing greater importance to the sub-index *Innovative and sophisticated factors* is a high correlation between this sub-index and GCI in SEE countries. This statement is confirmed by a value of Pearson correlation coefficient that is 0.793, which means that there is a high positive, statistically significant

Table 2 Scores of GCI and sub indices for Balkan countries in 2012

Country	GCI score	Sub index I	Sub index II	Sub index III
Albania	3.91	4.24	3.80	3.11
Bosnia and Herzegovina	3.93	4.33	3.75	3.28
Bulgaria	4.27	4.63	4.18	3.30
Croatia	4.04	4.68	4.01	3.39
Greece	3.86	4.13	4.05	3.37
Hungary	4.30	4.78	4.32	3.68
FYROM	4.04	4.52	3.85	3.13
Montenegro	4.14	4.49	3.39	3.57
Romania	4.07	4.22	4.12	3.20
Serbia	3.87	4.15	3.83	2.96
Slovenia	4.34	5.05	4.25	4.02
Turkey	4.45	4.75	4.42	3.79

Source: World Economic Forum, The Global Competitiveness Report (2012–2013)

Table 3 Descriptive statistics of GCI and sub indices for SEE countries in 2012

	Minimum	Maximum	Mean	Standard deviation
GDPpc	3992	27073	11143.67	7658.153
GCI score 2012	3.86	4.45	4.1017	0.19867
Sub-index I	4.13	5.05	4.4975	0.29036
Sub-index II	3.39	4.42	3.9975	0.28867
Sub-index III	2.96	4.02	3.4000	0.31040

Source: World Economic Forum, The Global Competitiveness Report (2012–2013), authors' calculations

Table 4 Correlation matrix between the sub-index and GCI

		GCI score	Sub index I	Sub index II	Sub index III
GCI score	Pearson Correlation	1			
	Sig. (2-tailed)				
Sub index I	Pearson Correlation	0.853[a]	1		
	Sig. (2-tailed)	0.000			
Sub index II	Pearson Correlation	0.618[b]	0.501	1	
	Sig. (2-tailed)	0.032	0.097		
Sub index III	Pearson Correlation	0.793[a]	0.819[a]	0.471	1
	Sig. (2-tailed)	0.002	0.001	0.122	

Source: World Economic Forum, The Global Competitiveness Report (2012–2013), authors' calculations

[a]Correlation is significant at the 0.01 level (2-tailed)

[b]Correlation is significant at the 0.05 level (2-tailed)

Table 5 Average GCI scores according to development stage

Development stage	N	Mean	Minimum	Maximum
Stage 2	7	4.0329	3.87	4.27
Transition 2–3	3	4.2633	4.04	4.45
Stage 3	2	4.1000	3.86	4.34
Total	12	4.1017	3.86	4.45

Source: World Economic Forum, The Global Competitiveness Report (2012–2013). Authors' calculations

Table 6 Chi-Square test results for dependence between competitiveness and development stage

	Value	Degrees of freedom	Asymp. Sig. (2-sided)
Pearson Chi-Square	21.143	20	0.389
Likelihood Ratio	20.258	20	0.442
Linear-by-Linear Association	0.838	1	0.360
N of valid cases	12		

Source: World Economic Forum, The Global Competitiveness Report (2012–2013), authors' calculations

correlation between GCI scores and scores of sub-index *Innovative and sophisticated factors* in these countries.

Bearing in mind the fact that stage of development determines the level of the GDP per capita, the data presented in Table 5 provide comparative view of the competitiveness level according to the stage development. Although it was expected that the countries at a higher development stage are more competitive, the results shown in Table 5 deny this expectation. The highest average GCI score is achieved by the countries in transition from the stage 2 to the stage 3.

In order to test the dependence between level of competitiveness and development stage Chi-square test has been performed. Results presented in Table 6 (significance 0.389) show that there is no dependence between competitiveness and development stage in observed countries in 2012.

4 Analysis of Innovative (In)activities of Enterprises in Serbia

Based on the analysis presented in the previous section, it is clear that one of the main reasons for low competitiveness scores of Balkan countries is stagnation of indicators that determine innovation. The indicators of innovation in Serbia are in significant decline. In comparison to the SEE countries, the scores of Serbia are below the average level (Fig. 2).

The score of pillar Innovation for Serbia is constantly declining during the period 2007–2012, except in 2008. This score for Serbia was above the average

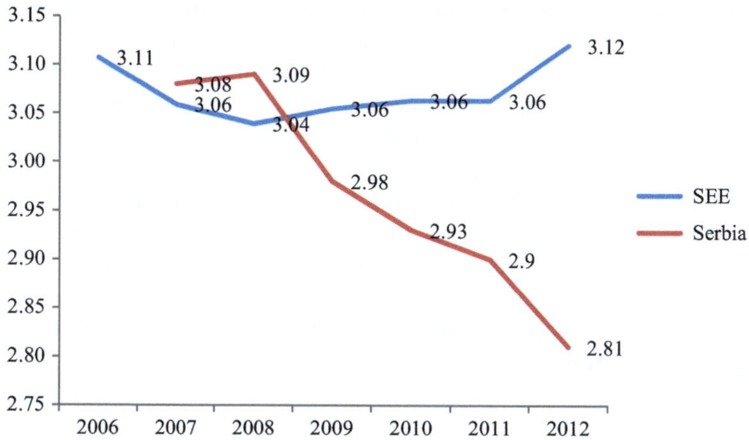

Fig. 2 Scores of pillar Innovation for Serbia and Balkan countries

Table 7 Scores of pillar innovation—comparative analysis

	Serbia	SEE	EU	World	Serbia/Balkan	Serbia/EU	Serbia/World
2006	n/a	3.11	3.99	3.41	n/a	n/a	n/a
2007	3.08	3.06	4.04	3.43	0.68 %	−23.76 %	−10.20 %
2008	3.09	3.04	3.99	3.40	1.67 %	−22.56 %	−9.12 %
2009	2.98	3.06	3.96	3.38	−2.45 %	−24.75 %	−11.83 %
2010	2.93	3.06	3.96	3.34	−4.35 %	−26.01 %	−12.28 %
2011	2.90	3.06	4.05	3.36	−5.33 %	−28.40 %	−13.69 %
2012	2.81	3.12	4.15	3.40	−9.94 %	−32.29 %	−17.35 %

Source: World Economic Forum, The Global Competitiveness Report (2012–2013), authors' calculations

score for SEE countries in 2007 and 2008, while it is 9.94 % lower in 2012. Compared to the EU and world average, the scores are very low (Table 7).

Although the lack of innovative activities causes low competitiveness at the national level, the causes should be sought through the analysis of innovative activities of enterprises. Namely, many authors (Baumol et al. 2007; Phelps 2008) put a heavy emphasis on entrepreneurship and private sector in explaining the virtues of developed and competitive economies. Even though not all entrepreneurs are innovators (Baumol and Schilling 2008), an extremely important group are the entrepreneurs engaged in the process of innovation. In economic theory, since Joseph Schumpeter's theory of development and the nature of capitalism, innovative entrepreneurship is seen as one of the driving forces of growth, development and improvement of competitiveness (Heertje 2006). Innovative entrepreneurship is a function, a role, which can be fulfilled by an individual alone or by teaming up with one or more partners, or with the support of a small firm. As well, a large enterprise can be treated as an entrepreneur in terms of fulfilling its role of innovative entrepreneur. The main point is that the entrepreneur is the one who brings together the necessary financial and personal conditions that the innovation calls for, in other words, the human resources, the physical instruments and financial resources essential to the activity (Baumol 2002). Moreover, one must not disregard the fact that the innovations are the result of decentralized initiatives, i.e. successful implementation of innovative solutions means that the innovators do not have to ask for permission from their superiors to work on a special direction of an innovative action (Acemoglu et al. 2007).

It can be concluded that in order to enhance the innovative activity at the national level, it is necessary to encourage private sector, entrepreneurs, human resources in R&D departments and every individual with an initiative.

In order to complete the analysis of the competitiveness of the Serbian economy, in the next part of the paper attention shall be paid to the research of innovative activities of enterprises in Serbia.

5 Research Aim and Results

The survey[1] of Serbian enterprises was conducted in 2012, with the aim to collect information about their opinion on a range of issues related to the problems and prospects of their business, but also to the role of institutions in creating a business friendly environment that would contribute to improving the competitiveness of enterprises. A part of the questionnaire was related to issues of innovation activities in enterprises, investments in research and development and human resource potential of these departments.

The research included 240 enterprises in Serbia with 23,564 employees. Enterprises in the sample belong to the following sectors: (1) industry, (2) construction and (3) service sector (Fig. 3). Most of the enterprises in the sample (71 %) belong to the field of industrial production. The ownership structure of the companies in the sample includes all forms of ownership that currently exist in Serbia (Fig. 3). The largest share of enterprises in the sample (66 %) is owned by private individuals.

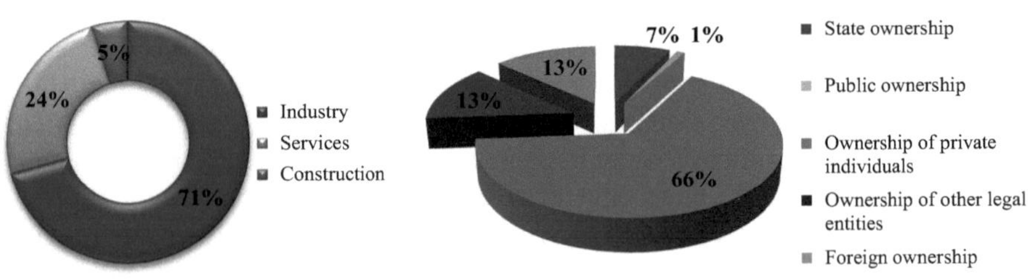

Fig. 3 The structure of the sample by branch and ownership

[1]The survey "BAS Poll—Opinion of the Business Community" was conducted in the organization of Society of Economists of Nis, Serbia and it was a project financed by LEDIB (Danish Programme for Local Economic Development in the Balkans) and City of Niš. The authors were the part of the research team and the data used in this paper are still unpublished part of the results. Project results are available at http://www.kler.ni.rs/index.php?language=en.

The key questions which have been analysed in this paper are:

- Do observed enterprises have a research department/department for new product development?
- Do interviewed managers think that their enterprise is competitive enough in the market?
- Doobserved enterprises have a need for using services of research centres, in order to increase productivity and competitiveness?

In the purpose of obtaining representative results it was necessary to:

- Explore the structure of the sample according to questions listed above;
- Test the significance of attitude differences between enterprises.

The methods which are used in order to conduct analyses are descriptive statistics and chi square test.

The answer to the first question (Do observed enterprises have a research department/department for new product development?) was provided by 232 respondents, which comprises 96.67 % of interviewed managers. Most of them responded negatively to this question (62.9 %), while only 19 % has a research department and 18.1 % is considering the creation of such a department. The structure of the answers according to the companies' ownership is presented in Table 8.

As it can be seen from Table 8, structure of the answers according to the ownership fits to the overall structure, except in case of public ownership where both enterprises have the research department. The number of these companies in sample is very small, so it is not possible to draw any relevant conclusions.

The answers given to the second question (Do interviewed managers think that their enterprise is competitive enough in the market?) support the finding that the

Table 8 Ownership/Research Department—cross tabulation

		Research Department			
Ownership		Yes	Considers	No	Total
State	Count	4	2	10	16
	% within Ownership	25.0 %	12.5 %	62.5 %	100.0 %
Public	Count	2	0	0	2
	% within Ownership	100.0 %	0.0 %	0.0 %	100.0 %
Private individuals	Count	27	29	98	154
	% within Ownership	17.5 %	18.8 %	63.6 %	100.0 %
Other legal entities	Count	4	7	20	31
	% within Ownership	12.9 %	22.6 %	64.5 %	100.0 %
Foreign	Count	7	4	18	29
	% within Ownership	24.1 %	13.8 %	62.1 %	100.0 %
Total	Count	44	42	146	232
	% within Ownership	19.0 %	18.1 %	62.9 %	100.0 %

Source: BAS Poll—Opinion of the Business Community database, authors' calculations

Table 9 Competitiveness/Research Department—cross tabulation

Research department		Competitive			Total
		No answer	Yes	No	
Yes	Count	4	28	12	44
	% within Competitive	11.1 %	19.4 %	23.1 %	19.0 %
Considers	Count	6	34	2	42
	% within Competitive	16.7 %	23.6 %	3.8 %	18.1 %
No	Count	26	82	38	146
	% within Competitive	72.2 %	56.9 %	73.1 %	62.9 %
Total	Count	36	144	52	232
	% within Competitive	100.0 %	100.0 %	100.0 %	100.0 %

Source: BAS Poll—Opinion of the Business Community database, authors' calculations

Table 10 Competitiveness/Services of research centres—Cross tabulation

Need of using services of research centers		Competitive			Total
		No answer	Yes	No	
No answer	Count	16	34	2	52
	% within Competitive	42.1 %	22.7 %	3.8 %	21.7 %
Yes	Count	6	40	8	54
	% within Competitive	15.8 %	26.7 %	15.4 %	22.5 %
No	Count	16	76	42	134
	% within Competitive	42.1 %	50.7 %	80.8 %	55.8 %
Total	Count	38	150	52	240
	% within Competitive	100.0 %	100.0 %	100.0 %	100.0 %

Source: BAS Poll—Opinion of the Business Community database, authors' calculations. World Economic Forum, The Global Competitiveness Report (2012–2013), authors' calculations

issue of competitiveness is not well known to the enterprises in Serbia, or it is not given adequate importance. The answer to this question was not provided by 38 respondents, which makes 15.8 % of all interviewed managers. Among the managers who answered to this question, 74.25 % of them think that their enterprise is competitive in the market, while 25.75 % have the opposite opinion.

Data presented in Table 9 show that 56.9 % of the observed enterprises that find themselves competitive in the market do not have a research department, while only 19.4 % have this department. On the other hand, only 3.8 % of enterprises that do not find themselves competitive in the market consider establishing that kind of department. The dependence between the answers to these two questions is confirmed by results of Chi-square test, with significance of 0.017.

The managers from Serbia were also asked if they have a need for using services of research centres, in order to increase productivity and competitiveness. The answer to this question wasn't provided by 21.7 % of respondents, only 22.7 % of managers answered positively and even 55.8 % answered negatively (Table 10).

6 Conclusion

Improving competitiveness is a central issue in contemporary economic literature, particularly in conditions of globalization and the economic crisis. For the Balkan countries this issue is even more important, given the fact that their score of competitiveness is far below indicators of EU countries and even below the world average.

Analysing the sub-indices of CGI, according to the latest Global Competitiveness Report 2012–2013, it can be concluded that the sub-index *Basic requirements* has the highest impact on the competitiveness of the Balkan countries, which relates to issues of institutions, infrastructure, macroeconomic stability and health and primary education (there is statistically significant correlation between GCI and sub-index *Basic requirements* of 0.853). Second most powerful influence on GCI has the sub-index *Innovative and sophisticated factors*, which includes issues of business sophistication and innovation (Pearson Correlation coefficient is 0.793). Key recommendations arising from these results are related primarily to the need of improvement of macroeconomic environment, including specifically infrastructure and institutions. As well, the issue of intensifying innovative activities is no less important. The stagnation in sub-index *Innovative and sophisticated factors* suggests that the Balkan countries invest little in improving the innovation infrastructure. The score of *Innovative and sophisticated factors* in 2006 was 3.11, and in 2012 is 3.12, which only a slight increase.

The results of the analysis of the competitiveness of Serbia indicate very low values, even in relation to the Balkan countries, so Serbia has found itself almost at the tail-end of Europe. The Global Competitiveness Index 2012–2013 rankings put Serbia to the 95th place and Greece is the only European country with lower rank. A special warning is a decline in the score of indicators related to innovation. Serbia has the score 3.08 for pillar *Innovation* in 2007 and until 2012 the decrease was 0.27, so the latest score amounts 2.81.

The results of innovative activities of enterprises in Serbia are very low. Only 19 % of observed enterprises have a research department and 18.1 % is considering establishment of such a department. It is an interesting fact that 56.9 % of observed enterprises, which find themselves competitive in the market, do not have R&D department. This is an alarming finding that indicates a lack of awareness about the need for innovative activities as one of basic mechanisms to improve competitiveness. The results indicate an urgent need for intensive work on improving the innovation infrastructure in enterprises and for promoting innovative entrepreneurship in Serbia.

References

Acemoglu D, Aghion P, Lelarge C, Van Reenen J, Zilibotti F (2007) Technology, information, and the decentralization of the firm. Q J Econ 122(4):1759–99
Balcerowicz L (1995) Socialism capitalism transformation. CEU Press, Budapest
Baumol WJ (2002) The free-market innovation machine: analyzing the growth miracle of capitalism. Princeton University Press, Princeton, NJ
Baumol W, Schilling M (2008) Entrepreneurship. The New Palgrave Dictionary Economics (online version 1–9)
Baumol WJ, Litan RE, Schramm CJ (2007) Good capitalism, bad capitalism, and the economics of growth and prosperity. Yale University Press, New Haven, CT
Cantwell J (2003) Innovation and competitiveness. In: Fagerberg J, Mowery DC, Nelson RR (eds) Chapter 21: Handbook of innovation. Oxford University Press, Oxford
Davila T, Epstein MJ, Shelton R (2006) Making innovation work. How to manage it, measure it, and profit from it. Wharton School, Philadelphia, PA
Dunn DMH (1994).Do nations compete economically? A critical comment on Prof. Krugman's Essay "Competitiveness: A Dangerous Obsession." Intereconomics Issue Nov-Dec:303–308
Golubovic N, Dzunic M (2012) Social determinants of competitiveness. University of Nis, Faculty of Economics, Nis
Heertje A (2006) Schumpeter on the economics of innovation and the development of capitalism. Elgar, Cheltenham
Kornai J (2010) Innovation and dynamism: interaction between systems and technical progress. Working paper No. 2010/33. United Nation University and World Institute for Development Economics Research, Helsinki, Finland
Krugman P (1994) Competitiveness. A dangerous obsession. Foreign Aff 73(3/4):28–44
Lankauskiene T, Tvaronaviciene M (2011) Interrelation of countries' developmental level and foreign direct investments performance. J Bus Econ Manag 12(3):546–565
Mowery DC, Nelson RR (1999) Sources of industrial leadership: studies of seven industries. Cambridge University Press, Cambridge
OECD (2008) Handbook on constructing composite indicators. Methodology and user guide. http://www.oecd.org/std/42495745.pdf. Retrieved 17 Apr 2015
Phelps E (2008) Understanding the great changes in the world: gaining ground and losing ground since World War II. In: Kornai J, László M, Roland G (eds) Institutional change and economic behaviour. Palgrave Macmillan, Basingstoke
Porter ME, Schwab K (2008) The Global competitiveness report 2008-2009. World Economic Forum, Geneva
Savic N (2012) Comparative analysis based on new competitiveness index. Panoeconomicus 1: 105–115
Schwab K (2009) The Global competitiveness report 2009-2010. World Economic Forum, Geneva
Schwab K (2010) The Global competitiveness report 2010-2011. World Economic Forum, Geneva
Schwab K (2011) The Global competitiveness report 2011-2012. World Economic Forum, Geneva
Schwab K (2012) The Global competitiveness report 2012–2013. World Economic Forum, Geneva
Society of Economists of Nis (2012) BAS Poll—opinion of the Business community. http://www.kler.ni.rs/index.php?language=en. In Serbian
Spence AM, Hazard HA (eds) (1988) International competitiveness. Ballinger, Cambridge, MA
Stiglitz JE, Sen A, Fitoussi J-P (2009) Draft summary. Commission on the Measurement of Economic Performance and Social Progress, Paris

Testing Uncovered Interest Parity for Structural Breaks: A Developing Country Perspective

Srđan Marinković, Ognjen Radović, and Željko Šević

Abstract This article is a single-country empirical study of uncovered interest parity. Uncovered interest parity (hereafter UIP) is a non-arbitrary condition well-known and widely tested in international finance. This test of UIP is based on high-frequency data. The most promising parts of the evidence are the EGARCH analysis of statistical properties of time series of deviations from UIP, and the Markov Switching model. EGARCH (1,1) delivers a model able to predict future volatility of the tested variable. Moreover, the model also describes the time-varying nature of volatility itself. The changing nature of volatility may arise due to the process of information arrivals or being liquidity driven, but can also be a consequence of some structural breaks. Namely, the time series remains homoscedastic in the short-term while heteroscedasticity appears in long-term horizons. The regime switching model is further employed in order to test if the smoothed probabilities along the sample reflect the main events through which the economy evolved over time. The model proved to be able to indicate correctly the *ex-ante* identified structural break that came from crisis incident, but failed to differ between pre- and post-liberalisation periods.

1 Introduction

Uncovered interest parity (hereafter UIP) is a non-arbitrage supported equilibrium condition that links the yields on two comparable assets denominated in different currencies. The basic issue in testing UIP directly is the necessity to operate with exchange rate expectations. Sometimes, if there is an active forward currency market, the forward exchange rate is taken to be a good proxy for expected future spot rate. Unfortunately, not only forward premium/discount misdirects exchange

S. Marinković (✉) • O. Radović
Faculty of Economics, University of Niš, Trg kralja Aleksandra Ujedinitelja 11, 18000 Niš, Republic of Serbia
e-mail: srdjan.marinkovic@eknfak.ni.ac.rs

Ž. Šević
University of Wales Trinity Saint David, Swansea Campus, Swansea SA1 6ED, Wales, UK

A. Karasavvoglou et al. (eds.), *Economic Crisis, Development and Competitiveness in Southeastern Europe*, Contributions to Economics,
DOI 10.1007/978-3-319-40322-9_8

rate movements (Froot and Thaler 1990; Sachsida et al. 2001; Engel 2014), but also survey data collected from the various sources (Kaminsky 1993). The latter regularity may come because even survey based forecasts appear to be informed or guided by UIP (Cuestas et al. 2015). The most frequently used approach is to assume rational expectation, and simply use *ex post* realised exchange rate changes as rationally predicted. Then we are able to test for UIP, according to the following equation:

$$\Delta s_{t+k} = \alpha + \beta\left(i_{t,k} - i^{*}_{t,k}\right) + \varepsilon_{t+k} \quad (1)$$

Where Δs_{t+k} is the percentage depreciation of the currency and $\left(i_{t,k} - i^{*}_{t,k}\right)$ is the current k–period interest rate differential between domestic interest rate and relevant foreign interest rate. For rather small changes in the exchange rate, it is acceptable to transform the dependent variable into a continuously compounded rate of return, expressing it as the difference in logs of exchange rate over k periods.

If the rational expectation hypothesis holds and two financial markets are perfectly integrated, then the estimate of intercept (α) must be equal to zero, and the estimate of slope coefficient (β) equal to one. The first condition implies that interest rate differential is built into exchange rate changes, while the second implies that there are no other explanatory variables that should be included in the model. The regression residual term (ε_{t+k}) should be stationary and orthogonal to information available at time t. Although the procedure is widely implemented, it contains critical flaws. Most variations in spot exchange rates are unanticipated (Chinn and Dooley 1995), notably where the trading (forecasting) window is short-term and the exchange rate is noisy.

2 Why Does UIP Frequently Fail

UIP could fail simply because a country does not work with a pure floating exchange rate regime. It is rarely seen, even in the most developed countries, that solely market forces, with no interventions, determine a pure floating exchange rate. It seems also that there is a kind of asymmetry in a way that the authorities react to correct market forces. If the market drives currency down, the authorities take contra-trend position (massive selling of reserve currency), if the market drives it up, they are not keen to do something. Calvo and Reinhart (2002) coined well known phrase "fear of floating", to describe a specific authorities' behavior. They found that countries that claim they allow their exchange rate to float mostly do not.

In the last 10 years, exchange rate policy applied in Serbia passed through several phases. From the very beginning of the reform, Serbia, de jure has followed a managed floating regime with explicit exchange rate targeting. However, it started de facto pegging its currency. Since the year 2003 the policy switched to the one most responsive to the market forces. The last phase of exchange rate policy starts in August 2006. It was then when NBS de facto shifted from the exchange rate targeting to the pure inflation targeting monetary strategy. Exchange rate was not anymore the variable of prime concern, and had to be managed only in order to prevent excess daily fluctuations (with no transparent threshold). The change of the policy into an independent floating regime, oriented to prevent excess daily fluctuations, inside the inflation targeting monetary framework was officially announced in August 2008. The shift in exchange rate policy coincides with the moment of de jure capital account liberalization. During almost the entire period the National Bank of Serbia was regularly present on the foreign exchange market. A notable exception is the third quarter of 2008, and the last three quarters of 2009.

In order to have UIP in place, perfect capital mobility is another necessary precondition. It means that the more open the economy is, the better the performing UIP will be, advocating the condition to be a good proxy for capital mobility. However, it is only one of several approaches proposed by theory to test the international mobility of capital. Montiel (1994), and more recently Kose et al. (2009), proposed several measures; capital controls in place, flow of funds and stock of funds measures, which are alternatives to measures that rely solely on financial return. The measures of capital mobility which rest on financial return (UIP) could fail because either effective or prospective capital controls constrain pricing arbitrage (Dooley and Isard 1980). Moreover, less developed financial markets are often not sufficiently deep to enable an efficient pricing arbitrage. The Republic of Serbia de jure introduced a liberalised capital account in 2006, but it did not abandon some of the old capital control measures. Amongst the measures that most severely constrain international capital mobility are mandatory reserves, which in the case of Serbia remain at all times prohibitively costly. Kose et al. (2009) stress that even such measures as prudential regulation applied to the banks in terms of limits of currency risk exposure can play a role similar to that of exchange rate controls, despite being ignored in many analyses. Anyway, empirical studies have mixed results in terms of the influence of capital account liberalization to the UIP. For instance, Francis et al. (2002) found the effect regionally specific. In some countries deviations from UIP decreased after the liberalization, but not for example in many studied Latin American countries. Interestingly, currency crises are seen as the events that move exchange rate away from the parity.

Ambiguous results come from testing UIP with data that differs in length of time. Some researchers found rather strong support of UIP when using overnight (Chaboud and Wright 2005) or even 1-month data (Lee 2013), contrary to econometric tests that mostly reject UIP conditions in long investment horizons (for a review see: Pasricha 2006). However, one should be cautious because tests with overnight trading horizon could include periods with a rather peculiar statistical nature, for instance currency under attack when the interest rate differential is used as a policy tool to fight against depreciation. This could plausibly explain why in some tests (Flood and Rose 2002; Bhatti 2014), UIP worked systematically better for countries that faced financial crisis. There is also novel research that relates higher explanatory power of UIP in predicting future exchange rates to the monetary volatility. For instance, Moore and Roche (2012) found that UIP better held with the countries and within the periods where the monetary growth was more volatile, even if controlled for inflation.

The fact in favour of short-term is also data availability. The data for the shorter time spans are readily available, even for emerging economies, while data on the long-term interest rates are frequently not as "clean" as data used for shorter horizons (Mehl and Cappiello 2009). Nevertheless, the empirical evidence questions the theoretical suggestions.

The majority of empirical investigations fail to support UIP, both for developed and developing countries. Among the most quoted papers is Froot (1990), which calculated the average value of slope coefficient over 75 published studies. Contrary to theory suggestions, he found it to be close to negative figure one (−0.88). However, some more recent empirical literature found significantly higher support of the UIP theory. For example, Lee (2013) studied a broad spectrum of currencies and found slope coefficients in the majority of cases supporting the UIP. According to the results, in many studied cases violations of the UIP came because of the various currencies are expressed against the US dollar and the other main currencies, that tend to appreciate even if they have higher interest rates. Moreover, UIP holds much better if one limits the research only to the cases of higher interest differential (Craighead et al. 2010). Authors explain that there is a zone of speculative (carry-trade) inactivity that corresponds to smaller interest differentials. On the contrary, higher differentials used to decay over time as a consequence of carry-trade, restoring UIP conditions. The same, Lothian and Wu (2011) find large interest differentials more promising in explaining movements in exchange rates of most developed economies over the time span of two centuries. The failure of small differentials to do the same effect is assigned to the noise surrounding small deviations, i.e. problems that traders face in extracting signals.

Nevertheless, the testing level of integration increasingly turns from testing if UIP holds to rather testing the statistical properties of deviations from it. Among the first empirical articles which tested the statistical nature of deviations from uncovered interest parity is Cumby and Obstfeld (1981). The authors rejected the assumption of randomness of the deviations. If exchange rate changes (i.e. daily exchange rate return) were random, it would be inconsistent with the uncovered interest parity. The presence of a nonzero interest rate differential will transform an otherwise pure random walk into a random walk with drift (Taylor 1995, p. 14). Since the interest rate differential is supposed to be changing over time, it can hardly be expected that it be identically equal to a constant.

If the degree of capital mobility varies through time, deviations from parity will also vary. The volatility of deviations is supposed to be higher in the period with more capital controls than in the period with a higher degree of integration (Faruqee 1992). From Eq. (1), it follows that any deviation from the parity condition is restated as:

$$y_{t,k} = (s_{t+k} - s_t) - \left(i_{t,k} - i^*_{t,k}\right) \tag{2}$$

Where $y_{t,k}$ denotes deviations (excess return), while lowercase letter s indicates logs of exchange rates. In the remainder of the article, we will carry out deviations to some statistical procedures to investigate their statistical nature.

3 Estimation Models: Statistical Properties of Data Set

The period covered by the analysis is from August 2005 to December 2009. The data set comprises 1078 daily data on referent foreign (EONIA) and local (BEONIA) overnight interbank interest rates and exchange rates. The data on the bilateral exchange rate was supplied by the National bank of Serbia, and were consequently sampled at the daily frequency. The Serbian dinar (RSD) vis-à-vis the Euro (EUR) exchange rate is expressed in terms of units of domestic currency per unit of foreign currency (direct quotation). The choice of overnight interbank rates is not rare in empirical studies (e.g. Baillie and Osterberg (2000) operated with overnight Eurocurrency deposit rates), and it may be superior to the choice of long-term/governmental bonds in many (above mentioned) respects. However, by using overnight interbank interest rates to test for UIP, a researcher brings the risk of incomparability of relevant foreign and domestic interest rates. The structure of the domestic banking industry has also been changed significantly, since the major reform was undertaken in 2001. Serbia opened the door of its market to the major regional banks. The data on structure of participants is not available, but it is reasonable to assume that it does not differ significantly from the structure of the relevant foreign interbank overnight market, leaving the difference in credit risk more or less irrelevant. Moreover, in tranquil times, interbank overnight rates are taken to be non-risky, which is a normally doubtful assumption for crisis-prone periods.

3.1 Descriptive Statistics of Data Set

Contained in Table 1 are the basic statistics of time series of interest rate differential, exchange rate changes and excess return. The last variable is also broken down into four sub-samples: the period before de jure liberalisation, the period after it and before the crisis, the crisis period itself, and finally the post-crisis period.

Theoretically, the currency that earns a higher rate of return should depreciate until the end of the holding period, so that statistically significant and persistent deviation (excess return) could indicate UIP failure. It is worth noting that the figures representing excess return are by no means actual earnings, since many costs

Table 1 Descriptive statistics

Series	Mean	Min	Max	SD	Skewness	Kurtosis	J–B[a]
$i_{t,k} - i^*_{t,k}$	0.0002	0.0001	0.0005	0.0001	0.2243	2.164	40.44 (5.93)
$s_{t+k} - s_t$	0.0001	−0.036	0.0489	0.0053	0.3385	15.410	6944.90 (5.93)
$y_{t,k}$							
2005:09–2009:12	−0.0143	−3.707	4.8805	0.5291	0.3276	15.476	7017.39 (5.93)
2005:09–2006:08	−0.0288	−1.237	0.8695	0.2446	−0.6949	8.438	299.35 (5.71)
2006:08–2008:10	−0.0348	−2.887	4.8804	0.5599	0.9987	16.533	4296.80 (5.87)
2008:10–2009:03	0.1649	−3.707	2.2730	1.0149	−0.8486	4.554	20.96 (5.40)
2009:03–2009:12	−0.0261	−1.011	0.9103	0.2760	0.0789	4.746	26.26 (5.68)
$dy_{t,k}$	−0.0000	−0.072	0.0487	0.0063	−1.2564	26.096	24244.5 (5.93)

Notes: J–B stands for Jarque–Bera test statistics
[a]in parenthesis are critical values for 5 % significance

Table 2 Autocorrelation test

	$i_{t,k} - i^*_{t,k}$	$s_{t+k} - s_t$	$y_{t,k}$
Autocorrelation of each series			
$\rho_{1,1}$	0.9250	0.2905	0.2909
$\rho_{1,2}$	0.8763	−0.0160	−0.0155
$\rho_{1,3}$	0.8468	−0.1401	−0.1396
$\rho_{1,10}$	0.7366	−0.0272	−0.0278
$\rho_{1,20}$	0.7572	−0.0313	−0.0320
$Q_1(24)$	1521.33 (0.00)	144.06 (0.00)	144.08 (0.00)
Autocorrelation of the square of each series			
$\rho_{2,1}$	0.9117	0.2994	0.3028
$\rho_{2,2}$	0.8536	0.1096	0.1078
$\rho_{2,3}$	0.8285	0.1196	0.1156
$\rho_{2,10}$	0.7158	0.0323	0.0327
$\rho_{2,20}$	0.7381	0.0759	0.0774
$Q_2(24)$	8246.17 (0.00)	446.15 (0.00)	437.90 (0.00)

impact the ultimate success of the speculative arbitrage strategy (rollover overnight positions).

Negative mean indicates that the daily interest rate differential was not fully offset by local currency depreciation, so that an arbitrager, by holding a short foreign and long domestic position, gains profit (allowing for transaction costs). The period of acute banking and currency disturbance solely has a differing nature of mean. In this period, the hypothetical arbitrager has lost the money, since the rollover of daily arbitrage, which starts from the very beginning of the period and continues until the end of the period, faced a severe drop in local currency value. The foreign exchange rate dropped more than required to offset all the positive differences between the domestic and corresponding foreign interest rate, so that the hypothetical arbitrager finished the period of arbitrage with a loss.

Although the method above is built on basic statistics, it brings a valuable insight of a time-varying nature of deviation from UIP. However, in order to employ correctly more sophisticated statistical methodology, time series should follow certain properties. The stationarity of time series is not only a necessary precondition if a researcher wants to proceed with more sophisticated methods, but also may have a specific economic interpretation. Namely, if deviation from the parity condition (excess return) is not a stationary process it will per se rule out UIP. If not, we could say that monetary integration between the pair of countries is reached to the level that excludes unbounded profit from the carry trade/uncovered interest arbitrage (Jiang et al. 2013).

3.2 *The Test of Unit Root*

We test for unit root using several statistical procedures. First, we calculated partial autocorrelations' coefficients for a different time lag. A statistical process is said to be stationary stochastic if the autocorrelation function either abruptly drops to zero at some finite lag or eventually tapers off to zero (Green 2003, p. 614). Instead of using the autocorrelation function, one can also compare the values of coefficients. As the lag becomes longer, the value of coefficient must decrease. The results clearly reject stationarity in the case of interest rate differential, contrary to the exchange rate and the deviations themselves (excess return), where the stationarity condition holds rather strong. The value of $Q(24)$ presents Ljung–Box statistics based on autocorrelation coefficients in the order of up to 24.

Table 3 presents the results from different tests of unit root. Tabulated critical values (not enclosed) depend upon both the number of observations (sample size) and the assumed statistical model. The variance ratio test assesses the null hypothesis that a univariate time series y is a random walk. The test delivers the vector of variance ratios (r ratio), with length equal to the number of tests. Each ratio is the ratio of the variance of the q-fold overlapping return horizon, where q times the variance of the return series. For a pure random walk, these ratios are asymptotically equal to one. For a mean-reverting series, the ratios are less than one, while for a mean-averting series the ratios are greater than one. The evidence rejects pure random walk (Table 3).

To continue we apply the Augmented Dickey–Fuller (ADF) as this test is considered to be more convincing with regard to the statistical property we are investigating. The Augmented Dickey and Fuller (1981) for unit root tests the null model:

Table 3 Test of stationarity

Variable	Variance ratio		ADF		DF–GLS	Ng–Perron	
	Stat	r	Stat	a	Stat	MZ_{α}	MZ_{t}
$i_{t,k} - i^*_{t,k}$	22.095[a]	1.92	−1.738	0.99	−0.631	−0.979	−0.607
$s_{t+k} - s_t$	4.160[a]	1.29	−8.330[a]	0.29	−24.317[b]	−493.328[a]	−982.692[a]
$y_{t,k}$							
2005:09–2009:12	4.167[a]	1.29	−8.360[a]	0.29	−24.322[a]	−493.387[a]	−15.705[a]
2005:09–2006:08	1.909	1.24	−11.846[a]	0.24	−2.404[b]	−4.386	−1.480
2006:08–2008:10	2.787[a]	1.25	−6.554[a]	0.25	−2.292[b]	−0.992	−0.350
2008:10–2009:03	2.251[b]	1.35	−6.437[a]	0.35	−0.741	−0.387	−0.226
2009:03–2009:12	3.699[a]	1.28	−10.083[a]	0.27	−1.140	−1.170	−0.706
$dy_{t,k}$	−2.887[a]	–	−12.709[a]	−0.28	−43.848[a]	−495.566[a]	−15.741[a]

Notes: ADF test uses the general to specific approach to select the number of lags. DF-GLS and Ng–Perron tests use modified information criteria (MIC)
[a]denotes rejection of null hypotesis of unit root at 1 % statistical significance
[b]denotes rejection of null hypotesis of unit root at 5 % statistical significance

$$y_t = y_{t-1} + b_1 \Delta y_{t-1} + b_2 \Delta y_{t-2} + \ldots + b_p \Delta y_{t-p} + e(t) \tag{3}$$

Against the alternative model:

$$y_t = a y_{t-1} + b_1 \Delta y_{t-1} + b_2 \Delta y_{t-2} + \ldots + b_p \Delta y_{t-p} + e(t) \tag{4}$$

The time series of interest rate differential, exchange rate changes and excess return are estimated as they belong to the random walk with drift (with constant/intercept). The estimate of AR(1) coefficient must satisfy the condition $a < 1$. In all series except the interest differential, it is significantly less than unit. Moreover, the test statistics for all series except interest differential stays below the tabulated critical values. Thus, according to the test, all series but the interest rate differential, clearly exhibit stationarity. Since the interest differential is nonstationary, or contains unit root, denoted $I(1)$, the excess return may also have unit root. It depends on which series overwhelms the other. If interest differential is predominantly responsible for changes in excess return, the statistical nature of the result series will contain unit root, otherwise it will share the statistical nature of the series of exchange rate changes. Since all series have a daily frequency, interest differential is expected to have a weak effect on excess return.

The last columns contain results given by Dickey–Fuller generalized least squares test (Ellliott et al. 1996) and Ng and Perron (2001) test based on two statistics, which are considered more rigorous than either Variance Ratio test or Augmented Dickey–Fuller. The tests' results are rather promising since for excess return (total sample time series) unit root property is rejected with confidence of more than 99 %, although Ng–Perron invariably rejected stationarity of all excess return series in shorter time spans (subsamples). Further analysis showed that according to Dickey–Fuller generalized least squares test (DF–GLS) even excess return series in third and fourth sub-samples are stationary up to the lag 5, and 21, respectively (albeit with 10 % statistical significance). Similar holds even for interest rate differential.

Since an excess return follows the stationary stochastic process, we will proceed with modelling its absolute value and volatility. All models were estimated by MATLAB, EViews or R software, alternatively.

4 Time Series Modelling Using ARMA(1,1)-GARCH(1,1) and ARMA(1,1)-E–GARCH(1,1)

4.1 ARMA(1,1)

Sometimes in modelling the statistical time series, the autoregressive moving-average process (hereafter ARMA) has the ability to explain variable dynamics, as well as complicated econometric models. An ARMA(p,q) process is the combination of AR(p) and MA(q) processes. The process has p autoregressive terms, or lagged dependent variable, and q lagged moving-average terms. The model has a most general form:

$$y_t = \mu + \phi_1 y_{t-1} + \phi_2 y_{t-2} + \ldots + \phi_p y_{t-p} + \varepsilon_t - \theta_1 \varepsilon_{t-1} - \ldots - \theta_q \varepsilon_{t-q} \quad (5)$$

Although it is assumed that the more extensive models have the ability to predict better, very often the simplest model, with no more than single autoregressive and moving-average terms, fits reality equally well. In the paper, we applied the most reduced form of general ARMA(p,q) model, i.e. ARMA(1,1).

$$y_t = \mu + \phi_1 y_{t-1} + \varepsilon_t - \theta_1 \varepsilon_{t-1} \quad (6)$$

The results, containing the value of relevant coefficients and t–statistics, are shown in Table 4. Log likelihoods are given jointly for the model of excess return and the model of volatility assigned to it. The volatility models are discussed next.

4.2 Volatility Modelling: GARCH Model

Using volatility models to assess the UIP condition has its own research history. Domowitz and Craig (1985) applied a model of autoregressive conditional heteroskedasticity (ARCH) and found expected future volatility unrelated to excess return (forward discount's bias). Recently, researchers have switched to the more sophisticated models. Sul (1999) tests the GARCH model and finds that conditional variance of excess return does not tend to depend on the degree of capital mobility, contrary to Goh et al. (2006), which finds Switching ARCH model enables diagnosing the influence of de facto capital liberalisation on the nature of deviations from UIP.

The assumption underlying the GARCH model is that volatility changes with the passage of time, what makes it suitable for modelling heteroskedastic processes. The rationale for using the GARCH model to test UIP is that changes in variable volatility point out structural breaks, by definition, a change in economy openness, and the presence of financial disturbances. Since the GARCH (1,1) model works without ex ante known breaks, it is a way to test whether the theoretically suggested breaks appear in the data.

The GARCH(1,1) model (see: Bollerslev 1986) assumes that volatility measured at any point in time, t, is under the influence of a long-run average variance rate, V_L, most recent observation of squared return u_{t-1}^2, and most recent estimate of the variance rate, σ_{t-1}^2. The model is still most widely used in forecasting volatility.

By solving the model, we obtain the weights scheme, or what weighting is to be assigned to any of those determinants: γ, α, and β respectively.

$$\sigma_t^2 = \gamma V_L + \alpha\sigma_{t-1}^2 + \beta u_{t-1}^2 \quad (7)$$

Setting $\omega = \gamma V_L$, the test model becomes:

$$\sigma_t^2 = \omega + \alpha\sigma_{t-1}^2 + \beta u_{t-1}^2 \quad (8)$$

Unfortunately, the tested ARMA(1,1)–GARCH(1,1) model did not deliver strictly stationary solution, since for that we require positive value of ω, and $\alpha + \beta < 1$. Namely, the sum of all weights must equal one. Since the sum of α and β is one, and ω is close to zero, the model belongs to the Exponentially Weighted Moving Average Model (EWMA) as a specific case of the GARCH (1,1) model, where the weight assigned to long-run average volatility is zero. This means that the variance rate of the excess return does not tend to be pulled back to a long-run average level, or it shows no mean reversion. Moreover, by comparing the weights assigned to the most recent (previous trading day) observations of daily variance rate (volatility persistence, or volatility clustering effect) and square of return, we see (Table 4) firstly that previous-day variance rate has strong impact on contemporaneous variance rate (α equals 76.58 %) and secondly, that daily volatility responds relatively fast to new information provided by the daily percentage change in excess return (β equals 23.41 %). The standard GARCH model successfully explains the volatility clustering, but it does not capture so called leverage effect, which is often recognized in various financial return time series. This is why we will proceed with another GARCH-type model able to capture leverage effect.

4.3 Exponential GARCH Model

The Exponential GARCH model (EGARCH) belongs to the same family of volatility models and differs in the way that it allows for asymmetrical impact of good versus bad news. It is also less susceptible to the above mentioned restriction. The only restriction is that the absolute value of coefficient β must be less that unit.

In this case, the ARMA(1,1)–EGARCH(1,1) model fits the sample data a bit better than the ARMA(1,1)–GARCH(1,1) model. The log likelihood function for this model is slightly higher (Table 4).

The value assigned to λ confirms that positive innovations are more destabilizing than negative ones. Since positive innovations, or positive excess return, by definition, mean that currency depreciates more than indicated by interest rate differential, it essentially declares that bad news for local currency generates more volatility than good news. However, the magnitude of λ coefficient, which is close to zero, indicates a not so strong asymmetry or the leverage effect.

Figure 1 presents the time series of conditional variance delivered by the ARMA (1,1)–EGARCH(1,1) model, which is a combination of the ARMA(1,1) model for the conditional mean and the GARCH(1,1) model for the conditional variance. We used here Hodrick-Prescott filter to smooth the trend, although some other procedures are available if a researcher want to separate permanent from transitory component of the conditional variance within the GARCH framework (Li et al. 2012). The graph clearly indicates that the time-varying nature of conditional variance coincides with ex ante indicated structural break that belongs to a crisis incident, but not to that of liberalisation.

Table 4 ARMA(1,1)–GARCH(1,1) and ARMA(1,1)–EGARCH(1,1) results

Parameter	ARMA(1,1)–GARCH(1,1)–*t*	ARMA(1,1)–EGARCH(1,1)–*t*
μ	−0.0001 (−1.2695)	−0.0001 (−1.1394)
φ_1	0.0439 (0.4548)	0.02609 (0.2694)
θ_1	0.2552 (2.6506)	0.2743 (2.8477)
ω	0.0000 (3.5110)	−0.4544 (−3.4501)
α	0.7658 (26.2116)	0.95738 (79.1911)
β	0.2341 (4.9825)	0.4846 (6.2451)
λ	–	0.0064956 (0.1742)
df	3.6083 (9.1719)	2.8764 (9.0617)
Log likelihood	4571.13	4462.50

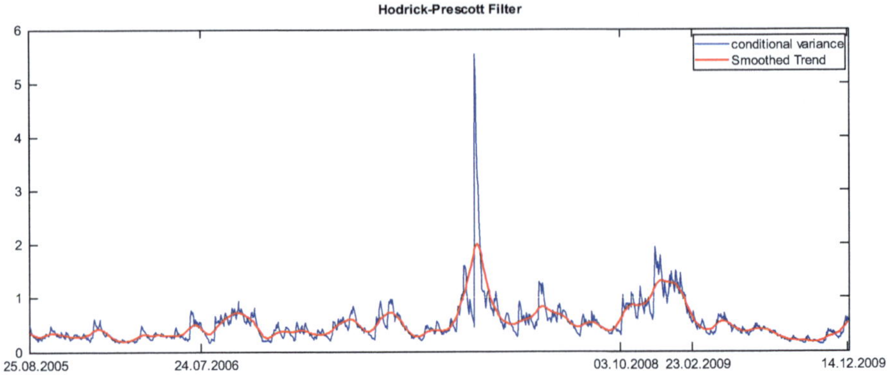

Fig. 1 Conditional variance

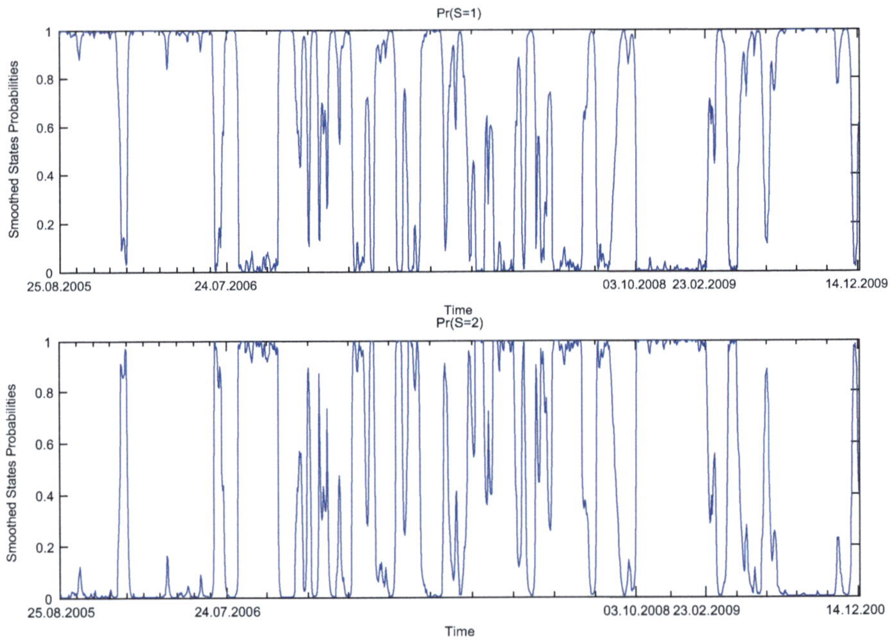

Fig. 2 Smoothed probability for state one (**a**) and two (**b**)

5 Regime Switching Modelling

There is a risk that statistical inference based on time series analysis, which does not take into account a switch in regime, leads to spurious results. Models which ignore any change in the ambience usually overestimate volatility persistence. Contrary to what was previously believed, Engel and Hamilton (1990) claim that the exchange

Table 5 Regime switching model (*t*–distribution)

	Low volatility regime (1)	High volatility regime (2)
Distribution parameters		
Variance	0.000002	0.000035
SE	0.0000	0.0000
df	4.6265	4.6535
SE	1.2712	1.0094
Regressors		
Value	−0.0003	0.0001
SE (*p*–value)	0.0001 (0.00)	0.0003 (0.70)
Probability of transition (SE)		
Stay the same (P_{11}; P_{22})	0.95 (0.03)	0.94 (0.03)
Shift to the other (P_{12}; P_{21})	0.05 (0.01)	0.06 (0.02)
Expected duration (periods)	22.20	15.66
Log likelihood		4500.11

rate follows the regime switch process, or the model of the exchange rate evolves over time. The switch of the regime that governs the exchange rate here is taken to include not only de facto changes in the exchange rate regime, but also changes in such a way that the exchange rate responds to its fundamental determinants. For example, in Beyaert et al. (2007) it was assumed that occasional and unpredictable shifts in monetary policy, currencies attacks and the liberalizations of capital flows govern shifts between regimes. Put that way, the regime switch framework is able to use more widely, e.g. for the floating regime.

Therefore, the next logical step is to incorporate an underlying assumption that some economic forces drive the market between different states. If the entire period contains sub-periods, which differ in the way the exchange rate responds to its fundamentals, it will be mirrored in volatility.

We have applied the Markov regime switching model to volatility of excess return. The model has the ability to portray the time evolving nature of volatility. We assume two states: low volatility (regime one) and high volatility state (regime two). According to the transition probability matrix (Table 5), the regimes seem highly persistent. The probability of regime one to stay in the same regime is close to one ($P_{11} = 0.95$), which is slightly higher than in the case of regime two.

The plots describe graphically the evolution of volatility. Time is portrayed on plots' abscise, with some points marked ex ante identified as significant. The plots do not show volatility itself but the probability that any period belongs to either of the two discrete states. If the probability comes close to one or zero, it means we can be fairly sure about the volatility feature of the period. The graphs are strongly conclusive about the volatility, since the smoothed probability is, more often than not, approaching its extremes.

The volatility difference between those two states is statistically significant. The variance in high volatility states is 17 times the variance in low volatility states. Unfortunately, the high volatility state switches to low volatility state, and vice versa, more frequently than we expected, meaning that the periods are rather short-lived. The expected duration of regime one (low volatility state) is just 22.20 days, while the expected duration of regime two is even shorter (15.66 days). The Markov switching model has log likelihood comparable to that of previously applied models.

Contrary to what was suggested by the theory, as well as some empirical studies (e.g. Beyaert et al. 2007), opening the capital account exhibits no clear stabilizing effect on the market. It produces no alignment of the exchange rate according to the interest rate differential. Excess return on domestic assets remained higher (expected depreciation of local currency on average did not offset for interest rate differential). From the very start, the major de jure liberalisation brings the market to a high volatility state. The excess return volatility increased. It follows several reversals to low volatility state. These reversals might be explained by the influence of foreign exchange interventions, which themselves could produce a switch between regimes. This regularity is clearly confirmed Taylor study (2005), but, for example, not in the case of bilateral the Bundesbank and the Federal Reserve System interventions that occurred around early nineties, which appeared to influence dollar excess returns over UIP but not on conditional variance of excess returns over UIP (Baillie and Osterberg 2000). During this period, the National Bank acted 46 times on both sides of the market with an amount that exceeded 10 % of daily interbank turnover. In any case, the National Bank was present in the market in 281 out of a total of 558 trading days. In less than 10 % of cases it was on the buying side. Bearing in mind the announced motivation for interventions, they clearly have the potential to explain the rather frequent switch to the low volatility regime. Some recent studies (Marinković 2014; Marinković and Radović 2016) indicated that direct interventions of National Bank of Serbia did have potential to decrease volatility of nominal exchange rate RSD/EUR.

Ex ante assumed intense period of crisis clearly and entirely belongs to a high volatility state. Interestingly, the period is also the sole period with a positive mean of excess return. This means that the market diverged from an awarding to a punishing short foreign-long domestic position, meaning that a hypothetical carry trader accrued loses. In the periods that preceded and followed the crisis, excess return had negative mean, which garnered speculative profit to actors sharing the same position. Therefore, the carry trade was profitable. To a very noticeable degree the findings comply with the findings of some recent studies of UIP that covered a group of less developed countries (Bhatti 2014).

6 Conclusion

The descriptive statistics indicates that statistical properties of time series of deviation from UIP evolutes significantly through time. The period that precedes de jure liberalisation, as well as the period that immediately follows, exhibits negative mean, which means that an increase in the differential drives the expected future value of the currency up. It is exactly what happened in all but the crisis periods. A parsimonious explanation for such development could be a shallow currency market. Import of speculative capital, driven by excess return (interest differential offset by exchange rate change) will itself drive the value of local currency up, just as capital reversal will drive it down. Massive capital inflow from abroad, driven by interest rate differential, ensures speculative arbitrage gain since it also helps local currency remain overvalued.

A plausible explanation for the apparent change in disparities during turbulent times could be an asymmetric response of monetary authorities on banking disturbances. The 'policy behaviour' argumentation is not novel in UIP empirical literature (McCallum 1994; Christensen 2000). In this case, the foreign authority decreases the rate whilst the local monetary authority responded in the opposite way. The combined influence of those undertakings further opened interest rate differential in favour of domestic rates. Nevertheless, the strike of funds outflow was one of unprecedented intensity and local currency depreciated much more than necessary to offset the change in interest rate differential. The change in deviations' mean and volatility, which happened during this period, supports the view that a failure of policy to fight against a speculative attack on currency by increasing interest differential, gains support of UIP in this special case.

EGARCH(1,1) model partially supports ex ante distribution of structural breaks. It indicates the impact of external shocks on the statistical nature of deviation from UIP. External shock took the form of capital reversals with a strong impact on the exchange rate, and a less obvious effect on the local interbank market.

What seems peculiar and does clash the theory, but is in line with some other empirical investigations, is the fact that de jure opening capital accounts in developing countries actually increased the volatility of deviation from UIP. In those countries, the capital account liberalisation probably would not trigger the convergence of local and foreign interest rates. On the contrary, it would expose the shallow foreign exchange market to short swings in the speculative capital flow.

Acknowledgement The authors are grateful to the Republic of Serbia Ministry of Education, Science and Technological Development for the funds and support that made this research possible.

References

Baillie R, Osterberg W (2000) Deviations from daily uncovered interest rate parity and the role of intervention. J Int Financ Mark Inst Money 10(3–4):363–379

Beyaert A, García-Solanes J, Pérez-Castejón JJ (2007) Uncovered interest parity with switching regimes. Econ Model 24(2):189–202

Bhatti HR (2014) The existence of uncovered interest parity in the CIS countries. Econ Model 40 (C):227–241

Bollerslev T (1986) Generalized autoregressive conditional heteroskedasticity. J Econ 31 (3):307–327

Calvo AG, Reinhart CM (2002) Fear of floating. Q J Econ 117(2):379–408
Chaboud PA, Wright JH (2005) Uncovered interest parity, it works, but not for long. J Int Econ 66 (2):349–362
Chinn M, Dooley M (1995) Asia–Pacific capital markets: integration and implications for economic activity. NBER Working paper No. 5280
Christensen M (2000) Uncovered interest parity and policy behavior: new evidence. Econ Lett 69 (1):81–87
Craighead W, Davis G, Miller N (2010) Interest differentials and extreme support for uncovered interest rate parity. Int Rev Econ Financ 19(4):723–732
Cuestas CJ, Filipozzi F, Staehr K (2015) Do foreign exchange forecasters believe in uncovered interest parity? Econ Lett 133:92–95
Cumby RE, Obstfeld M (1981) Exchange rate expectations and nominal interest differentials: a test of the Fischer hypothesis. J Financ 36(3):697–704
Dickey D, Fuller WA (1981) Likelihood ratio statistics for autoregressive time series with unit root. Econometrica 49(4):1057–1072
Domowitz I, Craig SH (1985) Conditional variance and the risk premium in the foreign exchange market. J Int Econ 19(1–2):47–66
Dooley PM, Isard P (1980) Capital controls, political risk, and deviations from interest–rate parity. J Polit Econ 88(2):370–384
Ellliott G, Rothenberg T, Stock J (1996) Efficient tests for an autoregressive unit root. Econometrica 64(4):813–836
Engel C (2014) Exchange rates and interest parity. In: Gopinath G, Helpman E, Rogoff K (eds) Handbook of international economics, vol 4. Elsevier, Amsterdam, pp 453–522
Engel C, Hamilton J (1990) Long swings in the exchange rate: are they in the data and do markets know it? Am Econ Rev 80(4):689–713
Faruqee H (1992) Dynamic capital mobility in Pacific Basin developing countries: estimation and policy implication. IMF Staff Pap 39(3):706–717
Flood PR, Rose AK (2002) Uncovered interest parity in crisis. IMF Staff Pap 49(2):252–266
Francis B, Hasan I, Hunter DM (2002) Emerging market liberalization and the impact on uncovered interest rate parity. J Int Money Financ 21(6):931–956
Froot AK (1990) Short rates and expected asset returns. NBER Working paper No. 3247, January
Froot AK, Thaler RH (1990) Anomalies: foreign exchange. J Econ Perspect 4(3):179–192
Goh KS, Lim GC, Olekalns N (2006) Deviations from uncovered interest parity in Malaysia. Appl Financ Econ 16(10):745–759
Green HW (2003) Econometric analysis, 5th edn. Prentice Hall, Upper Saddle River, NJ
Jiang C, Li X-L, Chang H-L, Su C-W (2013) Uncovered interest parity and risk premium convergence in Central and Eastern European countries. Econ Model 33(C):204–208
Kaminsky G (1993) Is there a peso problem? Evidence from the dollar/pound exchange rate, 1976–1987. Am Econ Rev 83(3):450–472
Kose MA, Prasad E, Jin Wei KRiS (2009) Finansijska globalizacija: Ponovna procena. Panoeconomicus 56(2):143–197
Lee B-J (2013) Uncovered interest parity puzzle: asymmetric responses. Int Rev Econ Financ 27 (1):238–249
Li D, Ghoshray A, Morley B (2012) Measuring the risk premium in uncovered interest parity using the component GARCH-M model. Int Rev Econ Financ 24:167–176
Lothian J, Wu L (2011) Uncovered interest-rate parity over the past two centuries. J Int Money Financ 30(3):448–473
Marinković S (2014) Non-parametric sign test and paired samples test of effectiveness of official FX intervention. Econ Ann 59(202):107–130
Marinković S, Radović O (2016) Market volatility and foreign exchange intervention. In: Anastasios K, Aranđelović Z, Marinković S, Polychronidou P (eds) The first decade of living with the global crisis: economic and social developments in the Balkans and Eastern Europe. Springer, Switzerland

McCallum B (1994) A reconsideration of the uncovered interest parity relationship. J Monet Econ 33(1):105–132
Mehl A, Cappiello L (2009) Uncovered interest parity at long horizons: evidence on emerging economies. Rev Int Econ 17(5):1019–1037
Montiel JP (1994) Capital mobility in developing countries: some measurement issues and empirical estimates. World Bank Econ Rev 8(3):311–350
Moore M, Roche MJ (2012) When does uncovered interest parity hold? J Int Money Financ 31 (4):865–879
Ng S, Perron P (2001) Leg length selection and the construction of unit root tests with good size and power. Econometrica 69(6):1519–1554
Pasricha GK (2006) Survey of literature on covered and uncovered interest parities. MPRA paper No. 22737
Sachsida A, Ellery R Jr, Teixeira JR (2001) Uncovered interest parity and the peso problem: the Brazilian case. Appl Econ Lett 8(3):179–181
Sul D (1999) Does *ex post* uncovered interest differential reflect the degrees of capital mobility? Appl Econ Lett 6(2):97–102
Taylor PM (1995) The economics of exchange rates. J Econ Lit 33(1):13–47
Taylor PM (2005) Official foreign exchange interventions as a coordinating signal in the dollar-yen market. Pac Econ Rev 10(1):73–82

Adult Education: A Vehicle for Economic Development

Pantelis Sklias and Giota Chatzimichailidou

Abstract In the present study, the issue under scrutiny is the contribution of adult education to economic development. More precisely this paper seeks to develop a more rigorous understanding of how adult education programs in several aspects of today's political, social and economic realms can empower individual actors, citizens, to involve in the societal evolution towards social cohesion, which consequently implies a transition to economic development. Transformative learning theory is such a tool to explain this empowerment to take action. What emerges from this paper is an alternative perspective on the benefits of adult education, differentiated from the dominant neoclassical approach framework of the Human Capital Theory, and relocated it in the methodological framework of International Political Economy. The latter serves as a tool of perceiving and understanding the existent complex context of political, economic and socio-cultural realities within European Union, coupled with the historical evolution of adult education. The upgrading of adult education standard is seen as central to the delivery of social cohesion and therefore to economic development.

1 Introduction

In this paper, we consider an analysis framework for interpreting certain aspects of today's complex political, social and economic reality, integrating the notion of adult education in economic development. We consider adult education as a development factor, not only in weak and developing countries, but also in the developed ones. In this paper the discussion revolves around European Union. It is of our strong belief that European Union's development policies and efforts may be heavily influenced by a European plan for promoting adult education programs in certain aspects of today's political, social and economic realms. Hence, adult education, especially through the prism of its dominant Transformative learning

P. Sklias • G. Chatzimichailidou (✉)
Department of Political Science and International Relations, University of Peloponnese, Aristotelous 1 and Athinon Ave, Corinth 20100, Greece
e-mail: psklias@hotmail.com; giotahatzi@gmail.com

A. Karasavvoglou et al. (eds.), *Economic Crisis, Development and Competitiveness in Southeastern Europe*, Contributions to Economics,
DOI 10.1007/978-3-319-40322-9_9

theory, might be a useful tool for both eliminating any disparities in the above realms and simultaneously empowering citizens' action towards social cohesion. The latter will successively boost economic development. On these grounds, we argue that adult education could serve as a vehicle for economic development. Hence, it is important to seek methodological tools that aim to capture the above parameters and reinterpret them in the development context. IPE seems to offer that methodological framework. Indeed, Pantelis Sklias (2001, 29) proposes that IPE includes a set of characteristics, which reveals that IPE is a singularized intellectual tool in furtherance of the study of social, economic and political relations.

There is a growing recognition that the transition to the knowledge economy requires continuous development of human capital, especially in work-related skills. Therefore, adult education has been intuitively grasped both by the policy makers around the world and the academic community. Moreover, the last two decades appeared many studies measuring the returns of education, in an attempt to analyze if future incomes of individuals are related to their past investments. Further study in this field has revealed that almost all of these studies lay on the Human Capital Theory (HCT), a dominant neoclassical theory introduced by Theodore Schultz (1972). Gareth Rees (2013, 200) comments that HCT provides a highly influential approach in understanding the role of adult learning in wider economic development, while, 'it also provides a means of addressing the determinants of individual behaviour in relation to participation in adult learning, in terms of individuals' capacities to make 'rational' calculations as to the instrumental benefits that will accrue to human capital formation' (Rees 2013, 200). The above studies that measure the benefits of education are classified in the field of Economics of Education. According to George Psacharopoulos (1996, 339) in this field emphasis is put on documenting the unit cost of education at different schooling levels and curriculum types, along with the learning and earning outcomes of education. Furthermore, the same research agenda involves efficiency assessment, i.e. cost-effectiveness analysis and cost-benefit analysis and equity assessment, i.e. costs incidence and benefits incidence (Psacharopoulos 1996, 340).

Those findings above reveal that almost all of these studies in the field of Economics of Education investigate the quantitative dimension of the role of education or schooling to economic growth. In effect, this was a disincentive for this paper's authors, whose main concern was to explore the qualitative dimension of the role of adult education to economic development. Moreover, literature review reveals that there are a few studies that measure the returns of lifelong learning, and all of them are based on neoclassical economics. A considerable attempt to survey the relation between adult education and development, within the context of IPE, is that of Frank Youngman (2000) in his study 'The political economy of adult education and development', who seeks to clarify the historical-structural constraints in the choices about adult education policies and programs in the South. However, to the best of authors' knowledge, no attempt was done to explore the potential of the contribution of adult education to economic development, within the framework of IPE in the developed countries and therefore in European Union. Hence, this paper was spawned from the lack of such a study.

Literature on economic development has very revealed that the term development encompasses a variation of approaches, measures and strategies. However, in this paper emphasis has very much given to the distinction between economic development and economic growth, especially in the framework of IPE (Gilpin 2002). Moreover, we should further explore the qualitative dimension of economic development. Sklias et al. (2013, 138), advocate the necessity to introduce a new qualitative dimension within the wider notion of economic development. In the field of adult education, a considerable amount of literature implies that there is a variety of definitions, not only across several studies, but also across countries. Many studies show a significant distinction between adult education and vocationally-oriented education. Further data on the above terms are presented in this paper.

Lastly, an analysis framework is proposed for the needs of this paper, which encapsulates the following perspectives:

- The historical reference framework of adult education.
- The basic reference framework of Transformative learning.
- The qualitative dimension of economic development.
- The features of a cohesive society.
- An analysis of the correlation between adult education and economic development.

Based on these perspectives, we attempt to investigate the contribution of adult education to economic development, within the methodological framework of IPE. Section 2 is devoted to the literature review on adult education and economic development. The methodological framework of IPE is presented in Sect. 3, whereas in Sect. 4 we present an analysis that explains the correlation between adult education and economic development.

2 A Literature Review on Adult Education and Economic Development

This section presents a literature review on adult education and economic development. The evolution of adult education within the 19th and 20th Century is presented in Sect. 2.1, whereas Sects. 2.2 and 2.3 are devoted to defining the terms adult education and economic development. In Sect. 2.4, the general framework of social cohesion will be discussed.

2.1 The Evolution of Adult Education Within Nineteenth and Twentieth Century

In expounding the economic achievement of the 19th and 20th centuries in several European countries, the contribution of better and more widespread education stands out very clearly. During 1880–1914 several European governments proceeded to the establishment of compulsory and free primary education -a previous traditional field of church's sovereignty- as a means of strengthening social cohesion. The industrialized countries had invested larger volumes of national resources for this purpose, in contrast to the countries of the South and East Europe. In 1911, in Germany, the investments for the national education have reached the level of 12 % of the total public spent, whereas in Great Britain 10 %, France 8 % and Spain only 1.5 % (Gaganakis 1999, 275). According to Berend (2013, 102), the emerging social and economic system of the 19th century required a certain minimum standard of general education and training in the masses in order to satisfy basic technical demands of modern industry. Moreover, modern education in Europe was not a response to Industrial Revolution, as it actually prepared it or in a certain sense it was a prerequisite for it. Science and its direct applications, especially technology achievements, had gained huge reputation after Second World War. Under those circumstances, Europe experienced a services revolution which reinforced the creation of a new category by millions of educated workers, those of the White Collar (Berend 2009, 335). Those rapid changes in the everyday life have also rised the demand to safeguard citizen's rights to equal education. By the same token, Karatzia-Stavlioti and Lambropoulos (2009, 633), note that in the post-Second World War period the need for world peace and social development has encouraged international organizations to contribute to the creation of a major international education discourse, whereas experts from international agencies were invited by politicians to advise on educational reforms and on how to borrow and invest money in education in order to achieve social and economic development.

Federighi (1999, 5) argues that the first state provisions promoting adult education in Europe accomplished in Norway, during the first half of the 18th century. At the end of the first half of the 19th century appeared the first historical studies on adult education in the United Kingdom, a practice which had already been exported overseas well before the independence of America, where a legislative transfer came into effect towards the end of the Elizabethan era (Federighi 1999, 5). Many scholars as Kokkos (2008, 59), Prokou (2008, 123) and Federighi (1999, 5) recommend that adult education has become a reality with the advent of industrial society. The necessity of modernization and constant improvement of non-formal (Rogers 2005) and informal systems learning (La Belle 1982, 159–175) emerges as a result of the globalization of the world economy in both national and European level. In the meanwhile, strengthening employment opportunities, reinforcing access to lifelong learning for all and diminishing social exclusion of the vulnerable groups are also issues of major concern that period (Kokkos 2008, 59).

In the middle of the 20th Century, UNESCO has invested considerable efforts in promoting adult's education value. In the 1950s, a unique experiment carried out by UNESCO in rural France to promote the contribution of the available technology to the development of popular culture and adult education, the "Télé-Clubs" (UNESCO Courier 1956, 4–6). The latters represent one of the early formations of collective television reception and discussion in Europe. The aim was to provide programs dealing with one of France's most serious national problems, the modernization of agriculture and the raising of rural living standard. Another innovation carried out by UNESCO, in 1950, in many countries around the world, Sweden among them, offered workshop in public libraries for professional librarians, especially interested in adult education (UNESCO Courier 1950a, 4). In the same way was the publication of an international list of selected films of universal interest in the field of adult education and coupled with the efforts to promote theatre for educational purposes. Such a practice took place in Western Germany, where the Ruhr Theatre Festival, under whose auspices by UNESCO and the Federation of German Trade Unions for Western Germany, presented plays, such as Shakespeare, that aimed to bring to the workers an understanding of European culture in its widest sense (UNESCO Courier 1950a, 4). The Co-operative Society or Movement, in 1950, was a group of men who were working together in order to serve their needs (UNESCO Courier 1950b, 3). Those men joined together, to produce and sell their products more efficiently and independently. Moreover, this team work served the needs of adult education, as through the team work the older men used to train the younger and through the benefits of education they were able to improve their living standards. Likewise, another UNESCO's innovation was the publication of the 'Guide Books', which were textbooks for adults, written in many languages, especially in Africa and Asia (UNESCO Courier 1950b, 3). Those textbooks aimed at helping people to improve their lives, through the study of several daily issues as crafts, hygiene, agriculture, nutrition and vocational subjects.

On 10 December 1948, the Universal Declaration of Human Rights, adopted by the UN General Assembly, education clearly stated as of right for everyone (The Universal Declaration of Human Rights 1948). The principles set forth in Article 26 advocate that everyone has the right to education and to participate freely in cultural, artistic and scientific life. Moreover, it recognizes that education shall be directed to the full development of the human personality and to the strengthening of respect for human rights and fundamental freedoms. A similar approach is supported in the Article 2 of Protocol No. 1 of the European Convention on Human Rights, signed on 20 March 1952 in Paris (The European Convention on Human Rights 1952), which declares that 'No person shall be denied the right to education'. Along similar lines the International Covenant on Economic, Social and Cultural Rights, adopted by the United Nations General Assembly, on 16 December 1966 (International Covenant on Economic, Social and Cultural Rights 1966), in Article 13, in addition to the aforementioned, it pays considerable attention to the notable education's ability to reinforce the full development of the human personality and the sense of its dignity, and to strengthen the respect of human rights and fundamental freedoms. Moreover, education develops human's opportunity to participate effectively in a free society, promotes understanding, tolerance and friendship among all nations and all racial, ethnic or religious groups and for the maintenance of peace. The Recommendation on the Development of Adult Education proceeded by UNESCO, while meeting in Nairobi from 26 October to 30 November 1976, becomes more specific to issues of adult education. It declares adult education as an integral part of life-long education that can contribute decisively to economic and cultural development, social progress and world peace of the entire community (Recommendation on the Development of Adult Education 1976). Furthermore, the Recommendation illustrates the contribution of adult education to develop a critical understanding of major contemporary problems and social changes and therefore this can provide the person with the ability to play an active role in the progress of society with a view to achieving social justice.

2.2 *Defining "Adult Education" and "Transformative Learning"*

The discussion of adult education should begin with the question 'Who is adult'. Alan Rogers (1998, 60) declares that the term 'adult' is usually equated to a specific age. However, there is not a specific age that determines who is adult, because both legal and social liabilities are activated in different ages (Rogers 1998, 60). UNESCO's Glossary (2011) identifies this term with focus on adult's position in the society:

> Education specifically targeting individuals who are regarded as adults by the society to which they belong to improve their technical or professional qualifications, further develop their abilities, enrich their knowledge with the purpose to complete a level of formal education, or to acquire knowledge, skills and competencies in a new field or to refresh or update their knowledge in a particular field. This also includes what may be referred to as 'continuing education', 'recurrent education' or 'second chance education'.

The literature reveals that many studies use the term 'lifelong learning' and others the term 'adult education'. There is obviously a variety of definitions, not only across several studies, but also across countries: Lifelong learning, adult learning, adult education, continuous education, vocational education and training, popular education, community education etc. This definition issue raises discussions whether all scholars talk about the same thing. In 1926, Alfred Lawrence Hall-Quest (1926) explained the difficulty in defining the term adult education 'Its sharp definition depends in part on accepted meanings of both adult and education'. Along similar lines, Alan Rogers (1998, 53) points out the difficulties in definitions' issue. Moreover, Rogers (1998, 60) puts forward the claim that the term adult education may refer to a few interpretations, such as: a stage in the human's life cycle, his social status, the acceptance by the society that the person has completed the compulsory education and is fully incorporated into the society or it may refer to a social subset, as adults as a distinct category from children, or finally it may include a set of ideals and values: adulthood. Paulo Freire (2005, 33), in his book 'Education for critical consciousness', in its first publication in 1973, perceives education as 'an act of love, and thus an act of courage'. Moreover, he stresses that education is not the transference of knowledge but it is the encounter of Subjects in dialogue in search of the significance of the object of knowing and thinking (Freire 2005, 126). Peter Jarvis (1999, 22), states that in United Kingdom the term lifelong learning has entered recently the British educational library and 'is used rather loosely to cover all forms of post-compulsory education including family education, community education, traditional adult education, further and higher education and continuing professional development. It is not a technical or legal term with precisely defined meaning but rather a cultural term denoting a new paradigm'. According to other scholars, such as Sutton and Kogan (Kokkos 2005), the term lifelong learning denotes the infinite and eternal nature of learning, it covers the lifespan and incorporates all forms of learning, both those provided by educational institutions and all forms of informal learning. A vital link between adult education and culture is provided by Talmadge Guy (1999, 5), who claims that every aspect of adult life is shaped by culture, which refers to shared values, attitudes, beliefs, behavior and language use within a social group. Adult education 'has served as a vehicle for defining the cultural values that people hold or that they view as central to being successful in their society' (Guy 1999, 5). Another issue to consider is culture's importance in shaping criteria for success or failure. Thus, a principal focus of culturally adult education is the reconstruction of learners' group-based identity from one that is negative to one that is positive (Guy 1999, 13).

A large body of literature has investigated the distinction between adult education and vocational education and training. In 1956, Jacob Bronowski (1956, 22), provided an example which identifies this distinction: a historian learns Medieval Latin in order to read documents and this is an example of education 'for a very specific purpose, and since this purpose often helps us to earn our living, I think of it as vocational education'. Additionally, a school-master who had just retired from teaching mathematics, who then learned Italian in order to read Dante, it obviously shows that he learned Italian for a specific purpose, thus this shouldn't be considered as vocational education. In a matter of fact 'The learner was fitting himself to derive from the work of Dante a larger, deeper sense of the many-sidedness of human life than had reached him in translation. At 65, he was fitting himself not to make a living but to live' (Bronowski 1956, 22). As stressed on the 5th Conference on adult education in Hamburg in 1997 'Adult education must involve people as actors who decide for themselves in the societal process of change, and give them the knowledge they require for this purpose, together with the skill to apply this knowledge responsibly'. According to the Recommendation on the Development of Adult Education by UNESCO (1976) the term adult education denotes:

> [. . .] the entire body of organized educational processes, whatever the content, level and method, whether formal or otherwise, whether they prolong or replace initial education in schools, colleges and universities as well as in apprenticeship, whereby persons regarded as adult by the society to which they belong develop their abilities, enrich their knowledge improve their technical or professional qualifications or turn them in a new direction and bring about changes in their attitudes or behavior in twofold perspective of full personal development and participation in balanced and independent social, economic and cultural development. Adult education, however, must not be considered as an entity in itself, it is a sub-division, and an integral part of, a global scheme for life-long education and learning.

In this study the foregoing discussion on the contribution of adult education to the empowerment of citizens to involve in the societal evolution towards social cohesion, lays on the dominant theory of Transformative learning. According to Kitchenham (2012, 1659) Transformational, or Transformative learning is an adult learning theory introduced by Jack Mezirow in the late 1970s (Mezirow 1978). The central core of the theory is the argument that adults experience is a catalyst that causes them to question their worldview, the disorienting dilemma, which leads to a fundamental change in the way that they view the world. Similarly, Edward Taylor (2007, 173) explains:

> Transformative learning offers a theory of learning that is uniquely adult, abstract and idealized, grounded in the nature of human communication. It is a theory that is partly developmental, but even more it is about where learning is understood as the process of using a prior interpretation to construe a new or revised interpretation of the meaning of one's experience in order to guide future action.

According to the Encyclopedia of the Sciences of Learning (Seel 2012, 3341), transformational learning is the process of deep, constructive, and meaningful learning that goes beyond simple knowledge acquisition and supports critical ways in which learners consciously make meaning of their lives. Along similar lines Dirkx (1998) identifies transformative learning as an ongoing, continuous process of re-constructing the meaning of our experience. Likewise, he continues that 'taken as narrative, this story reveals a sense of transformative learning as a heroic journey undertaken by a rational ego in pursuit of consciousness and enlightenment' (Dirkx 1998). Since the publication of Mezirow's theory, many scholars critiqued and elaborated on the theory, leading to theoretical development in a variety of new lenses (Taylor 2007, 174). Dirkx suggests four different lenses that have arisen from examining transformative learning theory: Daloz's developmental approach, Freire's emancipatory approach, Boyd's extrarational approach, and Mezirow's rational approach (Kucukaydin and Cranton 2012, 44).

For the needs of this paper, we argue that the term adult refers to a person that is regarded as adult by the society to which he belongs, and he is in that position to construe meaning upon his experience and revise interpretations in order to plan future actions. Moreover, we argue that adult education denotes the entire body of organized educational processes, within the framework on non-formal education, whatever the content, level and method. It actually covers the lifespan after the cessation of formal education and it serves both as a means of personal betterment and economic development. In essence, adult education, through the impact of

Transformative learning theory, may foster each citizen to develop critical review and understanding of major contemporary problems of his life, to reassess and interpret his experiences and therefore to react and communicate with other people and institutions and after all future action will be planed. Thence it arises that adult education develops citizens' ability to participate effectively in social cohesion, which consequently might contribute to the elimination of a few disparities in the political, social and economic realms. As a corollary, adult education will provide citizens with some patterns or help them to construct new patterns, which might be useful in order to react to future situations.

2.3 *Defining "Economic Development"*

Current research has indicated that there is no consensus view about what development means or what it implies, as highlighted also by Cherry Gertzel (O'Brien and Williams 2011, 394). Frank Youngman (2000, 240) supports that development, in the sense of 'the idea that deliberate action can be undertaken to change society in chosen directions considered desirable' is not an innovative idea, but its origin derives from 1940s. According to the economic historian Robert Heilbroner (Goulet 2002, 12) development is 'the first act of world history'. A closer look at the literature indicates many efforts to define this term. In 1969, Dudley Seers (1969, 1) highlighted the broader sense of the word development versus economic growth, as he argued 'We have all been aware that development consists of much else besides economic growth'. According to Seers (1969, 2), development is inevitably treated as a normative concept, as almost a synonym for improvement. The purpose of development is to reduce poverty, inequality and unemployment and if all of these have declined from high levels, then this has been a period of development for a country, whereas 'If one or two of these central problems have been growing worse, especially if all three have, it would be strange to call the result development, even if per capita income doubled' as Seers proposes (1969, 5). As highlighted by Sotiropoulos et al. (2005, 28), economic development is different than economic growth, whereas the purely economic conception of development implies an equalization of the latter to growth, which refers to the average annual growth rate, GDP, industrial production, etc. An economy can be enlarged by borrowing large sums of money or by exporting a single product whose control has a financial oligarchy. Simultaneously in the same economy, other sectors might be in deep crisis, whereas at the social level growing poverty, periodic hunger threat, degradation of the natural environment, ethnic conflicts and illiteracy might also appeared (Sotiropoulos et al. 2005, 28). Similarly, Goulet (2002, 12) clarifies that 'development does not deliver economic wellbeing to all nations and people: in its distribution of benefits, it is not just'. Similarly, Griffin (Goulet 2002, 19) implies that 'there is no best path to development'.

O'Brien and Williams (2011), perceive development both as a process and a state. Whereas Thomas and Reader (O'Brien and Williams 2011) propose that the term development refers to a multidimensional process that involves the transition from a less desirable to a more desirable societal situation. For Amartya Sen (Nafziger 2005, 1) development involves reducing deprivation or broadening choice. Deprivation represents a multidimensional view of poverty that includes hunger, illiteracy, illness and poor health, powerlessness, voicelessness, insecurity, humiliation, and a lack of access to basic infrastructure. Moreover, Sen suggests that development is 'a process of expanding the real freedoms that people enjoy' (Todaro and Smith 2012, 1). Development is the process of improving the quality of all human lives and capabilities by raising people's levels of living, self-esteem, and freedom, as also highlighted by Todaro and Smith (2012, 775). Thirlwall (2001, 20), identifies Goulet's work in broadening the notion of development in order to include economic and social objectives and values that every society strives for. Goulet (2002, 22), connotes that development, as pursued by the dominant economy, means maximum economic growth, whereas what it ought to be pursued is qualitative human betterment. Moreover, Goulet (Thirlwall 2001, 20) distinguishes three basic components or values of development:

1. Life-sustenance,
2. Self-esteem,
3. And freedom.

In this paper, we argue that economic development is both a process and a state. It is a process as it involves the means by which a society can be transformed towards an improvement of human lives and a state where citizens feel more satisfied, secure, they enjoy equal opportunities to work and to have access to basic infrastructure. In a nutshell, this is the state that people wish to stay for more. Lest the reader be led astray, we do not argue that economic development is separate from economic growth. Economic development declares a state in terms of growth, where measures like GDP per capita are also very useful.

2.4 The General Framework of Social Cohesion

According to OECD (2011, 17) a cohesive society works towards the well-being of all its members, fights exclusion and marginalisation, creates a sense of belonging, promotes trust, and offers its members the opportunity of upward mobility.

Figure 1 presents the triangle of social cohesion, which consists of three different, but equally important lenses: social inclusion, social capital and social mobility (OECD 2011, 17). According to the Routledge Dictionary of Economics (2002, 539), social capital refers to: (a) Assets collectively owned for the benefit of the community at large, (b) The benefits resulting from feelings of sympathy and obligation. These feelings underlie terms of trade, the provision of health and education, and access to goods and services. Social mobility implies the movement of individuals, families and groups from one class or status group to another (The Palgrave Macmillan Dictionary of Political Thought 2007, 644). Social inclusion

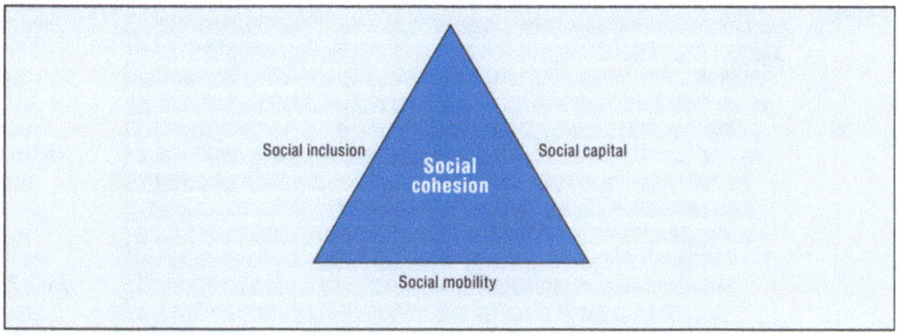

Source: OECD, 2011, 17

Fig. 1 The components of social cohesion

can be seen as the process by which societies combat poverty and social exclusion in order to create a "society for all" (United Nations—Analysing and Measuring Social Inclusion in a Global Context 2010, 1). According to Eleni Prokou (2011, 220), there is no one single process of inclusion, but there are a number of different forms of inclusion being promoted and then legitimised by society itself. The need to build an inclusive society constitutes one of EU's structural indicators. As highlighted in the Memorandum on Lifelong Learning (Commission of the European Communities 2000, 220), a framework of partnership should be achieved among member states in the field of lifelong learning in order to build an inclusive society which offers equal opportunities for access to quality learning throughout life to all people, and in which education and training provision is based first and foremost on the needs and demands of individuals.

OECD has introduced a few indicators to measure social cohesion, such as Life Satisfaction (OECD–Social Cohesion Indicators 2014, 134). Data on life satisfaction comes from the Gallup World Poll, which is conducted in more than 150 countries around the world based on a common questionnaire, translated into the predominant languages of each country. Life satisfaction is determined not only by economic development, but also by people's diverse experiences and living conditions. One could envisage that this measurement defines both social cohesion and economic development, because as mentioned in the previous chapter, the authors of this paper have introduced the framework of economic development which incorporates the state of self-satisfaction. Figure 2 presents the data from the survey conducted in 42 counties, which indicates the average points of life satisfaction in 2012. As can be seen, there are broad regional country groups of life satisfaction. On the top of the list are five Nordic countries, whereas it is obvious that continental Western and Eastern European OECD members are not particularly satisfied with their lives, with the notable exceptions of Switzerland, Austria and the Netherlands. On the other hand, Life satisfaction is deteriorated in European Mediterranean countries.

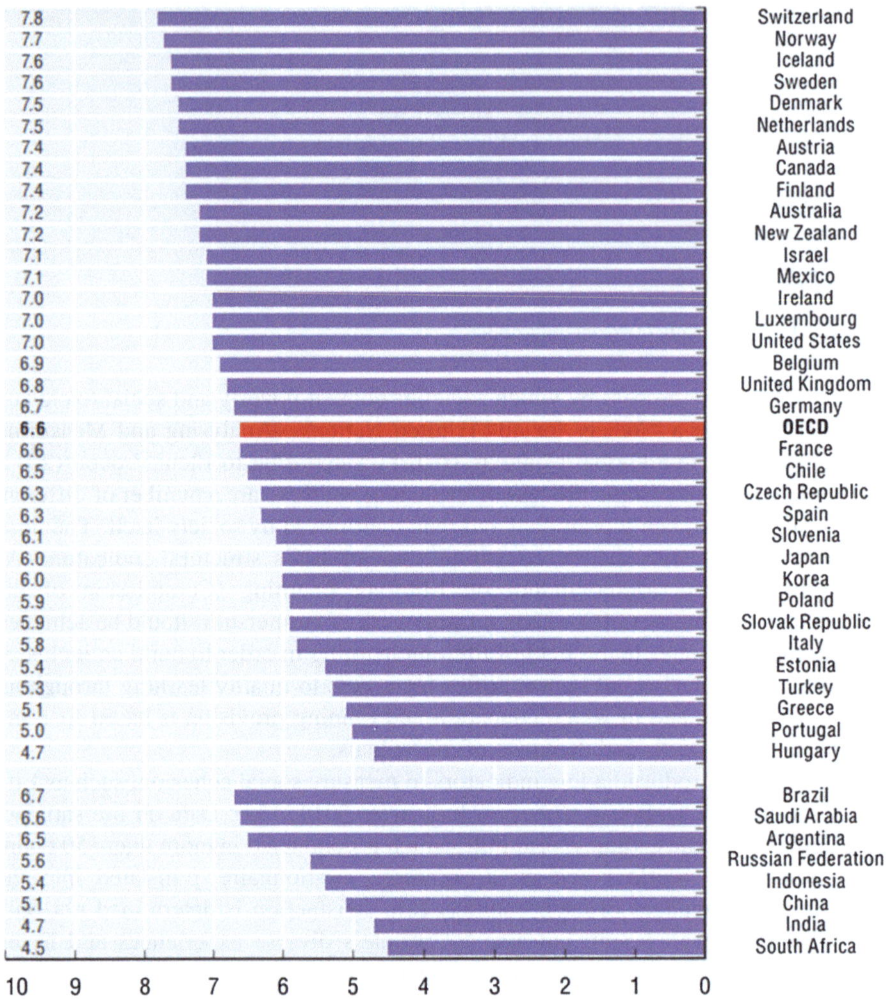

Source: OECD - Social Cohesion Indicators, 2014

Fig. 2 Average points of life satisfaction on an 11-step ladder from 0 to 10, 2012

3 The Methodological Framework of International Political Economy

As highlighted in the preface the majority of the studies that investigate the contribution of education to economic development lay on neoclassical economics and particularly on HCT. Emrullah Tan (2014) claims that HCT is a comprehensive approach to analyze a wide spectrum of human affairs in light of a particular mindset, however it has serious limitations in its analytic framework by which the neoclassical model attempts to explain social and economic phenomena. In the meanwhile, as mentioned above, HCT measures the quantitative dimension between education or schooling and economic growth. In effect, this was a disincentive for this paper's authors, whose main concern was to explore the qualitative dimension of economic development. Robert Gilpin (2002, 55) admits that neoclassical economics are being used by the majority of the economists, whereas several limitations in its framework, especially with regards to matters pertaining to social reality, are very clear. Sklias et al. (2013, 143) propose that initiating from the principles of neoclassical economics, then the developmental phenomenon and the formulation of development conditions are affected by internal factors and variables as well. On the basis of this point, adult education can be seen as one of the strongest links of the chain of development together with politics and economics.

The scientific approach of IPE appeared in mid-1970, as a result of the economic reality which was formed after the oil crisis of 1974 and the collapse of the financial system of Bretton Woods (Andrianos 2008, 81; Hancock and Vivoda 2014, 207). Murphy and Nelson (2001, 393) state that today's field of IPE can be traced back to 1971, when Susan Strange founded the International Political Economy Group (IPEG), which in its days focused on how to resuscitate the fixed exchange-rate system, as according to Fred Hirsch, comfortable middle-class people in the industrialized world would doubt the utility of further economic growth. The key to the institutionalization of IPE, by attracting funders, researchers, initiating graduate programs and creating ubiquitous undergraduate courses, was probably the 1973 October War in the Middle East with its first deployment of the oil weapon and the long recession that followed (Murphy and Nelson 2001, 394). Benjamin Cohen (2007, 10) declares that for some scholars, the moment of IPE's birth came with the publication of a seminal article by Strange in 1970, entitled 'International Economics and International Relations: A Case of Mutual Neglect', whereas for others it came a year later when Strange followed up her own call to action by forming an organized research network, the International Political Economy Group (IPEG).

IPE is an interdisciplinary field, which draws on many distinct academic schools, most notably Political Economy, Political Science and Economics, also Sociology, History, and cultural studies (Wikipedia 2015). This offers the opportunity to use tools from other disciplines. According to Hancock and Vivoda (2014, 206), IPE is a subfield of International Relations (IR) itself, one of the primary fields in Political Science. This argument actually derives from the agenda of the American school of IPE (Cohen 2007, 7). On the other hand, IR should be considered as a subdiscipline of IPE according to the British school of IPE (Cohen 2007, 10). Amanda Dickins (2006, 479) suggests that IPE emerged as the International Economy developed apace in the 1960s, sparking interest in the politics of the International Economy and drew upon diverse sources, including Economics and History as well as International Relations. The early development of IPE incorporates two types of IPE scholar, one type predominates in the United States, the rationalist species, *Ratiosaurus rex*, and the other in the United Kingdom and Canada, the diverse critical species, *Querimonia* (Dickins 2006, 480). Cohen (2007, 1) claims that beyond an interest in marrying international economics and IR, there is no consensus at all on what, precisely, IPE is about, because once born the field proceeded to develop along separate paths followed by quite different clusters of scholars.

As highlighted by Murphy and Nelson (2001, 395), there are two schools of IPE on both sides of the Atlantic: The American school or International Organization (IO) and the British school. Cohen (2007, 1) advocates that the dominant -the hegemonic- globally version of IPE is developed by the American school, where 'Analysis is based on the twin principles of positivism and empiricism, which hold that knowledge is best accumulated through an appeal to objective observation and systematic testing'. On the contrary, the British style of IPE is less wedded to scientific method and more to normative issues, also its supporting scholars are more receptive to links with other academic disciplines, beyond mainstream economics and political science (Cohen 2007, 2). Sklias et al. (2012, 18) claim that IPE is a renowned intellectual and methodological tool, suitable for the diachronic study of social, economic and political issues. Despite different views, opinions and approaches of IPE, researchers converge onto one point: there is an integration of economy and politics, also of domestic and international within IPE (Sklias et al. 2012, 18). In other words, it seems that those demarcation lines between both economy and politics, and 'internal' and 'external' do not exist anymore (Sklias et al. 2012, 21). Robert Gilpin (2002, 84), insists that IPE depends on the theory and the knowledge that arises from neoclassical economics. Nonetheless, IPE and neoclassical economics impose different questions, as both of them use different analysis framework. The discussion in this paper is premised on the analytical framework of the British school of IPE. According to Cohen (2007, 3), this school offers a broader field of study, concerned with all manner of social and ethical issues, identifying injustice, promoting social development and its driving ambition is to make the world a better place. Whereas, in the American school the core object of study is limited to questions of state behavior and system governance, its driving ambition is to explore possible solutions to challenges within the existing system and finally restricts itself mainly to mid-level theorizing-highlighting key relationships with larger stable structures (Cohen 2007, 3).

4 An Analysis of the Correlation Between Adult Education and Economic Development

In the current study we have investigated the origins and the role of adult education. We argue that adult education programs in current aspects of today's political, social and economic realms, might eliminate a few disparities in the above realms, enhance social inclusion, and simultaneously empower citizens' action towards a cohesive society. It is of great importance that education should not be seen as a self-constrained enterprise, but as a parameter in a complex context where education coexists and interacts with the political, social and economic realms. John

White (2013, 295) underlines philosophers' inclination forwards the linkage between education and some wider, ethical and political philosophical questions about the kind of life it is good for a human being and coexistence in a political community. In addition, it is of our belief that adult education very much determines the identity and quality of social cohesion towards economic development. Moreover, in this paper we propose the construction of a European plan for adult education, which might empower every member state to adopt/construct and promote specific programs for its citizens, concerning their needs, in order to accomplish the above targets for eliminating disparities and empowering citizens' action. This European plan should be voluntary, whereas a central authority of distinguished scholars would provide recommendations and any help to the member states upon best practices in adult education programs from around Europe. Moreover, those adult education programs will be put forward Transformative learning, through which every citizen will be reinforced to develop a critical understanding of major contemporary problems and social changes, and therefore his ability to participate effectively in a cohesive society will be developed. In the meanwhile, social cohesion strengthens the respect for human rights and fundamental freedoms, such as security, self-esteem, democracy, well-being and access to basic infrastructure for all citizens. Notwithstanding, we argue that this position is unlikely to achieve economic and social prosperity for all, although there are elements in the proposed program that are desirable.

Those adult education programs could be in branches as: (a) Domestic (Pan) European and international migration, in order to help people take advantage of the opportunities and tackle the challenges of increased cross-border mobility, (b) Enhancing Democratic participation and active citizenship, (c) Empowering vulnerable people, (d) Tackling political extremism, (e) Dealing with terrorism and the fear it spreads etc. All the above grounds threaten the fragments of a cohesive society. Moreover, these programs will reinforce EU's policies in the field of lifelong learning and adult education. According to Milana and Holford (2014, 1) European adult education has emerged within national contexts and only recently Europe has seen an attempt to build an unprecedented supranational polity. European Commission has encouraged member-states to share and exchange knowledge about their national systems in peer-to-peer activities, working groups and networks and therefore, all member states are now involved in debates—domestic and international—on the status and development of adult education (Milana and Holford 2014, 2). One issue to analyze further is whether adult education is re-positioned away from social policy framework towards vocational training. Vocational training is less oriented towards old-style social policy making in favor of organizations, NGOs etc. In 1999, Colin Griffin (1999) gave a comprehensive review of the scope and limitations of lifelong learning and the welfare state reform. In the first place Griffin describes the role and scope of lifelong learning up to his days, in the light of European Commission's approach. Then, he underlines that there is a shift away from education towards learning, which also connotes the abandonment of education as social policy in favour of individual learning as government strategy (Griffin, 431–432). Nowadays, according to Rees

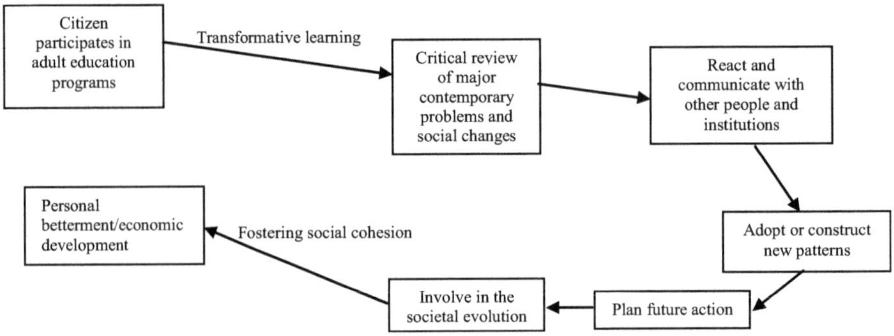

Fig. 3 The correlation between adult education and economic development

(2013, 200), 'governments, especially in the more developed economies, have prioritized vocational provision, often at the expense of other types of adult learning'. Adult learning has been defined in terms of its potential contribution to economic activity, hence, many national governments have shifted priorities for adult learning towards direct vocational provision (Rees 2013, 201). Further research will therefore concentrate on this shift towards vocational training, within European Union in the forthcoming papers.

Within the framework of the British school of IPE, we have the opportunity to approach the notion of economic development, within a broader qualitative framework. We support the idea, along with other scholars, of reinforcing the qualitative dimension of economic development which should incorporate citizens' action and opinion on their opportunities to well-being. Also, in this paper we argue that economic development is a state and a process that involves the means by which a society can be transformed towards an improvement of human lives and a state where citizens feel more satisfied, secure, they enjoy equal opportunities to work and have access to basic infrastructure. Within the chain of economic development, adult education may be one of the strongest links. The above assumptions provide further evidence that there is a correlation between a cohesive society and economic development. On these grounds we argue that adult education could serve as a vehicle for economic development in the developed countries.

A summary of these thoughts is included in Fig. 3.

5 Conclusion

The significance of this paper is the attempt to explore the potential of the contribution of adult education in economic development, within the framework of IPE in EU. Adult education and economic development strengthen one another. In this framework citizens play a vital role as they are reinforced to form and hold together with other people and the institutions, the fragments of a cohesive society towards economic development. The methodological framework of International Political Economy is adopted in this study in order to analyze the benefits of both economic development and adult education, differentiated from the dominant neoclassical approach framework of the HCT. Adult education may be one of the strongest links of the chain of economic development and it may very much determine the identity and quality of economic development. Further findings of this study will be presented in future papers. Considerably, more work will need to be done to determine the role of adult education to economic development.

References

Andrianos I (2008) The impact of cultural and social characteristics into economic development of Western Balkans. Unpublished Doctoral Dissertation. Democritus University of Thrace

Berend I (2009) An economic history of twentieth-century Europe. Gutenberg, Athens (In Greek)

Berend I (2013) An economic history of nineteenth-century Europe. Cambridge University Press, New York, NY

Bronowski J (1956) The educated man in 1984. http://unesdoc.unesco.org/images/0007/000781/078152eo.pdf#68667. Accessed 11 July 2015

Cohen B (2007) The transatlantic divide: why are American and British IPE so different? Lecture presented to the inaugural meeting of the International Political Economy Society, Princeton University, Princeton, New Jersey, 17 November 2006. https://escholarship.org/uc/item/28k8z2t4#page-2. Accessed 27 Sept 2015

Commission of the European Communities (2000) Commission staff working paper: a memorandum on lifelong learning, Brussels, 30.10.2000, SEC (2000) 1832

Dickins A (2006) The evolution of international political economy. Int Aff 82(3):479–492

Dirkx JM (1998) Knowing the self through fantasy: toward a mytho-poetic view of transformative learning. Paper presented at the 39th Annual adult education research conference. http://www.adulterc.org/Proceedings/1998/98dirkx.htm. Accessed 11 July 2015

Federighi P (1999) Glossary of adult learning in Europe. European Association for the Education of Adults (EAEA) and UNESCO Institute for Education. http://www.unesco.org/education/uie/pdf/glossary.pdf. Accessed 11 July 2015

Freire P (2005) Education for critical consciousness. Continuum, London

Gaganakis K (1999) Social and economic history of Europe. Hellenic Open University, Patra (in Greek)

Gilpin R (2002) Global political economy: understanding the international economic order. Poiotita Publishers-Princeton University Press, Athens (in Greek)

Goulet D (2002) What is a just economy in a globalized world? Int J Soc Econ 29(1/2):10–25

Griffin C (1999) Lifelong learning and welfare reform. Int J Lifelong Educ 18(6):431–452

Guy TC (1999) Culture as context for adult education: the need for culturally relevant adult education. New Dir Adult Contin Educ 1999(82):5–18

Hall-Quest LA (1926) The university afield. http://babel.hathitrust.org/cgi/pt?id=mdp.39015004281351;view=1up;seq=24. Accessed 10 July 2015

Hancock KJ, Vivoda V (2014) International political economy: a field born of the OPEC crisis returns to its energy roots. Energy Res Soc Sci 1:206–216

Jarvis P (1999) Lifelong learning. In: Federighi P (ed) Glossary of adult learning in Europe. European Association for the Education of Adults (EAEA) and UNESCO Institute for Education. http://www.unesco.org/education/uie/pdf/glossary.pdf. Accessed 11 July 2015

International Covenant on Economic, Social and Cultural Rights (1966) http://www.ohchr.org/EN/ProfessionalInterest/Pages/CESCR.aspx. Accessed 9 July 2015

Kitchenham A (2012) Jack Mezirow on transformative learning. In: Seel MN (ed) Encyclopedia of the sciences of learning. Springer, New York, NY
Kokkos A (2005) Adult education methodology. Hellenic Open University, Patra (In Greek)
Kokkos A (2008) Adult education in Greece. Convergence 42(2/3):59–73
Kucukaydin I, Cranton P (2012) Critically questioning the discourse of transformative learning theory. Adult Educ Q 63(1):43–56
La Belle TJ (1982) Formal, nonformal and informal education: a holistic perspective on lifelong learning. Int Rev Educ 28(2):159–175
Milana M, Holford J (2014) Adult education policy and the European Union. https://www.sensepublishers.com/media/1971-adult-education-policy-and-the-european-union.pdf. Accessed 12 July 2015
Mezirow J (1978) Perspective transformation. Adult Educ Q 28(2):100–110
Murphy CN, Nelson DR (2001) International political economy: a tale of two heterodoxies. Br J Polit Int Relat 3(3):393–412
Nafziger EW (2005) From seers to Sen: the meaning of economic development. http://www.rrojasdatabank.info/widerconf/Nafziger.pdf. Accessed 11 July 2015
O'Brien R, Williams M (2011) Global political economy. Papazisis Publishers, Athens (In Greek)
OECD (2011) Perspectives on global development 2012: executive summary. http://www.oecd.org/site/devpgd2012/49067839.pdf. Accessed 11 July 2015
OECD–Social Cohesion Indicators (2014) http://www.oecd-ilibrary.org/docserver/download/8113171ec027.pdf?expires=1435769266&id=id&accname=guest&checksum=6BFE53602B0ED7FEF10AE13FA5AF8BF6. Accessed 11 July 2015
Prokou E (2008) A comparative approach to lifelong learning policies in Europe: the cases of the UK, Sweden and Greece. Eur J Educ 43(1):123–140
Prokou E (2011) The aims of employability and social inclusion/active citizenship in lifelong learning policies in Greece, The Greek Review of Social Research, Special Issue 136 C', pp 203–223
Psacharopoulos G (1996) Economics of education: a research agenda. Econ Educ Rev 15(4):339–344
Recommendation on the Development of Adult Education (1976) http://portal.unesco.org/en/ev.php-URL_ID=13096&URL_DO=DO_TOPIC&URL_SECTION=201.html. Accessed 11 July 2015
Rees G (2013) Comparing adult learning systems: an emerging political economy. Eur J Educ 48(2):200–212
Rogers A (1998) Teaching adults. Metaixmio, Athens (In Greek)
Rogers A (2005) Non-Formal education. Flexible schooling or participatory education? Springer, New York, NY
Routledge Dictionary of Economics (2002) http://down.cenet.org.cn/upfile/33/2009522115641174.pdf. Accessed 8 July 2015.
Schultz T (1972) The economic value of education. Papazisis Publishers, Athens
Seel MN (2012) Encyclopedia of the sciences of learning. Springer, New York, NY
Seers D (1969) The meaning of development. https://www.ids.ac.uk/files/dmfile/themeaningofdevelopment.pdf. Accessed 11 July 2015
Sklias P (2001) Global political economy. Papazisis Publishers, Athens (In Greek)
Sklias P, Koutsoukis N-S, Roukanas S (2013) Culture, politics and economics: dynamics, mechanisms and processes for sustainable development. Int J Sustain Soc 5(2):133–145
Sklias P, Roukanas S, Maris G (2012) The politics of International and European economic relations. Papazisis Publishers, Athens (In Greek)
Sotiropoulos DA, Huliaras A, Roussos S, Sklias P (2005) Third world: politics, society, economy, international relations. Papazisis Publishers, Athens (In Greek)
Karatzia-Stavlioti E, Lambropoulos H (2009) Education and economic development: evaluations and ideologies. In: Cowen R, Kazamias AM (eds) International handbook of comparative education. Springer, New York, NY, pp 633–650
Tan E (2014) Human capital theory: a holistic criticism. Rev Educ Res 84(3):411–445

Taylor E (2007) An update of transformative learning theory: a critical review of the empirical research (1999–2005). Int J Lifelong Educ 26(2):173–191

The Palgrave Macmillan Dictionary of Political Thought (2007) 3rd edn. http://text-translator.com/wp-content/filesfa/Dictionary-of-political-thoughts.pdf. Accessed 11 July 2015

The Universal Declaration of Human Rights (1948) http://www.un.org/en/documents/udhr/. Accessed 11 July 2015

The European Convention on Human Rights (1952) http://conventions.coe.int/Treaty/en/Treaties/Html/009.htm. Accessed 11 July 2015

Thirlwall AP (2001) Growth and development. Papazisis Publishers, Athens (In Greek)

Todaro MP, Smith SC (2012) Economic development, 11th edn. http://eco.eco.basu.ac.ir/BasuContentFiles/57/57304a77-1269-4081-bd5b-4c66b84b06a4.pdf. Accessed 11 July 2015

UNESCO Courier (1950a) Libraries—a neglected resource. http://unesdoc.unesco.org/images/0008/000815/081543eo.pdf#81543. Accessed 11 July 2015

UNESCO Courier (1950b) Struggle against ignorance and inertia. http://unesdoc.unesco.org/images/0007/000749/074977eo.pdf#74977. Accessed 11 July 2015

UNESCO Courier (1956) What's wrong on French farms. http://unesdoc.unesco.org/images/0007/000781/078152eo.pdf#68667. Accessed 11 July 2015

UNESCO Glossary (2011) Adult education. http://glossary.uis.unesco.org/glossary/en/term/1944/en. Accessed 11 July 2015

UNITED NATIONS—Analysing and Measuring Social Inclusion in a Global Context (2010) http://www.un.org/esa/socdev/publications/measuring-social-inclusion.pdf. Accessed 11 July 2015

Youngman F (2000) The political economy of adult education and development. Zed Books, London

White J (2013) Philosophy, philosophy of education and economic realities. Theory Res Educ 11 (3):294–303

Wikipedia (2015) International political economy. https://en.wikipedia.org/wiki/International_political_economy. Accessed 11 July 2015

Pantelis Sklias is a professor of International Political Economy (IPE) at the Department of Political Science and International Relations of the University of Peloponnese, Corinth Greece. He was also a visiting lecturer at the Department of International and European Studies of the University of Macedonia and visiting lecturer and assistant professor from 2002 to 2007 at the Department of International Economic Relations and Development of the Dimocritus University of Thrace. Since 2002, he has taught at the Hellenic Open University. From 1999 to 2002, he was a visiting research fellow at the Postgraduate Centre for Culture, Development and the Environment (CDE) of the University of Sussex. His research interests include institutions, international development, and civil society.

Giota Chatzimichailidou is a PhD Candidate at the Department of Political Science and International Relations of the University of Peloponnese. She writes a PhD thesis with the title "The contribution of Adult Education to Economic Development". Her research interests include Adult Education, International and European Political Economy, Development and Governance.

MIX
Papier aus verantwortungsvollen Quellen
Paper from responsible sources
FSC® C105338

If you have any concerns about our products,
you can contact us on
ProductSafety@springernature.com

In case Publisher is established outside the EU,
the EU authorized representative is:
Springer Nature Customer Service Center GmbH
Europaplatz 3, 69115 Heidelberg, Germany

Printed by Libri Plureos GmbH
in Hamburg, Germany